Bahrain

WORLD BIBLIOGRAPHICAL SERIES

General Editors:
Robert L. Collison (Editor-in-chief)
Sheila R. Herstein
Louis J. Reith
Hans H. Wellisch

VOLUMES IN THE SERIES

VOLUME 49

Bahrain

P. T. H. Unwin
Compiler

CLIO PRESS

OXFORD, ENGLAND · SANTA BARBARA, CALIFORNIA
DENVER, COLORADO

© Copyright 1984 by Clio Press Ltd.

British Library Cataloguing in Publication Data

Unwin, P. T. H.
Bahrain. – (World bibliographical series; 49)
1. Bahrain – Bibliography
I. Title   II. Series
016.953'65   Z3028.B34

ISBN 0-903450-86-0

Clio Press Ltd.,
55 St. Thomas' Street,
Oxford OX1 1JG, England.

ABC-Clio Information Services,
Riviera Campus, 2040 Alameda Padre Serra,
Santa Barbara, Ca. 93103, U.S.A.

Designed by Bernard Crossland
Typeset by Berkshire Publishing Services
Printed in Great Britain by
Billing and Sons Ltd., Worcester

THE WORLD BIBLIOGRAPHICAL SERIES

This series will eventually cover every country in the world, each in a separate volume comprising annotated entries on works dealing with its history, geography, economy and politics; and with its people, their culture, customs, religion and social organization. Attention will also be paid to current living conditions — housing, education, newspapers, clothing, etc. — that are all too often ignored in standard bibliographies; and to those particular aspects relevant to individual countries. Each volume seeks to achieve, by use of careful selectivity and critical assessment of the literature, an expression of the country and an appreciation of its nature and national aspirations, to guide the reader towards an understanding of its importance. The keynote of the series is to provide, in a uniform format, an interpretation of each country that will express its culture, its place in the world, and the qualities and background that make it unique.

SERIES EDITORS

Robert L. Collison (Editor-in-chief) is Professor Emeritus, Library and Information Studies, University of California, Los Angeles, and is currently the President of the Society of Indexers. Following the war, he served as Reference Librarian for the City of Westminster and later became Librarian to the BBC. During his fifty years as a professional librarian in England and the USA, he has written more than twenty works on bibliography, librarianship, indexing and related subjects.

Sheila R. Herstein is Reference Librarian and Library Instruction Coordinator at the City College of the City University of New York. She has extensive bibliographic experience and described her innovations in the field of bibliographic instruction in 'Team teaching and bibliographic instruction', *The Bookmark*, Autumn 1979. In addition, Doctor Herstein co-authored a basic annotated bibliography in history for Funk & Wagnalls *New encyclopedia*, and for several years reviewed books for *Library Journal*.

Louis J. Reith is librarian with the Franciscan Institute, St. Bonaventure University, New York. He received his PhD from Stanford University, California, and later studied at Eberhard-Karls-Universität, Tübingen. In addition to his activities as a librarian, Dr. Reith is a specialist on 16th-century German history and the Reformation and has published many articles and papers in both German and English. He was also editor of the *American Society for Reformation Research Newsletter*.

Hans H. Wellisch is Associate Professor at the College of Library and Information Services, University of Maryland, and a member of the American Society of Indexers and the International Federation for Documentation. He is the author of numerous articles and several books on indexing and abstracting, and has also published *Indexing and abstracting: an international bibliography*. He also contributes frequently to *Journal of the American Society for Information Science, Library Quarterly,* and *The Indexer*.

Contents

Contents

Preface

This bibliography covers a wide range of material published on Bahrain but does not aim to be conclusive or definitively comprehensive, thus not everything that has ever been published in English on Bahrain is mentioned. The two criteria used for the inclusion of material have been its availability and its relevance, with availability being interpreted in a fairly wide sense. Many of the references are thus only available in specialist libraries on the Middle East, the British Library, or locations on Bahrain itself. The main bookshop on Bahrain is the Family Bookshop, Shaikh Isa Al Kabir Rd., situated near the American Mission Hospital. There are surprisingly few books or articles written exclusively on Bahrain, although the country is mentioned in many general texts on oil and the British involvement in the Gulf. The large number of publications in these fields necessitates a degree of subjectivity in the choice of those to include in this bibliography. Consequently only publications that provide important background material or more than a passing reference to Bahrain have normally been included. Certain sections, such as those on languages, education, sports and recreation, and the arts, nevertheless remain poorly represented. This directly reflects the lack of works published in English on these topics. The number of government publications has been kept to a minimum, but where it has been felt that they provide important information not available elsewhere they have been listed.

The historical British involvement in the Gulf has meant that the majority of non-Arabic works on Bahrain are written in English. The present bibliography, however, also includes some material published in Danish, French, German and Italian. The extensive archaeological work on Bahrain undertaken by Danes in the 1950s and 1960s necessitates the inclusion of a number of Danish publications, but it should be noted that many of these have English summaries. Material in other European languages is also important because of the different light that it sheds on the islands of Bahrain, devoid of colonial sentimentality.

Preface

Traditionally the region in which Bahrain lies has been known as the Persian Gulf, and hence most writers refer to it as such, despite the Arab use of the phrase Arabian Gulf. In an attempt to remain as impartial as possible the simple word Gulf has been used wherever possible in the present work.

Transliterations from Arabic present considerable problems, and the approach used in the annotations has normally been to follow the method used by the author of the work in question. This has the advantage that it clearly illustrates the changing use of terminology. While *al-Baḥrain* is a more correct transliteration for the name of the country, *Bahrain* is in common usage and has therefore been used in the title and introduction. Tribal names also present particular difficulties. In the Gulf *Al-* for the names of tribes, and *al-* for individuals within the tribe, are now in general usage in both government and other circles, and for pragmatic reasons the introduction therefore follows this method, thus referring to the ruling family of Bahrain as Al-Khalifah and to individual members of it as, for example, Shaikh Ahmed al-Khalifah. Dates, as well as names, have been cited in the annotations as given in each work in question.

Numerous people have helped me in my compilation of this bibliography. I am particularly grateful to the Committee of the Hayter Travel Fund of the University of London for providing me with financial assistance to visit sources of material on Bahrain. In England the following people deserve special thanks: Pat and Brian Adams; Valerie Allport, for obtaining copies of many obscure references for me through the inter-library loan scheme, despite the restrictions placed on the operation of this service by the government cuts in education; my colleagues in the departments of geography at Bedford College (University of London) and the University of Durham; the staff of the Middle East Documentation Centre at the University of Durham; and the many unknown assistants in libraries who have provided me with the bulk of the material on which this bibliography is based. I also remain very grateful to the following people in Bahrain: Helen and John Martin, for providing wonderfully welcome hospitality to a complete stranger; Robert Jarman, for suggestions of often fairly obscure references connected with early travellers in the region; Bill Williams, for providing access to the Bahrain Historical and Archaeological Society's extensive collection of material; Tom Nightingale for references on the flora and fauna of the region; Mr. and Mrs. H. B. Bending of the British Council, for their advice and hospitality; Mr. H. R. Cade of the Family Bookshop; and Mustapha al-Khatib of the Ministry of Information. Most of

Preface

all, though, I must thank my wife Pam for her overall support and also for her help in undertaking the very tedious task of checking my manuscript for errors.

Tim Unwin
Englefield Green
14 February 1984

Introduction

Located in a central position in the Gulf, the islands of Bahrain have played an important commercial role in the region since prehistoric times. Traditionally, the economy was dominated by pearling and trade, but more recently, and particularly since the discovery of oil in 1932, the islands have undergone a rapid economic transformation. The pace of this change increased appreciably following independence from Britain in 1971 and the 1974 rises in oil prices. Bahrain today, though, still retains parts of its rich cultural heritage, and old and new are to be found together in marked juxtaposition. Bounded by the sea, Bahrain nevertheless maintains close contacts with its neighbours, particularly Saudi Arabia 24 kilometres to the south-west.

Geography and geology
The archipelago of Bahrain consists of 35 islands, totalling an area of approximately 675 square kilometres. Only six of the islands are inhabited, with most of the population being found on Bahrain Island and al-Muharraq. The other principal islands are Sitra, Jidda, Umm Nassan, Nabih Salih, and the Hawar Islands adjacent to the coast of Qatar. The largest of the islands, Bahrain, on which the capital al-Manamah is situated, is approximately 48 kilometres long and 16 kilometres wide at its broadest point, and it is connected to al-Muharraq to its north-east by a 2.4 kilometre long causeway, construction of which began in 1929. Another causeway joins Bahrain Island to Sitra, and a new causeway is being constructed from the west coast to the eastern shoreline of Saudi Arabia.

Geologically Bahrain consists of an oval-shaped centre of Eocene carbonate rocks which is surrounded by unconsolidated Pleistocene and more recent sediments. The Eocene succession, which can be divided into seven formations, mostly consists of limestones which have been extensively dolomitized and dedolomitized through time. In terms of structure, the island is dominated by a broad asymmetrical pericline, which has a north-south trend. The relief is determined largely by this

Introduction

structure and geology with coastal plains giving way to a gently sloping dipslope, and escarpment zone, the interior basin, and then the central Jabal Dukhan, which reaches a highest point of 122.4 metres.

The climate is generally harsh, being both hot and humid, with little rainfall. Three characteristic seasons can be identified. The months from December to March are normally the coolest, with monthly average temperatures varying from $19°C$ in January to $25°C$ in March. Virtually all of the annual rainfall, normally less than 10 centimetres, falls in this period. This season is also dominated by the moist north-west wind, known as the Shamal. From March the temperatures rise rapidly reaching a maximum in the month of August when the mean monthly temperature is normally around $36°C$. Occasionally in June the temperatures are moderated by the Bara, a cool north wind, but this relief is only temporary. Apart from the Shamal the other dominant wind to occur is the hot, sand-bearing wind from the south known as the Qaws. The summer remains hot until October when the temperature begins to fall rapidly. Humidity throughout the year remains high, with the figures for the summer being slightly lower than those of the winter.

The low rainfall has meant that settlement and agriculture in the islands have been restricted largely to the areas where groundwater is easily accessible. One of the reasons for Bahrain's past prosperity was indeed the abundance of freshwater springs to the north of the island, and many writers have noted the practice of diving for fresh water which was known to well up at various locations on the sea bed. This occurrence has given rise to one of the suggested derivations of the name Bahrain, meaning 'two seas', the one being salt water and the other fresh water. It now seems evident that the aquifers of Bahrain are a continuation of those underlying eastern Saudi Arabia, and that they can be divided into three, the A, B and C systems, approximately corresponding to the Alat and Khobar-Alveolina members of the Dammam Formation and the Umm er Radhuma-Rus carbonates. The periclinal fold of Bahrain Island provides a structural weakness which has concentrated upward flow of groundwater from these aquifers. Traditionally most water was obtained from springs, known as *ains*, but with increased demand these have been replaced by wells. The recently increased abstraction has led to a serious decrease in both the quality and quantity of the water available. The only major source of low-salinity groundwater is found in the Khobar aquifer, but even this has salinity levels of approximately 3,000 mg/l of TDS. Since the 1920s this Khobar aquifer appears to have suffered from increased salinity due to upward flow from the much more saline Umm er Radhuma system, as well as very recent sea encroachment. In addition, the Alat system has apparently been entirely destroyed, and abstraction of water has also led to the complete salinization of the aquifers in the region around Sitra due to salt water incursion. These changes have recently begun to place severe constraints on both agricultural improvements and also the provision of 'fresh' water for domestic purposes. Consequently the increased production of desalinated water has become a major priority of the government.

History

For much of the period between the 3rd and 16th centuries the name Bahrain, in its various spellings, was used to refer to the whole coastal region of eastern Arabia between Kuwait and Qatar. In this period the main island of modern Bahrain was known as Uwal. However, at the time of the Portuguese intervention in the Gulf the name Bahrain itself became restricted in its meaning to the offshore islands coterminous with the present state.

Of all the states of the Arabian peninsula and southern Gulf, Bahrain has perhaps fascinated archaeologists the most. This interest stems largely from the occurrence on the islands of somewhere in the region of 100,000 burial mounds, now considered to date mostly from between 2600 and 1800 BC. These attest to Bahrain's prehistoric importance, but it was not until the various Danish expeditions to the islands, beginning in the 1950s, that its prehistory began to be unravelled in detail. The findings of Sumerian cuneiform inscriptions towards the end of the 19th century mentioning the name Dilmun, an important trading centre situated somewhere in the Gulf, also gave rise to speculation that Dilmun was Bahrain and that the islands did indeed have a glorious past. Bahrain's archaeological record is far from complete, but it now seems that in the third millenium BC the islands were an important commercial centre in the heart of an extensive cultural complex stretching out into mainland Arabia, and that in all probability this was Dilmun. Prior to this it is apparent from the evidence of small encampments and flint working sites that the islands were occupied during the Palaeolithic period, but little is really known about these early hunter inhabitants of Bahrain. From 3000 BC the archaeological record becomes more detailed, and although most of the burial mounds appear to have been robbed in antiquity it is possible to piece together much about life on the islands at this time. Of particular importance are three sites investigated by the Danish archaeological expeditions: the temple complex at Barbar, the tel at Qala'at al-Bahrain (the Portuguese fort), and a small temple at Ain Umm Es-Sujur.

During the third millenium BC Bahrain seems to have served two main roles: as a point of trans-shipment and trade, and as a religious and burial centre. Apparently copper, precious stones and timber were brought by people from Dilmun from places known as Magan and Meluhha to the east and then traded with the peoples of Mesopotamia. However, by about 2000 BC Dilmun declined rapidly in importance, probably due to the Aryan invasions and destruction of the Indus Valley civilization with which Dilmun had traded. Bahrain at this period had few of its own resources and was consequently unable to sustain the impact of the loss of supply of the raw materials of its trade. Following a period when life on the islands was at low ebb, Bahrain again achieved some degree of prosperity during the first millenium BC when the Assyrians, Babylonians and then the Persians in turn claimed sovereignty over the islands. Little is known of Bahrain after the Persian conquest in the middle of the 6th century BC, but when Alexander the Great sent ships into the Gulf two of them reached Tylos, which has since been identified as Bahrain, and which apparently was then governed by an independent ruler. In the ensuing Seleucid period Bahrain's wealth seems to have returned to something of its former glory as commercial links were strengthened.

During the 4th century AD the Persian Sassanid king Shappur I annexed eastern Arabia, including Bahrain, to his empire, and placed it under the jurisdiction of the king of Hira. From this time until the arrival of Islam little is heard of Bahrain. In 630 Al-'Ala bin Abdulla al-Hadrami, the envoy of the Prophet Mohammed, called on the Rabia tribe, the people of Bahrain, to submit to Islam, and from this date the history of the islands became inexorably linked with that of the emergence and spread of Islam. Following the death of Mohammed it appears that many of the Rabia rejected his teachings, but they were quickly defeated by the forces of the Caliph, and a succession of governors was installed. In the following centuries Bahrain was influenced on several occasions by radical Islamic movements such as the Al-Zinj and Al-Khawarij, but in the 9th century a more significant change took place when Abu Said Al-Jannabi declared the rule of the Carmathians in the islands. Despite attempts by the Caliphs to subdue the revolt, Carmathian rule survived until 1058 when Abu al-Bahlul overthrew the dynasty and for a short while established himself as the ruler of Bahrain.

From the 11th to the 16th centuries Bahrain became subject to the ebb and flow of different regional power bases, some times retaining a quasi-independent status and at others being under the control of the rulers of Qatif, Hasa, Hormuz or Oman. In 1487, following the Omani invasion of Bahrain, Umar bin al-Khattab was appointed governor of the islands, but already external forces from beyond the region were beginning to make themselves felt. In 1498 the Portuguese rounded the southern tip of Africa, and thus paved the way for European sea-based empires to interfere for the first time directly with the turbulent waters of the Gulf.

Early in the 16th century Bahrain again appears to have been under the influence of the kings of Hormuz, and when Afonso de Albuquerque conquered Hormuz and installed there a puppet king the Portuguese immediately confirmed the existing treaty relations between the shaikh of Bahrain and the erstwhile king of Hormuz. A short while later Mukarram, the king of Hasa, seized Bahrain from Hormuz and began interfering with Portuguese trading interests in the Gulf. Consequently the Portuguese under Antonio Correa attacked Bahrain in 1521 and after a brief struggle defeated Mukarram. The Portuguese then installed a succession of governors in the islands, but a number of revolts in the ensuing decades ensured that their rule was not easy and that at least on a couple of occasions independent rulers controlled Bahrain. In 1602 Portuguese rule of the islands eventually came to an end when the governor was murdered and the people involved in his demise then placed themselves under Persian protection. Following the loss of Bahrain and then the loss of Hormuz to the English, the king of Spain and Portugal continued to attempt to recapture his possessions in the region. This culminated in the sending of a fleet from India in 1645 with orders to capture both Hormuz and Bahrain. Before the fleet could even reach the Gulf, though, it was attacked and destroyed by a hostile Omani fleet, thus ending one and a half centuries of direct Portuguese involvement in the Gulf.

Although the Persians dominated the rule of Bahrain from the beginning of the 17th century to the arrival there of the British, their hold on the islands was by no means always secure. In 1718 the islands were conquered by Oman, and the Persians could only buy them back several years later. A second Omani invasion occurred in 1738 and it seems that as a result of these two incursions many of the traditional Shi'ah population of the islands fled to the neighbouring mainland of Arabia. During this period of unrest in the Gulf another tribal movement, later to be of great significance to Bahrain, was emerging. At the beginning of the 18th century the three families of the Utub tribe, the Al-Khalifah, Sabah and the Jalahima, began to settle in Kuwait, and soon developed a particular interest in the pearl trade. By the 1760s this interest had taken the Al-Khalifah to the settlement of Zubarah in the north-west of Qatar. Zubarah rapidly grew into an important trading centre and the competition that it posed for Bahrain gradually drew the Persians there into conflict with the Al-Khalifah. After several unsuccessful skirmishes the Al-Khalifah, under Shaikh Ahmed al-Khalifah, later known as al-Fatih, the conqueror, then captured Bahrain in 1783, establishing the dynasty which continues to rule the islands to this day. Their control over Bahrain in the early years was not, though, without its problems. In 1799 the Imam of Muscat occupied Bahrain and Shaikh Sulman bin Ahmed together with his brother Abdullah, who had succeeded their father as joint rulers in 1796, were forced to flee to Zubarah. By this date the Wahhabi movement on mainland Arabia had gained considerable strength, and Shaikh Sulman bin Ahmed in 1809 turned to the Wahhabi ruler Abd al-Aziz to help him to regain Bahrain. The Wahhabis willingly agreed, driving the Omanis out of Bahrain, but instead of restoring the Al-Khalifah they installed their own governor on the islands. The Al-Khalifah, nevertheless, eventually managed to regain control of the islands, and by the second decade of the 19th century, when the British first began to play a significant role in this part of the Gulf, the Al-Khalifah shaikhs had fully regained power.

In 1816 the British Resident in Bushire, apparently without the authority of the Indian Government, signed a draft treaty of friendship with the Al-Khalifah shaikhs. Although this never came into force, it paved the way for the signing in 1820 of a General Treaty of Peace, which followed the British defeat of the so-called Qawasim 'pirates' of Ras al-Khaimah. By this treaty the ruler of Bahrain would not allow into his country produce obtained by piracy and would be party to the treaty signed with the Qawasim. In 1825 Sulman bin Ahmed died, and he was succeeded by his son Khalifah, who continued as joint ruler with his uncle Abdullah bin Ahmed. On the death of Khalifah bin Sulman in 1834 internal conflicts within the Al-Khalifah then led to a period of instability. In 1842 Abdullah bin Ahmed expelled Khalifah's son Muhammad with whom he had jointly ruled for eight years. Muhammad bin Khalifah then returned to Bahrain in 1843 and in his turn deposed his great uncle Abdullah.

In 1856 a further agreement aimed at the reduction of slavery was signed between the ruler of Bahrain, Muhammad bin Khalifah, and the British. This was followed by the much more important Friendly Convention of 1861 in which the ruler of Bahrain agreed to the cessation of all maritime warfare in return for British protection. Soon after this, further rivalries in the Al-Khalifah family again came to the fore, and the British, fearing growing interest by Turkey and Persia in the islands, took increased military and diplomatic action. Thus, when in 1867 Muhammad bin Khalifah, who had apparently solicited aid from both Turkey and Persia, attacked Qatar, the British denounced him as a pirate and deposed him as a punishment for contravening the 1861

Introduction

convention. In his place they installed his brother Ali as ruler. Later, in 1869, Muhammad bin Khalifah returned to Bahrain, killed his brother, and again took over the reins of power. During this period both Turkey and Persia continued to involve themselves in the internal conflicts of the island in attempts to reassert their territorial claims. The British, however, soon captured Muhammad bin Khalifah, and then in his place declared Isa bin Ali, the son of the killed ruler, who was at that time living in Qatar, as shaikh.

It seems that Shaikh Isa bin Ali, either through his own volition or through British pressure, resisted the overtures of both Turkey and Persia, and was prepared to associate his country more closely with British rule. Consequently two more agreements were signed between Bahrain and the British government in 1880 and 1892. By these the shaikh agreed not to enter into negotiations or make any kind of treaty with any state or government other than the British without the consent of the British government. The shaikh also agreed not to part with any of his territory save to the British government. Despite the increased British influence over Bahrain at this time, a number of other events occurred in the reign of Shaikh Isa which were to have important consequences in later years. Firstly, in 1890 Shaikh Isa gave refuge to Ibn Saud and his family when they fled from Riyadh following the capture of that city by the Rashidis. Close ties between Bahrain and Saudi Arabia emerged from this offer of hospitality, and these have seen their most recent expression in the start in 1982 of the construction of the causeway joining the two countries. Secondly, in 1900 a British Political Assistant was stationed at Bahrain for the first time, to be replaced in 1904 by the first British Political Agent, Capt. F. B. Prideaux. Bahrain therefore grew in political importance, and its central administrative role also had increased commercial and economic benefits. In 1946 the British Political Residency in the Gulf was transferred from Bushire to Bahrain and this further centralization in Bahrain of British administration in the eastern Gulf meant that its political and economic importance therefore grew relative to the other states of the region. Thirdly, in 1913 the British and Ottoman governments signed a convention by which the Turks recognised Bahrain's independence, and in 1916 Ibn Saud signed a treaty agreeing to refrain from aggression towards Bahrain. By these agreements all claims other than those by Persia and Britain itself to Bahrain's territorial integrity were removed.

In 1923 internal troubles within Bahrain led to the abdication of Shaikh Isa and the succession of his son, Shaikh Hamad, who ruled for 12 years as deputy ruler and then on the death of his father in 1936 for a further 7 years as Shaikh of Bahrain.

Introduction

Political development in the 20th century

In any discussion of the emergence of Bahrain as an independent state in the 20th century it is far from easy to separate the political from the economic changes that have taken place. Nevertheless, to give a brief introduction to these changes some aspects of the political development of the state will first be summarized here, before examples of the economic changes that have taken place are given in the ensuing section.

In 1926 Charles Belgrave, later Sir Charles, took up the position of Adviser to Shaikh Hamad. At this time there was little formal government administration, and for the next three decades Sir Charles Belgrave played an important role in moulding the shape of the government. A year earlier in 1925 Major Frank Holmes, of the Eastern and General Syndicate, had begun a well-drilling programme ostensibly to increase water supplies for Shaikh Hamad. Nevertheless, he had also obtained an exclusive oil exploration permit. The oil discoveries in the 1930s consequent on this concession then provided the means by which the government was able to expand its activities. Before it was possible to undertake extensive changes, though, a renewed political offensive by Persia in 1927 brought into the foreground the peculiar nature of the relationship between Britain and Bahrain. For the previous half-century Persia had, on the whole, acquiesced in its claims to the islands, but when in May 1927 the king of Saudi Arabia signed the treaty of Jiddah with the British, agreeing to maintain friendly relations with Bahrain, which was then in special treaty relations with the British government, the Persian government responded by arguing that Bahrain was a Persian possession and that the treaty therefore constituted an infringement of the territorial integrity of Persia. The British emphatically denied the Persian claims, but in 1928 a further exchange took place with Persia reasserting its claims to the islands and Britain rejecting them. This dispute remained unsettled until 1970, and over the forty year period of continued British involvement in Bahrain it was to provide more than one occasion of disagreement. The 1970 agreement with Iran brought to an end the major international territorial claims to Bahrain. Nevertheless, the Iranian revolution of 1979 has produced an air of uncertainty, with the possibility of future Iranian claims being made on Bahrain. In addition, neighbouring Qatar has laid claim to the islands of Hawar. In 1936 Bahrain posted a military garrison on the Hawar Islands, and this gave rise to a complaint by Shaikh Abdulla bin Qasim al-Thani of Qatar to the British Political Resident. After evidence had been presented from both sides, the British Political Resident argued that Bahrain possessed a *prima facie* claim to the

Introduction

islands through the presence of its garrison, and consequently in 1939 he awarded the islands definitively to Bahrain. Since then, however, Qatar has not accepted this verdict, and the dispute remains unsettled. Following the discovery of oil in 1932 increased revenues enabled the shaikh and his advisers to develop the government administration and to expand the provision of social services. In 1931, a Department of Education had been established, and during the 1930s considerable infrastructural developments, in the form of road, telephones and electricity installations, were set in progress. In addition government departments for public health, medicine, public works, labour affairs, and minors' estates were soon established. In association with these a number of committees relating to such matters as trade disputes, diving regulations, agriculture, and religious endowments were created, supposedly to enable the people of Bahrain to take an increasing part in their own government.

In 1942 Shaikh Hamad died, and was succeeded by his son Shaikh Sulman bin Hamad al-Khalifah. The developments begun by his father were continued and by the early 1950s the growth of the country's administration and commercial facilities had made Bahrain possibly the most 'modern' of the states of the southern Gulf. Nevertheless, although the social services provided free medicine and education, and although political expression was to some extent enabled through the various committees, the first signs of political unrest became visible in 1952. In response to this the ruler agreed to the establishment of further committees and councils. The first of these to be created was the Labour Law Advisory Committee, which eventually drafted the Labour Law in 1957. In 1955 the partially elected Councils of Health and Education were formed, and in March 1956 a Council of Administration, dominated by members of the royal family, was established. However, it appears that these measures were insufficient to satisfy the demands of certain sectors of the population, and in 1956 at the time of the Suez crisis considerable rioting occurred and a state of emergency was declared. This was partly directed at the British, and in particular the visit of the British Foreign Secretary, and consequently one result thereof was the 'retirement' of Sir Charles Belgrave.

By 1961 when Shaikh Isa bin Sulman al-Khalifah succeeded his father some reforms had indeed been introduced, but during the first decade of his reign major political changes took place associated with the final British withdrawal from the region. In January 1968 the Labour government of Britain declared its intention to withdraw all British forces east of Suez, and thus set in motion the processes by which the states of the Gulf would achieve full independence. That same year saw widespread activity in the Gulf as the rulers, together with the British government, tried to find a formula which would ensure political stability and security following the departure of the British forces. The initial aims were to unite Bahrain, Qatar and the seven emirates of the Trucial States into a single federation, and in February 1968 a summit meeting of the rulers of all of these states produced a declaration of unity advocating the creation of such a federation with both a Higher Council of the rulers and a Federal Council for administration. However, in a meeting in May 1969 the rulers failed to reach any major agreements, and it seemed clear from then that both Bahrain and Qatar were likely to go their own separate ways at independence.

In January 1970 Shaikh Isa took the first steps towards creating Bahrain as a separate independent state when he established a Councl of State to replace the Advisory Council. The new Council was also to include a smaller proportion of members of the royal family. Additionally, other decrees halved the number of government departments, bureaus and agencies, and established a new set of ministries. On 15th August 1971 Bahrain was formally declared independent, and soon afterwards it was admitted to the Arab League and the United Nations. The Council of State was then replaced by a Council of Ministers, with a Cabinet composed of ministers from the following ministries: the Bahrain Defence Force (established in 1968), Public Security, Foreign Affairs, Finance and National Economy, Education, Labour and Social Affairs, Municipalities, Health, Information, Justice, Development and Engineering Services, and Agriculture. Further political changes were to come in 1972, when Shaikh Isa issued a decree permitting elections for a Constitutional Assembly which would establish a new draft constitution. Elections for the 22 Constitutional Assembly seats took place in December 1972 and 88.5 per cent of the electorate participated. The new constitution was eventually promulgated in June 1973, and it adopted a generally democratic stance, dealing with such controversial issues as women's and trade union rights and the authority of the elected representatives to grant concessions relating to Bahrain's resources. It also stipulated that a National Assembly of 30 delegates should be created, which together with the 12 members of the Council of Ministers, would form the main legislative assembly of the country. Elections for the National Assembly took place in December 1973, and although over 100 meetings of the Assembly were held, its activities came to a halt in May 1975 following growing confrontations between the government and the Assembly. In August 1975 the Assembly was eventually dissolved.

Introduction

At the same time as these internal political changes were taking place, Bahrain's external relations also took on a new form. In particular, as a result of a United Nations Security Council resolution of May 1970, following an investigative mission by a Personal Representative of the Secretary General to the islands in March/April 1970, the Iranian government finally relinquished its claim to Bahrain. The mission had concluded that the overwhelming majority of the people of Bahrain wished to gain recognition of their identity as a fully independent and sovereign state, and the Iranians consequently acceded to these wishes. In addition, at independence in 1971, all political and military treaties relating to the special relations with Britain were terminated, and subsequently the two countries signed a new treaty of friendship. This search for political stability is likely to become more pressing as signs of increased tension within Bahrain are making themselves felt. The extent of Iranian involvement in attempts to ferment political instability in the Arab countries of the Gulf remains unclear, but the discovery of a plot apparently by members of the Shi'ah community to overthrow Bahrain's monarchy in December 1981 indicates that all is not well. According to the Ministry of the Interior the 73 defendants, all of whom were given prison sentences, planned to produce an Iranianstyle Islamic republic, and although Iran denies the charge that it was behind the plot relationships between Bahrain and Iran remain uneasy.

The most recent changes in Bahrain's external political relationships came when in 1981, together with Kuwait, Oman, Qatar, Saudi Arabia and the United Arab Emirates, it was involved in the founding of the Gulf Co-operation Council (GCC). The main aims of the six states involved in the GCC are initially to achieve economic integration through the abolition of customs tariffs, the exchange of goods and services, and the erection of taxation barriers to protect local industries. It is also, though, concerned with maintaining stability within its member states, and therefore it is of considerable political significance.

The economy

In the 19th century Bahrain's economy was dominated by pearl fishing and trade. To be sure, fishing played an important part and limited agriculture, restricted by the harsh physical environment, was also practised, but the mainstay of the economy remained as it had done for millenia in the collection and selling of pearls, with Bahrain's offshore banks reported to be the best in the region. However, at the end of the 19th century the pearl industry declined, with estimates of the numbers

Introduction

of boats involved falling from 1,500 in 1833 to 900 in 1896 and 509 in 1930. During the 1930s first the 'world recession' and then the Japanese development of cultured pearls hit hard at the pearling economy, and in 1948 following the Second World War it is estimated that only 83 boats were involved in pearl fishing. Traditionally agriculture was dominated by the production of dates along the north coast of the main island, with irrigation water being provided by springs and wells. Several underground canal systems also took water to parts of the island where it was difficult to obtain other water sources for irrigation. Shipbuilding, pottery and handicrafts made up the remainder of the traditional industrial structure of the islands.

At the same time as pearling declined, though, Bahrain began to reap the advantages of the developing exploitation of its oil reserves. Undoubtedly the extra income available to those working in the oil industry when compared with the wages to be obtained from pearl diving also led to the further decline of pearling, but the additional revenues obtained from oil paved the way for a dramatic transformation of the economy. British oil companies had shown little interest in taking up exploration rights for oil in Bahrain, and in 1927 Holmes eventually interested an American corporation, the Eastern Gulf Company, in a two-year exploration option. After several discussions and negotiations Eastern Gulf then assigned its option to the Standard Oil Company of California who in 1930 assigned it to its fully owned, Canadian registered, subsidiary the Bahrain Petroleum Company Ltd. (BAPCO). The various treaty relations between Bahrain and Britain had necessitated that BAPCO be registered in Canada to give it the status of a British company. Immediately consequent on the 1930 concession exploration and drilling operations began, and in 1932 the first production well came on stream. By 1935 there were 16 producing wells, and in order to process the oil it was decided to set up a small refinery near Sitra Island. This began production in 1936. By 1937 its capacity had been increased to 25,000 barrels per day (b/d), and with plans to further increase its capacity above the production levels of the Bahrain field it was decided to lay a pipeline from the Saudi Dammam field to Sitra where the Saudi oil could then be refined.

Although Bahrain was the first state on the Arab side of the Gulf to produce oil, its resources are among the smallest of the region. Between 1940 and 1965 Bahrain's crude oil production rose from 19,300 b/d to 57,000 b/d, and then to 76,639 b/d in 1970. Since then, though, output has declined steadily to a level of only 46,411 b/d in 1980. Current estimates suggest that its oil reserves are likely to last at present extraction levels only until 2010. Despite this depletion of oil

Introduction

reserves Bahrain's gas output is expected to last for at least 50 years production at 1980 extraction levels.

The increases in oil output until the 1970s and the changes in the participation agreements meant that the state revenue from oil production has increased dramatically. In 1952 an agreement between Shaikh Sulman and BAPCO provided for a half-and-half profit sharing arrangement, greatly increasing government revenue, but unlike other Gulf states Bahrain was relatively slow to take its hydrocarbon industry fully into its own hands. In November 1974 the government signed an agreement to acquire a 60 per cent share in BAPCO's oil and gas exploration and production activities, excluding the refinery, and this became effective in July 1975. In March 1976 the Bahrain National Oil Company (BANOCO) was established to manage the state's participation in the oil industry, and in 1978 BANOCO took over the marketing and distribution of oil products in Bahrain. At the end of 1979 BANOCO eventually took over full ownership of BAPCO's exploration and production rights, and in 1980 it acquired a 60 per cent share in the Sitra refinery. In the mid-1970s this refinery had a rated capacity of 250,000 b/d with Bahrain providing only about one quarter of the crude oil output. The recent slump in oil demand has, though, meant that output of the refinery was running at only about 150,000 b/d in mid-1982.

In 1979 the Bahrain National Gas Company (BANAGAS) was created to administer the country's gas industry. There are two non-associated gas fields, the Khuff field and the far smaller and nearly exhausted Arab-zone field. Associated gas production levels, unlike the non-associated gas, have, however, increased over recent years and are now playing an increasingly important role. A liquefied petroleum gas plant was opened in 1979, and this now processes about 120 million cubic feet per day of associated gas.

The small size of Bahrain's hydrocarbon reserves has forced the government to take a much more immediate concern with ways of diversifying the economy than has been the case in many other countries of the region. Consequently two major industrial projects have been established since independence, and a further four are currently under construction.

The first of these major industrial concerns to take shape was the aluminium smelter, Aluminium Bahrain (ALBA). In 1969 a group of British, Swedish, French and US companies formed a consortium with the Bahrain government to build and operate a 120,000 tonne a year aluminium smelter. This began production in 1971. In 1975 the government acquired a majority shareholding in the company, and a reshuffling

Introduction

of the other shareholders has left Saudi Arabia with 20 per cent, the US's Kaiser Aluminium with 17 per cent, and West Germany's Breton Investments with 5.1 per cent. An extension consisting of two potlines was completed in 1981 and this raised the capacity to 170,000 tonnes a year. The early 1980s have, though, seen a stagnation of world aluminium demand, and ALBA's stockpiles have increased as their marketing agency is now finding difficulties in disposing of their increased production. The government has nevertheless continued to emphasize its commitment to this sector of the economy and three major secondary industries related to aluminium now exist. The oldest, Bahrain Atomisers, was set up in 1973 with 51 per cent government ownership, and in 1981 produced 2,600 tonnes of powder. A second company, the Bahrain Aluminium Extrusion Company, which is fully state owned, was established in 1977 specifically to produce for the local market and in 1981 its output was 3,500 tonnes of products. The third aluminium user is Midal Cables Ltd., which is privately owned and was set up in 1978 to produce 25,000 tonnes a year of aluminium rods and conductors. In all, it is estimated that these three companies use about 15,000 tonnes of ALBA's output annually.

The second scheme to get off the ground was the Arab Shipbuilding and Repair Yard (ASRY) Company's drydock, which was opened in 1977 under the operation of the Portuguese company Lisnave. Financed by the member countries of OAPEC, ASRY has a capacity of 450,000 tonnes dwt, and can therefore handle the largest oil tankers in the world. Nevertheless, the slump in the oil market, the Iran-Iraq conflict, and the competition presented by other drydocks such as that at Dubai, have meant that ASRY, which has run at a loss every year since its inauguration, is having increasing difficulties in attracting business.

Despite some problems with industries already established, Bahrain has recently had much success in attracting other joint Arab projects, which have yet to reach completion. Thus work is currently in progress on the construction of a petrochemical plant for the Gulf Petrochemical Industries Company (GPIC), which is equally owned by Bahrain, Kuwait and Saudi Arabia. When completed this should have a daily capacity of 1,000 tons of methanol and 1,000 tons of ammonia. A second project is the Gulf Aluminium Rolling Mill Company's plant, which was begun in 1981. This is the first project to be developed by the Qatar-based Gulf Organisation for Industrial Consulting. The third recent example of the investment of Gulf capital in new heavy industry in Bahrain is the iron pelletization plant. This was also started in 1981 and it is being built for the Arab Iron and Steel Company. Finally, Bahrain, Kuwait and Saudi Arabia founded the Heavy Oil Conversion

Introduction

Company in 1981 to construct a fuel oil cracker in Bahrain with a proposed capacity of 80,000 b/d.

In association with these major projects other smaller industries have also been developed in recent years so that Bahrain now boasts a number of medium-sized companies involved in the production of supplementary gas, asphalt, prefabricated housing, plastics, soft drinks, air conditioning equipment, paper products, and ship servicing and repairs. Increasing government legislation is now enforcing the use of locally produced materials, and, while this acts as an incentive for the expansion of local industries, it is also likely to hit hard at the numerous commercial traders of Bahrain who have developed their livelihoods based largely on the importation of goods not produced locally. Much of the development that has taken place was enabled so to do through the expansion of the port facilities at Mina Sulman, which were originally built in 1966 with facilities for berthing six ships at one time. Expansion in the 1970s enabled a further six berths as well as a container terminal to be constructed. This container terminal with two roll-on-roll-off berths is seen as being particularly important since an increasing amount of the region's trade is being handled in this fashion. The establishment of a free trade area around the port has also meant that it has acted as a focus for the attraction of a number of light industries to the country.

While Bahrain has therefore seen an extensive amount of industrial development for a country of its size in the last decade, this must not overshadow other alterations in the economy. Of particular importance have also been the changes in the banking sector. Prior to independence there had only been three banks in Bahrain. In 1965 the Bahrain Currency Board had been established to trade the newly created Dinar against other currencies, but its activities were fairly limited. Following independence in 1971 the first Bahraini banks, the National Bank and the Bank of Bahrain and Kuwait, came into operation, and in 1973 the Currency Board became the Bahrain Monetary Agency, which now functions as a Central Bank. By 1981 the number of full commercial banks in Bahrain had risen to 19, with there also being two special banks, namely the Housing Bank and the Bahrain Islamic Bank, 46 Representative Offices, and 9 Investment Banks. The major change in Bahrain's financial sector, though, was the government's decision in 1975 to permit offshore banking units to operate from Bahrain. Following the 1974 increases in the oil revenues of the Gulf states a number of banks were attracted to the region in response to the need to recycle this money back into the world economy. To take advantage of this situation, and in an attempt to make Bahrain a major world financial

Introduction

centre the Bahrain Monetary Agency encouraged many foreign banks to take out licences for offshore banking units, and from the first 18 when the scheme commenced the number of such units had risen to 65 by March 1981.

The development of Bahrain as an important financial market, together with its industrial diversification, albeit heavily dependent on the hydrocarbon sector for both power and feedstocks, has meant that just over a decade after independence the country's economy is much less restricted and limited than it was in 1971. The increased oil revenues have also enabled the government to embark on extensive infrastructural development and widespread expansion of welfare and social service provision necessitated by a significant growth in population and thus demand. Bahrain's population has not increased as rapidly as that of some of its neighbours, but it has nevertheless risen from a figure of 143,213 in the 1959 census to 350,798 in 1981, an increase of 245 per cent in 22 years. Over the period 1950-81, though, the proportion of the population that was indigenous fell from about 80 to 68 per cent. This clearly reflects the increases in foreign labour that have been required in order to undertake the ambitious industrial projects outlined above.

Both the increases in industrial demand and the growth of the country's population have required a major expansion of power and water provision. The islands' first power station began operating in 1931, and within two years its load had risen to 300 KW. Since then further power stations have been constructed so that in the early 1980s there were four in operation: the oldest at Mahooz with a capacity of 115 MW of gas turbines; a 35-MW gas turbine station at al-Muharraq; a steam-powered 120-MW station at Sitra; and a gas turbine station at Rifa'a producing 250 MW. Increasingly, though, the government has tended to concentrate on the joint production of both power and water, with the focus of its attention being the Sitra power and water desalination complex. The first multi-stage flash desalination project at Sitra was completed in 1976 with two units producing 5 million gallons per day. Desalinated water is pumped from here to West Rifa'a where it is blended with underground water to produce water for domestic use. Although the aim is to provide water with a final salinity of 500 ppm, the high demand and the relatively low output of desalinated water means that the actual quality is nearer 1,500-2,000 ppm. Work is currently in progress on the construction of a further three units at Sitra, each of which will produce an additional 5 million gallons per day. These are due to be completed in 1984 and 1985, and as well as their water provision they will also add a considerable amount of

Introduction

additional power to the electricity grid. Other projects for increasing water supply include a 10 million gallon per day reverse osmosis plant at Ras Abu Jarjur, and the proposed 10 million gallon per day multistage flash unit at Ad Dur. In addition to these water and power facilities, all of the major industrial complexes, such as the refinery and ALBA, have their own desalination units. Most of the fuel for the new power/desalination complexes is to be provided by gas feedstocks, but as noted earlier these only have a limited lifespan and some other energy source will therefore have to be found to ensure Bahrain's continued prosperity.

In addition to increasing the demand for power and water, the rapid growth of population has also caused an acute housing shortage in Bahrain. The first major scheme to be undertaken to relieve this pressure was the construction of Isa Town to the south-west of al-Manamah. This new town received its first inhabitants in 1968 and because the Amir Shaikh Isa bin Sulman donated the land and the state provides free public services, residents now only have to repay the costs of house construction. In the early 1980s its population was estimated at 22,000, and it is expected that when Isa Town is completed it will have a total population of about 35,000. In 1974 the Ministry of Housing was created in order to tackle the growing housing shortage, and a three pronged approach was implemented. This advocated an island-wide house building programme, the provision of building plots and a home loan scheme. The first housing plan was launched in 1976, and over its three year period government figures indicate that 4,200 dwellings were constructed, 2,000 loans totalling BD 17.5 million were disbursed, and 1,500 housing plots were allocated. To implement the distribution of loans more efficiently a Housing Bank was established in 1979, and this provides the entire cost of housing to individuals at varying interest rates. Current plans envisage the development of additional residential colonies at Arrad, Hidd, Jiddafs, A'ali, Damistan, East and West Rifa'a, and Sanabis, and there are also proposals to develop a major new township in the Sakir area running parallel to the west coast of the island. In association with these housing developments the Works Directorate is undertaking the improvement of the island's road network. Currently the capital, al-Manamah, experiences severe road congestion, but this has been partially alleviated by the construction of a ring-road system and the development of multi-storey car park facilities. The construction of the causeway to Saudi Arabia will also be associated with a major reorientation of Bahrain's road system, as the four-lane highway enters the west of Bahrain Island from the offshore island of Umm Nassan and then heads east to the capital.

Introduction

In addition to the above infrastructural developments there have also been extensive changes in the provision of social services. The first modern school to be established was built in 1919 in al-Muharraq, and by the end of the 1950s 11,000 boys and 5,000 girls were being educated in the 46 government schools in Bahrain. Since then a system of five different types of school has been developed, divided into the following categories: primary and religious schooling (6-12 age group); intermediate schooling (13-15); secondary streaming (16-18); technical streaming (16-18); and commercial streaming (16-18). By 1981, although education was not yet compulsory, the annual school enrolment had reached 62,000 children, of whom 55 per cent were boys. In 1968 the Gulf Technical College was founded to provide the opportunity for students to undertake further technical training, but currently only about 15 per cent of Bahrainis choose to follow a technical education. This lack of interest by the local population in developing skilled labour has acted as an important constraint to indigenous economic change, and has been one of the main factors leading to the importation of foreign labour. The government is nevertheless still striving for educational advances, and plans are currently being implemented for the development of a university sector.

As with education, free health service provision has also expanded rapidly, and with 24 health centres together with a hospital capacity of 1,124 beds in 1981, there is now good provision of both primary and secondary medical facilities on the islands. Recently Bahrain's largest hospital, the Sulmaniya Medical Centre, has undergone a modernization and expansion programme, and in 1982 a new maternity wing with 95 beds was opened. In 1976 a College of Health Science was established by the Ministry of Health to cater for the provision of nurses, pharmacists, radiologists and laboratory technicians, and by the end of the 1970s approximately 150 students were graduating from here each year. Further medical and health facilities are also provided by a small, and expensive, private medical sector.

Prospects

At a time of increased political tension in the Gulf, resulting from the continued war between Iran and Iraq which began in 1980, as well as the wider tensions currently emanating from Lebanon, Bahrain's continued prosperity seems less assured than it did during the first decade following independence. Likewise, the attempted *coup* in 1981, whether or not it was inspired by Iran, reflects a further source of tension arising from the traditional divisions between the Shi'ah and Sunni elements of Bahrain's population. Consequently, in seeking

8 **Bahrain.**
Bahrain: Ministry of Information, n.d. [late 1970s]. unpaged.
An illustrated introduction to the following aspects of Bahrain: geography and natural history, tradition and culture, communications, trade and economy, finance and banking, construction and development, commerce and industry, welfare and social affairs, and sport and recreation.

9 **Bahrain: the businessman's map and guide.**
Manama: Falcon Publishing, n.d. 40p.
Provides lists of information concerning the major areas of business in Bahrain, in addition to details on emergency services, government ministries, embassies and recreational facilities. There are detailed maps of Bahrain island, northern Bahrain, Al Muharraq, Al Jufayr, and Al Manamah.

10 **Bahrain – offshore centre of the Gulf: a special report.**
The Times (London), 16 Dec. 1980, p. I-VIII.
A report on the financial world of Bahrain, paying particular attention to the role of foreign banks, the Bahrain Monetary Agency, insurance, communications, and accommodation.

11 **Bahrain: a special report.**
The Times (London), 6 Feb. 1980, p. I-VIII.
A report assessing the political, business and social climate in the emirate of Bahrain, together with a two-page economic briefing. Particular attention is paid to finance, agriculture, energy, industrial diversification, property, communications, and the causeway to Saudi Arabia.

12 **Bahrain: a special report.**
The Times (London), 15 Dec. 1982, p. I-IV.
A report on the political and economic mood in Bahrain a year after the discovery of a plot to overthrow the government. Specific attention is paid to banking, oil, agriculture, education, wildlife, and tourism.

13 **Basic data on the economy of Bahrain, Qatar, Muscat and Oman, and the Trucial States.**
Overseas Business Reports (US Department of Commerce), vol. 22 (March 1968), p. 1-14.
An account of the geography, demography, economy, politics and trade of the countries in the title in the 1960s.

14 **Bahrain.**
C. Dalrymple Belgrave. *Journal of the Central Asian Society*, vol. 15, no. 4 (Oct. 1928), p. 440-45.
A short description of the geography, history and politics of Bahrain prior to the late 1920s. Particular attention is paid to pearling.

The Country and Its People

15 **Bahrain: from dhow to discoteque.**
Charles Belgrave. *Mid East*, vol. 8, no. 3 (May-June 1968),
p. 32-37.
Highlights some of the major developments in Bahrain between the mid-1920s
and mid-1960s. Covers such issues as social and economic change, educational
developments and health.

16 **Personal column.**
Charles Belgrave. London: Hutchinson, 1960. 248p.
The autobiography of the adviser to the Shaikh of Bahrain from 1926 to 1957. It
provides interesting insights into all aspects of life on the islands during that
period, and in particular on the subjects of government administration, pearling
and socio-economic change.

17 **Bahrain.**
James H. D. Belgrave, pictures by Bernard Gerard. Paris: Editions
Delroisse, 1974. 144p.
A well-illustrated introduction to Bahrain in English, French and German. It is
divided into sections on history, development, the people, Manama, boat building,
Muharraq, Isa Town, BAPCO, ALBA, agriculture and pottery, but it includes a
wealth of other information on the culture, history and economy of Bahrain.

18 **Welcome to Bahrain.**
James H. D. Belgrave. Manama: Augustan Press, 1st ed. 1953,
9th ed. 1975. liii + 208p. 3 maps. bibliog.
In the 1950s and early 1960s no official guide book to Bahrain had been
produced, and this publication served as the main guide to the country. The first
part includes chapters on the country, the people, the state, development,
commerce and industry, communications, the oil industry, pearls, traditional
industries, prehistory, antiquities, natural history, horses, religious occasions and
local customs, and Bahrain's stamps. Part 2 is on the history of Bahrain's islands,
part 3 provides a guide to numerous places in the country, and part 4 contains
useful information on recreations, gardening and other social activities. It includes
numerous photographs, and is a useful, if slightly dated, introduction to the
country.

19 **Kuwait and the rim of Arabia.**
Gilda Berger. New York, London: Franklin Watts, 1978. 64p.
An introduction to the Arabian peninsula for children. After three introductory
chapters on the peninsula, life in the Arab world, and a history of the peninsula,
each country is described in turn, with details of Bahrain being given on p. 27-31.

20 **Le Golfe persique: mer de légende – reservoir de pétrole.** (The Persian Gulf: sea of legend – reservoir of oil.)
Jean-Jacques Berreby. Paris: Payot, 1959. 228p. 4 maps. bibliog.

A French introduction to the Gulf in which Bahrain is mainly discussed in chapter 12, where mention is made of the country's pearl industry and relations with Britain and Iran. Elsewhere some details of Bahrain's oil industry in the 1950s are given.

21 **La péninsule arabique. Terre sainte de l'Islam, patrie de l'arabisme et empire du pétrole.** (The Arabian peninsula. Holy land of Islam, fatherland of Arabism and empire of oil.)
Jean-Jacques Berreby. Paris: Payot, 1958. 270p. 4 maps. bibliog.

A French guide to Arabia, including several scattered references to Bahrain, which is described as the Pearl of the Gulf. Details of the country, its economy, and the development of its oil industry are summarized on p. 211-18.

22 **The Arab Gulf Journal.**
Edited by Bill Charlton, May Ziwar-Daftari. London: MD Research and Services, Oct. 1981- . biannual.

One of the few journals specifically on the Gulf, paying particular attention to agricultural, demographic, economic and industrial changes.

23 **The Persian Gulf states.**
General editor Alvin J. Cottrell, editors C. Edmund Bosworth, R. Michael Burrell, Keith McLachlan, Roger M. Savory. Baltimore, Maryland; London: Johns Hopkins University Press, 1980. 695p. 6 maps. bibliog.

This detailed volume is concerned with the whole of the Gulf region. It is divided into five main sections: the history of the Gulf, economics and urban development, cultural background, arts and society, and finally twelve appendixes. A number of chapters, in addition to providing general observations on the Gulf, are subdivided into sections on each country within the region. Bahrain is discussed particularly in connection with agriculture, its relations with Britain, education, industry, oil, pearl fishing, religious structure, and urbanization. The appendixes provide a wealth of summarized information on such aspects as climate, flora, demography, industrial development, and the agricultural sector. Each chapter and appendix has its own selected bibliography. It provides one of the most comprehensive introductions to the wider region of which Bahrain is a part.

24 **Crossroads. Land and life in southwest Asia.**
George B. Cressey. Chicago, New York, Philadelphia: J. B. Lippincott, 1960. 593p.

A traditional 'regional geography' of southwest Asia. Bahrein is mentioned in several places mainly in connection with its oil industry.

25 **Bahrain: language, customs & people.**
Jerry L. Curtis. Printed by Tien Wah Press, Singapore, no publication details [Bahrain 1977]. 256p. 3 maps. bibliog.
An introduction to Bahrain divided into six chapters. The first includes sections on the place, the people, the men, the women and the children of Bahrain; the second is on holidays and customs; the third includes 35 Bahraini and Arab recipes; the fourth is on general information for the foreigner, covering subjects such as banks, currency, customs regulations, passports, taxis, hotels and restaurants, embassies, cinemas, post, shops, churches and museums; the fifth is a 119p.-section on language; and the sixth includes a genealogy of the ruling family and a short bibliography. It includes numerous photographs of the land and its people.

26 **The Persian Gulf.**
G. Dalyell. *Scottish Geographical Magazine*, vol. 57, no. 2 (1941), p. 58-65.
An account of the Gulf by the late Political Agent in Bahrain. It describes Bahrain's pearl trade, oil industry, and sepulchral mounds.

27 **Al-Bahrain islands.**
Mahmoud Ali Al-Daoud. *Iraqi Geographical Journal*, vol. 2 (June 1964), p. 21-26.
This paper provides a brief historical and geographical introduction to Bahrain. It notes the nationalistic movement which began to take form in 1956 in a Committee of National Union, but which was dissolved after strikes in 1957, and it asserts that Arab nationalism was playing an active part in Bahrain during the early 1960s.

28 **Bahrain, Kuwait, Qatar and United Arab Emirates: official standard names approved by the United States Board on Geographic Names.**
Defense Mapping Agency Topographic Center. Washington, DC: US Government Printing Office, 1976. 145p. map.
A list of places and their spellings as approved by the US Board on Geographic Names, including 835 places in Bahrain.

29 **The Arab of the desert: a glimpse into Badawin life in Kuwait and Sau'di Arabia.**
H. R. P. Dickson. London: George Allen & Unwin, 1949. 648p. 9 maps.
This detailed study of the lifestyle of the badawin includes several mentions of Bahrain, in particular in connection with pearling.

30 **Kuwait and her neighbours.**
H. R. P. Dickson. London: George Allen & Unwin, 1956. 627p.
6 maps.

Although mainly on Kuwait, this book provides many scattered mentions of Bahrain. The author was Political Agent at Bahrain from just after the First World War until 1920, and then Political Agent at Kuwait from 1929 to 1936. The migration of the Al Khalifah to Zubara and then Bahrain is mentioned in a section on the early history of the region, and brief details of the islands are given in a chapter on the districts and villages near Kuwait. The early 19th-century occupation of Bahrain by the Wahabis under Ibn 'Ahfaisan, the arrival of Major Frank Holmes in Bahrain in 1922 in search of oil for Ibn Sa'ud in Qatif, Shaikh 'Isa Ibn 'Ali Al Khalifah's deposition in 1923, and the discovery of oil in Bahrain are all noted.

31 **Bahrain 1979: a MEED special report.**
Nigel Dudley. *Middle East Economic Digest*, July 1979. 68p.

This report concentrates on banking, oil and gas, construction, the causeway to Saudi Arabia, the aluminium industry, the ASRY (Arab Shipbuilding and Repair Yard) shipyard, Mina Sulman, cold storage facilities, tourism, telecommunications, social services, insurance, trade, agriculture and training. Concluding sections cover basic data and statistics relating to the period 1972-78.

32 **About people in Bahrain.**
Pieter J. Feteris. New York, Washington, Hollywood: Vantage Press, 1972. 84p.

A series of sixteen sketches on life in Bahrain, reflecting the author's experiences there. It covers such subjects as a beach party, Rhamadan, and the New Bahrain from a distinctly 'American' point of view.

33 **The encyclopaedia of Islam: new edition.**
Edited by H. A. R. Gibb, J. H. Kramers *et al.* Leiden, the Netherlands: E. J. Brill; London: Luzac, vol. 1, 1954-60; vol. 2, 1960-65; vol. 3, 1965-71; vol. 4, 1973-78.

The definitive encyclopaedia of the Islamic world. Volume 1 contains a description of the islands of Bahrain and volume 4 provides details of the Al-Khalifa ruling family of Bahrain.

34 **A handbook of Arabia.**
Great Britain. Admiralty War Staff, Intelligence Division.
London: HM Stationery Office, 1916-17. 2 vols. 5 maps.

Provides much useful information on the tribes of Arabia and their allegiances at the time of the First World War. Volume 1 is concerned with a physical and social survey of Arabia, and Bahrein is discussed in detail in chapter 9, section C (p. 311-24). Details are given of the archipelago's area, physical characteristics, climate, population, industries and trade, currency, weights and measures, government and administration, recent history and politics, and it concludes with a description of the main islands.

The Country and Its People

35 **The Arab states of the Persian Gulf and south-east Arabia.**
Great Britain. Central Office of Information, Reference Division.
London: HM Stationery Office, 1962. 28p. 3 maps. (R.5322).
This paper includes details of Britain's relationships with the Gulf area and information concerning each of the Arab states forming its littoral. Bahrain is specifically discussed on p. 19-22, with sections on political life, economic life, the oil industry, education, medical services, electricity, development schemes, and municipal and rural affairs.

36 **Gulf Diary.**
Manama: Al Hilal Publishing and Marketing Group, 1980- . annual.
In addition to a 2-days-a-page diary this gives information of relevance to visitors, useful words, a shopping guide, and a guide to each of the countries in the Gulf.

37 **Gulf facts.**
Middle East Forum, vol. 38, no. 7 (July-Sept. 1962), p. 16-30.
A description of the countries of the Gulf in the early 1960s. It notes Bahrain's archaeological heritage, its traditional importance as a centre of the pearl trade, its recent expansion in educational facilities, its oil industry, and the short-lived Higher Executive Committee formed in 1954.

38 **Gulf guide and diary, 1982.**
Saffron Walden, England: Middle East Review Company, 1981.
134p. + diary. map.
In addition to a week-by-week diary this volume includes an introductory section on each country in the Gulf. Bahrain is described on p. 17-30, where details are given on its political organization, geography, population, principal towns, history, oil, industry, agriculture and fishing, infrastructure, banking and finance, hotels, restaurants, transport, and tourist attractions. It also includes a short section on Gulf Arabic.

39 **The Gulf handbook.**
Bath, England: Trade and Travel Publications, 1979. 3rd ed. 772p.
8p. of maps.
A useful guide to the Gulf for business travellers and other visitors. An introductory section on the region as a whole covers general information, essential courtesies in the Gulf, business, desert travelling, health precautions, Islam, and women in the Gulf. Bahrain is discussed in detail on p. 49-107, where information is provided on its geography, climate, plants and wildlife, communications, social background, constitution, history, economy, banking, foreign exchange, oil and gas, industry, infrastructure, agriculture and social services. There is also a guide to Bahrain covering such items as hotels, restaurants, discotheques, bars, transport facilities, leisure, hospitals, banks, ministries, newspapers, churches, and useful addresses. A further section provides details of places outside Manama and Muharraq and a concluding section gives further general information.

40 **Persian Gulf states.**
Rupert Hay. Washington, DC: Middle East Institute, 1959. 160p.
After introductory chapters on geography, historical background, the British
Residency, the shaikhs and their administrations, the people, general economy
and communications, and oil, each of the countries of the Gulf is surveyed in
turn with Bahrain being described in chapter 8. Mention is made of the country's
fresh water supply, agriculture, population, government, oil operations, entrepôt
trade, and economic change.

41 **Al Hilal Guide to Living and Working in Bahrain.**
Manama: Al Hilal Publishing and Marketing Group, 1982-. annual.
c.200p.
A useful guide for businessmen travelling out to Bahrain. Has sections on the
government, history, crafts and industries, oil, economy and trade, geography, the
role of women, Islam and festivals, as well as providing informaion on day-to-day
work and leisure in Bahrain.

42 **Iraq and the Persian Gulf.**
London: Admiralty, Naval Intelligence Division, 1944. 682p.
97 maps. (Geographical Handbook Series, BR 524).
Bahrein is described mainly in chapter 3 on the coasts of the Persian Gulf. Information is given on the islands' geography, geology, agriculture, fishing, archaeology,
transport, demography, industry and trade. It is also discussed in the context of
British foreign relations in the Gulf.

43 **Bahrain: a moden Dilmun.**
Molly Izzard. Manama: Intergraphics, 1982. 128p.
A lavishly illustrated introduction to the state of Bahrain. It is divided into three
sections on the place, the people and the achievement.

44 **Gulf states.**
Robert G. Landen. In: *The Middle East: its governments and
politics.* Edited by Abid A. Al-Marayati. Belmont, California:
Duxbury Press, 1972, p. 295-316.
An account of the historical background, economic and social environment,
political structure, political processes, oil-related problems, foreign policy and
political prospects of the Gulf states.

The Country and Its People

45 **The Gulf emirates: Kuwait-Bahrain-Qatar-United Arab Emirates.**
M. Philippe Lannois. Geneva: Nagel Publishers, 1976. 191p.
13 maps. bibliog. (Nagel's Encyclopedia-Guide).

After a general introduction covering geography, population, history, customs and
traditions, literature and architecture, the traditional economy, and oil, each state
is described in turn. Bahrain's recent history, administration, economy, and social
and intellectual background are discussed on p. 77-88, and there is then a section
on Bahrain for the tourist, covering the town of Manama, the surroundings of
Manama, the island of Bahrain, an archaeological itinerary, the *qanats* (underground water channels), the island of Muharraq, and the other islands. The
volume concludes with sections on practical information, vocabulary, and hotels.

46 **Dunhill guide to living and working in Bahrain.**
Edited by Angela Leslie. Manama: Al Hilal Publishing and
Marketing Group, n.d. 246p. 2 maps.

Provides an introduction to the government, history, crafts and industries, oil,
industrial development, economy and trade, geography, festivals, food and fauna
of Bahrain, in addition to extensive information on day-to-day living covering
such topics as home maintenance, carpentry, supermarkets, jewellery, opticians
and insurance. There are also sections on arriving in the islands, working there,
and leisure activities. Appendixes provide information on Islam and on the
major hotels of Bahrain.

47 **The Persian Gulf: an introduction to its people, politics, and
economics.**
David E. Long. Boulder, Colorado: Westview Press, 1976. 172p.
2 maps. bibliog. (Westview Special Studies on the Middle East).

A general survey of the Gulf concentrating on politics, the significance of oil, and
the relations between the USA and the various states of the region. Bahrain is
discussed individually in the chapters on the land and people (p. 14-15), the
political dynamics of the Gulf states (p. 32-33), the regional politics of the Gulf
(p. 63), and on economic prospects in the Gulf (p. 117-19).

48 **The new Arabians.**
Peter Mansfield. Chicago: Ferguson, 1981. 274p.

An account of the emergence of the 'New Arabians' and their prospects for the
future. Bahrain is discussed mainly in chapter 14, where information is given on
its history, economic development, immigrant labour, government organization,
oil, pearl industry and religious conflicts.

49 **The Middle East and North Africa.**
London: Europa Publications, 1948- . annual.

After an introductory general survey and details of regional organizations, the
countries of the Middle East are described in turn. Annually revised notes on
Bahrain cover its geography, history and economy, and there is also a section on
statistics in addition to a directory of the state.

10

50 **Middle East Annual Review.**
Saffron Walden, England: Middle East Review, 1974- . annual.

After introductory sections on politics, trade, industry, civil engineering and construction, services, and finance in the Middle East, each country is surveyed in turn. The chapter on Bahrain provides information on politics, the economy, development, banking and infrastructure, and some statistics are also given.

51 **The Middle East Yearbook.**
London: IC Magazines, 1977- . annual.

After two introductory sections on politics and society, and economy and business in the Middle East, this publication gives a country-by-country account of the region. The chapter on Bahrain covers general economic change, historical development and current issues, and also provides some statistics.

52 **Two oil sheikhdoms.**
John Midgley. *Geographical Magazine*, vol. 29 (1956), p. 143-48.

A largely pictorial account of the development of Kuwait and Bahrain following the discovery of oil.

53 **A pictorial survey of Bahrain – small nation: big future.**
Claud Morris. *Middle East International*, no. 6 (Sept. 1971),
p. 21-28.

An illustrated account of Bahrain celebrating its entry as the 128th state in the United Nations.

54 **Area handbook for the Persian Gulf states.**
Richard F. Nyrop. Washington, DC: US Government Printing
Office, 1977. 448p. 9 maps. bibliog.

After introductory chapters on the general overview of the societies, the historical setting, religious life, social structure, and the oil industry, each of the Gulf states is then described in turn. For Bahrain (p. 207-37) detailed information is provided on its geography, demography, labour force, living conditions, education, the economy, agriculture and fishing, industry, foreign trade and balance of payments, budget and fiscal policy, money and banking, government and politics, legal system, mass communications system, foreign policy, armed forces and internal security.

55 **Bahrain: a MEED special report.**
Edmund O'Sullivan, edited by John Whelan. *Middle East
Economic Digest*, Sept. 1981. 72p.

An economic report on Bahrain divided into two main sections on the government at work and the private sector. It provides information on the causeway to Saudi Arabia, the Gulf Petrochemicals Industries Company, the Arab Iron and Steel Company, the Gulf University, the Arab Shipbuilding and Repair Yard Company's drydock, Aluminium Bahrain, water and power, Mina Sulman, Gulf Air, and banking. There is a short concluding section on basic data.

56 **Bahrain: a MEED special report.**
   Edmund O'Sullivan, Michael Petrie-Ritchie. *Middle East Economic Digest*, Sept. 1982. 64p.

Provides detailed information on Bahrain's economy, agriculture, oil and gas, industry, aluminium, contracting, services, private sector, infrastructure and leisure. It concludes with a brief section on basic data.

57 **An island survey.**
   D. W. Price. *Royal Engineers Journal*, vol. 56 (Dec. 1942), p. 288-95.

An account of the survey of Bahrain which began with an aerial survey of the island by the Royal Air Force in 1935 and resulted in a ground survey undertaken by the Desert Survey Party during the winter of 1936-37.

58 **Bahrain.**
   Michael Rice & Co. Bahrain: Ministry of Information, n.d. [1971]. 48p.

An introduction to the state of Bahrain published to celebrate the first ten years of the rule of Shaikh Isa bin Sulman Al-Khalifa and Bahrain's independence. It has sections on the ruler, Bahrain today, administration, finance, currency, international trade, industry and the economy, public utilities, security and the armed forces, agriculture, education, public health, local government, Isa Town, communications, sports, cultural life, and archaeology.

59 **Die arabische Halbinsel: Saudi Arabien, Yemen, Südyemen, Kuwait, Bahrain, Qatar, Vereinigte Arabische Emirate, Oman; Reiseführer mit Landeskunde.** (The Arabian Peninsula: Saudi Arabia, Yemen, South Yemen, Kuwait, Bahrain, Qatar, United Arab Emirates, Oman; guidebook with national studies.)
   Wigand Ritter. Buchenhain vor München, GFR: Volk und Heimat, 1978. 278p. 20 maps.

Bahrain is discussed on p. 192-203 of this useful German guide to Arabia. Details are given of its physical environment, history, current economy and social welfare, and the section concludes with some practical advice for visitors.

60 **Arabian Studies.**
   Edited by R. B. Serjeant, R. L. Bidwell. London: C. Hurst; Totowa, New Jersey: Rowman & Littlefield, for the Middle East Centre, University of Cambridge, England, 1974- . annual.

A multi-disciplinary journal covering all aspects of the Arabian peninsula.

61 **A practical guide to living and travel in the Arab world.**
Nancy A. Shilling. Dallas, Texas: Inter-Crescent Publishing, 1978.
295p.

Introductory sections of this guide provide background information on Arab culture and religion, business attitudes, social customs, business customs and courtesies, the Arabic language, professional considerations, the status of women, Islamic law, and other useful advice for the would-be traveller. Bahrain is discussed in detail on p. 95-108, where further information is provided on the country, the people, travel, hotels, restaurants, housing, servants, shopping, education, recreation, health facilities, churches, salaries, costs, female employment, business customs and courtesies, tipping, business hours, holidays in 1978, and useful telephone numbers.

62 **The Middle East.**
Edited by Alice Taylor. Newton Abbot, England: David & Charles in co-operation with the American Geographical Society, 1972.
224p. 23 maps. (Focus Series).

Bahrain is discussed mainly in Alexander Melamid's chapter in this book written to inform young adults in the United States of America about the Middle East.

63 **This is Bahrain.**
Manama: Gulf Public Relations (Bahrain), 1975- . quarterly.

Each issue contains a number of short articles on various aspects of life in Bahrain. In addition there is a useful section on general information, hotels, banks, airlines, cabinet ministers, diplomats and clubs, and there are maps of Manama, Muharraq, and the islands of Bahrain. Circulation 13,000.

64 **Les émirats du golfe Arabe: le Kowëit, Bahrëin, Qatar et les Emirats Arabes Unis.** (The Arab Gulf emirates: Kuwait, Bahrein, Qatar and the United Arab Emirates.)
Jean-Jacques L. Tur. Paris: Presses Universitaires de France, 1976.
125p. 10 maps. bibliog. (Que Sais-je?).

An introduction to the Gulf in French, which includes numerous mentions of Bahrein. It is divided into four main chapters on the geographical and historical background of the region, the revolution brought about by oil, the alternatives offered by diversity and tribalism, and the contrasting options of solidarity and federalism. Bahrein's social and economic changes are described in particular on p. 83-88.

65 The social and economic evolution of Bahrein, Qatar, Muscat and Oman.
John J. Vianney. *Levante*, vol. 15, nos. 1-2 (1968), p. 37-42.

A brief account of the influence of the discovery and exploitation of oil on the societies and economies of Bahrein, Qatar, Muscat and Oman. It notes that Bahrein's traditional economy was based on trade, fishing and pearl diving, and that its retail and wholesale trade was dominated by Iranians and Indians in the 1960s. The importance of its oil refinery, and its new role as a major British base following the evacuation of Aden are also mentioned.

66 Area handbook for Saudi Arabia.
Norman C. Walpole, Alexander J. Bastos, Frederick R. Eisele, Alison Butler Herrick, Howard J. John, Tura K. Wieland. Washington, DC: US Government Printing Office, 1966. 371p. 8 maps. bibliog.

Although specifically on Saudi Arabia, Bahrein is mentioned in connection with boundary disputes, its historic relations with Britain, and oil shipments from Saudi Arabia to Bahrein for refining.

67 The Arabian Year Book 1978.
Edited by Rashid Wazaifi. Kuwait: Dar Al Seyassah Press, 1978. 964p.

This year-book provides general information on each country of Arabia, together with a country-by-country guide to commercial and industrial establishments, a list of world suppliers in the region, and a who's who in the Gulf. General information on Bahrain's government, finance, industry, communications, newspapers, social services and customs regulations, together with an alphabetical list of companies operating in the country, is provided on p. 9-82.

68 Bahrain.
John Whelan. *Middle East Economic Digest,* special report, March 1978. 68p. 2 maps.

Provides details on the following aspects of Bahrain: banking and finance, oil and gas, industry, construction and property, housing, manpower, trade, utilities, the port of Mina Sulman, food, telecommunications, social affairs, expatriate life, doing business, basic data and contracts during 1977. It also has a section on statistics.

69 Bahrain: a MEED practical guide.
Edited by John Whelan. London: Middle East Economic Digest, 1983. 190p. map. bibliog.

A thorough introduction to Bahrain. It is divided into six sections. The first provides general background information; the second gives practical advice on travel to, and accommodation in, Bahrain; the third provides information for expatriates living in the state; the fourth is on the economy; the fifth discusses doing business; and the last is a guide to the main towns and areas of interest in Bahrain.

70 **Bahrain 1980: a MEED special report.**
John Whelan, Simon Procter, edited by Wilfred Ryder.
Middle East Economic Digest, Sept. 1980. 68p.

A review of Bahrain's economy paying particular attention to links with Saudi Arabia, oil, offshore companies, industry, shipping services, air transport, banking, and government spending. It concludes with a section on basic data.

71 **Bahrain: port of pearls and petroleum.**
Maynard Owen Williams. *National Geographic Magazine*, vol. 89, no. 2 (Feb. 1946), p. 195-210.

A description of the economy of Bahrain in the mid-1940s, providing some information on pearling, its freshwater springs, its many burial mounds, and recent economic changes. It includes a number of photographs of the island and its people.

72 **A periplus of the Persian Gulf.**
Arnold Wilson. *Geographical Journal*, vol. 69, no. 3 (March 1927), p. 235-59.

A description of the Gulf based on a variety of secondary sources. It mentions Bahrain's pearl trade, ancient tumuli, and the work of the American missionaries based on the island.

73 **Die Arabische Halbinsel: Länder zwischen Rotem Meer und Persischen Golf.** (The Arabian peninsula: lands between the Red Sea and the Persian Gulf.)
Eberhard Wohlfahrt. Berlin, Frankfurt, Vienna: Ullstein, 1980. 1,276p. bibliog.

After a general introduction on the physical environment, religion, peoples and economy of the Arabian states, each country is surveyed in turn. Details are given of Bahrain's pearling, environment, history, people, oil and economic change. Appendixes include brief historical outlines and statistical surveys of each country.

74 **Bahrain: Middle East Economic Digest special report.**
Marcus Wright. *Middle East Economic Digest*, Sept. 1983. 80p.

A detailed report on the current economic position of Bahrain, with major sections on hydrocarbons, industry and contracting, banking and finance, infrastructure and services, contracts, and basic data. It also includes an interview with the Minister of Finance and National Economy, Ibrahim Abdel-Karim. It notes that Bahrain's oil reserves are expected to be exhausted by 1996, and it investigates the ways in which the government is handling the growing economic crisis.

75 **Arabia: the cradle of Islam. Studies in the geography, people and politics of the peninsula with an account of Islam and mission-work.**
   S. M. Zwemer. New York: Fleming H. Revell, 1900. 2nd rev. ed. 437p. 8 maps. bibliog.

Bahrein is described in chapter 10, on the pearl islands of the Gulf, in this early guide to Arabia. It mentions the physical nature of Bahrein, its springs, the pearl industry which used 900 boats at the end of the 19th century, other aspects of its economy, early archaeological investigations on the island, and its contact with 'western civilization'.

Geography and Geology

76 **The marine terraces of the Bay of Kuwait.**
T. Al-Asfour. In: *The environmental history of the Near and Middle East since the last Ice Age.* Edited by William C. Brice. London, New York, San Francisco: Academic Press, 1978, p. 245-54.
Notes that a minus-3-metre submarine platform has been observed off Bahrain.

77 **Bahrain contract: survey and mapping of the State of Bahrain.**
Fairey Surveys Newsletter, no. 16 (Nov. 1976), p. 1.
Report on the contract signed between Fairey Surveys and the State of Bahrain to carry out photography, geodetic surveys and photogrammetric mapping of the islands.

78 **The Middle East: a geographical study.**
Peter Beaumont, Gerald H. Blake, J. Malcolm Wagstaff. London: John Wiley & Sons, 1976. 572p. 100 maps. bibliog.
Bahrain is mentioned several times in this geographical introduction to the Middle East, mainly in connection with the discovery of oil and the changes that it has brought about. It notes that oil was discovered in 1932, but that Bahrain's real importance is as a refinery centre. It also mentions Bahrain's ship repair yard and aluminium smelter.

79 **The petroleum geology and resources of the Middle East.**
Z. R. Beydoun, H. V. Dunnington. Beaconsfield, England: Scientific Press, 1975. 99p. 5 maps. bibliog.
Provides information on the geomorphic divisions, tectonic framework, stratigraphy, and economic mineral deposits of the Middle East, and also an account of the petroleum resources of the area. It includes many scattered references to Bahrain.

Geography and Geology

80 **South-west Asia.**
William C. Brice. London: University of London Press, 1966.
448p. 72 maps. bibliog. (Systematic Regional Geography, vol. 8).

There are several mentions of Bahrain in this traditional 'regional geography' of the area stretching from Pakistan to Egypt and the USSR to Ethiopia. It is noted mainly in connection with the oil industry, with oil being first tapped commercially in 1932. The traditional economy of its pearl fishing fleet and Iran's claim to the island are also mentioned. Its population in the mid-1960s is estimated at 162,000 on an area of 231 square miles.

81 **Soils of the State of Bahrain.**
E. M. Bridges, C. P. Burnham. *Journal of Soil Science*, vol. 31, no. 4 (Dec. 1980), p. 689-707.

A survey and discussion of the soils of Bahrain, which can be divided into four groups: Solonchaks, Regosols, Yermosols, and Fluvisols. It notes that the Solonchaks of the northern plain contain unprecedented amounts of gypsum which, in the absence of leaching, give rise to a variety of morphological features. The distribution of Regosols, Yermosols and Fluvisols can be related closely to physiographical location throughout the country.

82 **Bahrain Surface Materials Resources Survey.**
Edited by D. Brunsden, J. C. Doornkamp, D. K. C. Jones.
State of Bahrain: Ministry of Works, Power and Water, 1976.
7 vols. text (i.e. vols 1-6, plus vol 4 in 2 parts), 5 vols. maps.

A geological regional memoir forming the final report of the Bahrain Surface Materials Resources Survey. The six volumes of text cover summary and recommendations, introduction, geology, geomorphology and superficial materials, hazards associated with salt weathering in Bahrain, and a reconnaissance survey of soils and land capability for agriculture. This, the most complete account of Bahrain's geology and geomorphology to date, is summarized in *Geology, geomorphology and pedology of Bahrain* (q.v.).

83 **The Bahrain Surface Materials Resource Survey and its application to regional planning.**
Denys Brunsden, John C. Doornkamp, David K. C. Jones.
Geographical Journal, vol. 145, no. 1 (March 1979), p. 1-35.

This paper describes the State of Bahrain, its physical environment, the surface materials resources, environmental degradation, and the hazards for construction. It results from the Bahrain Surface Materials Resource Survey undertaken by the authors between 1974 and 1976 at the request of the (then) Ministry of Development and Engineering Services, Government of Bahrain, and provides much useful material on Bahrain's geology, relief, drainage, geomorphology, soils, land use capability, and areas of salt hazard.

84   Change and development in the Middle East: essays in honour of
      W. B. Fisher.
      Edited by John I. Clarke, Howard Bowen-Jones. London, New
      York: Methuen, 1981. 322p. 26 maps.

A collection of essays by staff and research students of the Department of Geography, University of Durham, as a *Festschrift* in honour of the retiring head of department Professor W. B. Fisher. It concentrates on the changes that have taken place over the last thirty years. The papers by Keith McLachlan, Gerald H. Blake, John I. Clarke, and William J. Donaldson make particular reference to Bahrain.

85   Organisms as producers of carbonate sediment and indicators of
      environment in the southern Persian Gulf.
      M. W. Hughes Clarke, A. J. Keij. In: *The Persian Gulf: Holocene
      carbonate sedimentation and diagenesis in a shallow epicontinental
      sea.* Edited by B. H. Purser. Berlin, Heidelberg, New York:
      Springer-Verlag, 1973, p. 33-56.

A discussion of the principal carbonate-producing and environmentally significant organisms of the Gulf, aimed at facilitating the interpretation of certain fossil assemblages. It notes that planktonic and nectonic animals are scarce, but that benthonic life is abundant. Increasing restriction seems to be clearest where salinities attain 50 grams per litre. Imperforate Foraminifera are the dominant assemblage around Bahrain.

86   An empty quarter.
      R. U. Cooke. London: Bedford College (University of London),
      inaugural lecture, 1976. 20p. 2 maps.

A report on some aspects of research into desert geomorphology. It notes a study of building material disintegration in Bahrain, which resulted in a salt-weathering hazard map of the state.

87   Middle East − review and bibliography of geomorphological
      contributions.
      R. U. Cooke, A. S. Goudie, J. C. Doornkamp. *Quarterly Journal
      of Engineering Geology*, vol. 11 (1978), p. 9-18.

A paper providing engineers with some background information and bibliographic sources to geomorphological studies relating to arid areas, especially the Middle East. Bahrain is seen as being part of a physiographic region of desert plains with limestone inselbergs.

Geography and Geology

88 **Urban geomorphology in drylands.**
R. U. Cooke, D. Brunsden, J. C. Doornkamp, D. K. C. Jones, with contributions by J. Griffiths, P. Knott, R. Potter, R. Russell.
Oxford, England: Oxford University Press on behalf of the United Nations University, 1982. 324p. bibliog.

An analysis of the urban applied geomorphological problems of desert lands. The work undertaken by the authors for the Bahrain Surface Materials Resources Survey is extensively used as an example of the way in which geomorphological research can be used by urban planners.

89 **Routine computation of monthly upper air statistics using an electronic computer.**
D. Dewar. *Metereological Magazine*, no. 1,063, vol. 90 (Feb. 1961), p. 52-58.

Provides details of wind, temperatures and humidity at 100 millibar intervals above Bahrain in October 1958.

90 **Geology, geomorphology and pedology of Bahrain.**
J. C. Doornkamp, D. Brunsden, D. K. C. Jones. Norwich, England: Geo Abstracts, 1980. 443p. 62 maps. bibliog.

A thorough and detailed account of the soil and rock materials found at the surface within the State of Bahrain, arising out of the work of the inter-disciplinary team forming the Bahrain Surface Materials Resources Survey which worked in the country in December 1974 and April 1975. Chapters cover the following aspects of Bahrain: the physical setting, structural and sedimentary setting, stratigraphy, structure, dolomitization and askarization, geological history, Pleistocene and recent setting, rocks, weathering and relief, fluvial geomorphology, aeolian landforms and deposits, relict mantles, the coastal plain and offshore islands, groundwater, pedology, the impact of man on landforms and Quaternary history. Six folded maps illustrate Bahrain's geology, geomorphology and superficial materials, drainage, soils (provisional), land capability for agriculture (provisional), and the geomorphology and superficial materials (provisional) of the Hawar Islands.

91 **Water resources and land use in the Qaṭif oasis of Saudi Arabia.**
Charles H. V. Ebert. *Geographical Review*, vol. 55, no. 4 (Oct. 1965), p. 496-509.

An analysis of the extensive freshwater reserves on the Arabian coastline opposite Bahrayn. It suggests that it takes 18,000 years for water to migrate from its source region in the Jabal Tuwayq to the wells of Al Qaṭif.

92 **Oxford regional economic atlas: the Middle East and North Africa.**
Economist Intelligence Unit with the Cartographic Department of Clarendon Press. Oxford, England: Oxford University Press, 1960. 135p. 64p. of maps. bibliog.

Includes maps on agriculture, oil, industries and communications, in addition to general geographical and geological maps. Bahrain is also mentioned in the section on supplementary notes and statistics with which the volume concludes.

93 **Sediments and water of Persian Gulf.**
K. O. Emery. *Bulletin of the American Association of Petroleum Geologists,* vol. 40, no. 2 (1956), p. 2,354-83.

An evaluation of the findings of a two-week survey of the sediments and water characteristics of the Gulf undertaken in 1948.

94 **Persian Gulf.**
Graham Evans. In: *Encyclopedia of oceanography.* Edited by R. W. Fairbridge. New York: Reinhold Publishing, 1966, p. 689-95.

An account of the dimensions and bathymetry, climate, oceanography, geology, geomorphology, marine geology and sedimentology of the Gulf. It argues that the modern Gulf is a good model for the interpretation and understanding of the older deposits of the Middle East.

95 **The recent sedimentary facies of the Persian Gulf region.**
G. Evans. *Philosophical Transactions of the Royal Society of London,* series A, vol. 259 (1965-66), p. 291-98.

The Gulf is seen as an excellent model for the interpretation of the older sedimentary deposits of the Middle East.

96 **The Middle East: a physical, social and regional geography.**
W. B. Fisher. London: Methuen, 1978. 7th ed. 615p. 142 maps. bibliog.

A thorough introduction to the Middle East divided into three sections on physical geography, social geography and regional geography. Bahrain is mainly mentioned in chapter 16 on the Arabian peninsula, where its long agricultural heritage, its oil developments, urbanization and immigration are briefly discussed.

97 **Soil map of the world 1:5,000,000. Volume VII: South Asia.**
Food and Agriculture Organization of the United Nations. Paris: Unesco, 1977. 117p. 8 maps.

In addition to a soil map and maps of the regional divisions of climate, vegetation, geology, geomorphology and lithology in the Indian subcontinent and Arabian peninsula, this useful volume provides information on environmental conditions, land use and soil capability.

98 **The Nearer East.**
   D. G. Hogarth. London: William Heinemann, 1902. 296p.
   60 maps. (Regions of the World).

An early 'regional geography' covering the eastern Mediterranean, Arabia and
Persia. Bahrein is noted mainly in the context of its importance as a pearl fishery.

99 **Reminiscences of the map of Arabia and the Persian Gulf.**
   F. Fraser Hunter. *Geographical Journal*, vol. 54, no. 6 (Dec.
   1919), p. 355-63.

An account of the compilation of the map to accompany Lorimer's gazetteer
(q.v.). It recounts the story of the 1906 dispute between the shaikhs of Bahrain
and Qatar over a valuable pearl fishery found off Musandam Island.

100 **Géographie d'Edrisi.** (Edrisi's geography.)
   Translated from the Arabic into French by P. Amédée Jaubert.
   Paris: Imprimerie Royale, 1836-40. 2 vols. 3 maps.

This translation of Edrisi's geography, which was originally finished in 1154,
includes several mentions of Bahrein, but mainly just as a point of reference.

101 **The structural and geomorphic evolution of the Persian Gulf.**
   P. Kassler. In: *The Persian Gulf: Holocene carbonate sedimentation and diagenesis in a shallow epicontinental sea.* Edited by
   B. H. Purser. Berlin, Heidelberg, New York: Springer-Verlag,
   1973, p. 11-32.

This paper notes that the Gulf is a tectonic basin of late Pliocene to Pleistocene
age. Pleistocene sedimentation subdued the tectonically controlled morphology,
but was locally rejuvenated by Quaternary adjustments. In the Pleistocene the
sea level fell by 120 metres. The post-glacial Flandrian marine transgression began
about 18,000 years BP.

102 **The Holocene geological history of the Tigris-Euphrates-Karun
   delta.**
   C. E. Larsen, G. Evans. In: *The environmental history of the
   Near and Middle East since the last Ice Age.* Edited by William
   C. Brice. London, New York, San Francisco: Academic Press,
   1978, p. 227-44.

Notes that deposits found 1 metre above the present sea level in Bahrain suggest
that there may have been a higher relative sea level in the region during the
Holocene period.

103 **Mapping Arabia.**
   John Leatherdale, Roy Kennedy. *Geographical Journal*,
   vol. 141, no. 2 (July 1975), p. 240-51.

A study of surveying techniques in the deserts of Arabia with particular reference
to the contributions being made by Hunting Surveys Ltd.

104 **The physical geography of south-eastern Arabia.**
G. M. Lees. *Geographical Journal*, vol. 71, no. 5 (May 1928),
p. 441-70.

Although essentially concerned with south-east Arabia, appendix 1 of this paper
discusses the nature of the water supply of Bahrein, and argues that the ultimate
source of the fresh water to be found on the islands is in the highlands of Nejd.

105 **Recent movements in the Middle East.**
G. M. Lees. *Geologische Rundschau,* vol. 43, no. 1 (1955),
p. 221-26.

Argues that the head of the Persian Gulf is now advancing and that extensive areas
which were under irrigated cultivation until the 13th century AD have since been
inundated. Bahrain is noted on a general map in which its geology is indicated as
being Palaeogene and Mesozoic.

106 **The Middle East: a social geography.**
Stephen H. Longrigg. London: Gerald Duckworth, 1963.
2nd rev. ed., 1970. 291p. 4 maps. bibliog.

In this evaluation of the Middle East Bahrain is noted as having a recent history of
oil development, of good administration but political suppression, and of economic
and social progress – but not of serious constitutional advance, since the Al
Khalifa family declined to share its power.

107 **Distribution and ultrastructure of Holocene ooids in the Persian
Gulf.**
J.-P. Loreau, B. H. Purser. In: *The Persian Gulf: Holocene
carbonate sedimentation and diagenesis in a shallow epicon-
tinental sea.* Edited by B. H. Purser. Berlin, Heidelberg, New
York: Springer-Verlag, 1973, p. 279-328.

This paper notes that most ooids are formed in agitated environments, such as
tidal flats and the tidal bars situated in wide channels between islands like Bahrain
and the mainland. Significant quantities are also being formed within lagoons. The
oolitic tidal bars between Bahrain and the mainland measure up to 10 kilometres
in length and have amplitudes of 5 metres.

108 **Natural resources and development in the Gulf states.**
Keith McLachlan. In: *Social and economic development in the
Arab Gulf.* Edited by Tim Niblock. London: Croom Helm, 1980,
p. 80-94.

A consideration of the dilemma facing the Gulf states – that they are generally
rich in hydrocarbon deposits but poor in most other natural resources. It provides
some statistics relating to Bahrain's population and resources, and it notes that
the country has striven to create new assets, such as its aluminium smelter, and
to reinforce its existing business, entrepôt and service functions.

Geography and Geology

109 The mollusca of the Persian Gulf, Gulf of Oman and Arabian
Sea as evidenced mainly through the collections of Mr. F. W.
Townsend, 1893-1900; with descriptions of new species. Part 1.
James Cosmo Melvill, Robert Standen. *Proceedings of the
Zoological Society of London* (May-Dec. 1901), p. 327-460.
A thorough, if early, catalogue of the species of mollusca to be found in the Gulf.

110 The mollusca of the Persian Gulf, Gulf of Oman, and Arabian
Sea as evidenced mainly through the collections of Mr. F. W.
Townsend, 1893-1906; with descriptions of new species. Part 2:
Pelecypoda.
James Cosmo Melvill, Robert Standen. *Proceedings of the
Zoological Society of London* (May-Dec. 1906), p. 783-848.
A continuation of the previous entry.

111 Die arabischen Länder. (The Arab lands.)
Edited by von Gunter Nötzold. Leipzig, GDR: V. E. B. Hermann
Haack, 1970. 352p. 17 maps. bibliog.
A geographical and historical introduction to the Arab states. Bahrein's geography,
history, economy and industrial structures are discussed on p. 244-47.

112 The geology of the Persian Gulf and the adjoining portions of
Persia and Arabia.
G. E. Pilgrim. *Memoirs of the Geological Survey of India*,
vol. 34, no. 4 (1908), p. 1-177.
A report on the geology of the Gulf based on the author's eight months of field
research in the region from November 1904 to June 1905. The first part is divided
into two chapters on physical factors and geological formations. Part 2 provides
detailed descriptions of each part of the area, with the islands of Bahrain being
described in chapter 5 (p. 112-25). Pilgrim argued that its rocks could be divided
into three divisions: limestones and marls of Eocene age; miliolitic formations,
probably Pleistocene; and Sub-recent sands, coral limestones, and littoral conglom-
erates. The numerous freshwater springs are also noted.

113 The Persian Gulf: Holocene carbonate sedimentation and
diagenesis in a shallow epicontinental sea.
Edited by B. H. Purser. Berlin, Heidelberg, New York: Springer-
Verlag, 1973. 474p. 76 maps. bibliog.
A collection of 22 papers on Holocene sedimentation and diagenesis in the Gulf.

114 The principal environmental factors influencing Holocene sedimentation and diagenesis in the Persian Gulf.
B. H. Purser, E. Seibold. In: *The Persian Gulf: Holocene carbonate sedimentation and diagenesis in a shallow epicontinental sea.* Edited by B. H. Purser. Berlin, Heidelberg, New York: Springer-Verlag, 1973, p. 1-10.
A summary of the physical environment of the Gulf, which is seen as separating the two major geological provinces of the Arabian Foreland and the Iranian Fold. Abnormally high salinities are caused by evaporation and partial isolation from the Indian Ocean. The Gulf has an average depth of 35 metres and a maximum depth of 100 metres near its entrance.

115 Sedimentation around bathymetric highs in the southern Persian Gulf.
B. H. Purser. In: *The Persian Gulf: Holocene carbonate sedimentation and diagenesis in a shallow epicontinental sea.* Edited by B. H. Purser. Berlin, Heidelberg, New York: Springer-Verlag, 1973, p. 157-78.
This paper on bathymetric highs in the Gulf argues that certain shoals, such as Abu Thama and Naiwat Arragie, north of Bahrain, are of sedimentary origin. Most attention, though, is paid to the Gulf east of Qatar.

116 Quaternary period in Saudi Arabia. 1: sedimentological, hydrogeological, hydrochemical, geomorphological, and climatological investigations in central and eastern Saudi Arabia.
Edited by Saad S. Al-Sayari, Josef G. Zötl. Vienna, New York: Springer-Verlag, 1978. 334p. bibliog.
Bahrain is mentioned briefly in the chapters by R. W. Chapman on geology, E. Schyfsma on climate, D. H. Johnson on the geology of the Gulf coastal region, and C. Job, H. Moser, W. Rauert and W. Stichler on the chemistry and isotope content of some wadi groundwater, of this book on the Quaternary in Saudi Arabia.

117 Gazetteer of Arabia: a geographical and tribal history of the Arabian peninsula.
Edited by Sheila A. Scoville. Graz, Austria: Akademische Druck-u. Verlagsanstalt, vol. 1, 1979. 733p.
A very detailed volume based on 'a 1917 British gazetteer' of Arabia. It covers entries from A to E, with Bahrain Island and Bahrain Principality being described on p. 408-49. The completed work will be in four volumes.

118 Marine mollusca from Bahrain Island, Persian Gulf.
Kathleen R. Smythe. *Journal of Conchology*, vol. 27, no. 7 (1972), p. 491-96.
A list of marine mollusca collected in 1971 from thirteen localities in Bahrain.

Geography and Geology

119 **Seashells of the Arabian Gulf.**
Kathleen R. Smythe. London: George Allen & Unwin, 1982.
123p. map. bibliog. (Natural History of the Arabian Gulf).

After a general introduction on the classes of molluscs found in the Gulf and how to collect, clean and store seashells, this well-illustrated guide provides details of all of the seashells to be found in the region.

120 **The Tornatinidae and Retusidae of the Arabian Gulf.**
Kathleen R. Smythe. *Journal of Conchology*, vol. 30 (1979), p. 93-98.

This paper discusses the Tornatinidae and Retusidae of the Arabian Gulf. It notes that *Retusida trunculata* (Brugière) occurs frequently in shell sand in Bahrain, although no record of its occurrence has been published previously.

121 **Holocene sediment types and their distribution in the southern Persian Gulf.**
C. W. Wagner, C. van der Togt. In: *The Persian Gulf: Holocene carbonate sedimentation and diagenesis in a shallow epicontinental sea.* Edited by B. H. Purser. Berlin, Heidelberg, New York: Springer-Verlag, 1973, p. 123-56.

Fourteen major units of the Holocene sediments, twelve of which are mainly carbonate in compositon, are identified on the basis of textures and grain types. The paper notes that towards the centre of the basin of the sea floor there is increased protection from wave action, and that the sediments therefore grade from skeletal, oolitic and pelletoidal sands and fringing reefs, through irregular compound grain sands, into basin centre muds.

122 **Some ideas on winter atmospheric processes over south-west Asia.**
J. M. Walker. *Meteorological Magazine*, no. 1,139, vol. 96 (June 1967), p. 161-67.

A discussion of the weather and climate of south-west Asia in relation to the subtropical jet stream and polar front jet streams over the region.

123 **Geology of the Arabian peninsula – Bahrain.**
R. P. Willis. *U.S. Geological Survey Professional Paper*, 560-E, 1967, p. E1-E4.

This paper on Bahrain's geology notes that the principal outcropping rocks on the main island are of Eocene age, with Miocene and younger rocks on the periphery. It observes that the anticlinal structure is clearly discernible in the rimrock that encircles the central part of Bahrain Island.

An island survey.
See item no. 57.

The geographical part of the 'Nuzhat-al-qulūb' composed by Ḥamd-Allāh
Mustawfī of Qazwīn in 740/1340.
See item no. 150.

Memoir on Bahreyn.
See item no. 777.

Travel and Exploration

124 **L'Arabie contemporaine avec la description du pèlerinage de la Mecque et une nouvelle carte géographique de Kiepart.** (Contemporary Arabia, with a description of the Mecca pilgrimage and a new geographical map by Kiepart.)
Adolphe d'Avril. Paris: E. Maillet & Challamel Ainé, 1868. 313p. map.

A 19th-century French guide to Arabia mentioning British treaty relations with Bahrein and the pearl fisheries to be found there.

125 **The pirate coast.**
Charles Belgrave. London: G. Bell & Sons, 1966. 200p. map. bibliog.

A description of the Gulf states of Arabia based on the diary of Francis Erskine Loch written between 1818 and 1820. There are numerous mentions of Bahrain in connection with Dilmun, Portuguese activity in the area, its pearl fleet, the move there of the British Residency in the Gulf in 1946, and other aspects of its history and economy.

126 **Southern Arabia.**
Theodore Bent, Mrs. Theodore Bent. London: Smith, Elder, 1900. 455p. 6 maps. bibliog.

The account of the Bents' travels in Arabia. The first chapter records their visit to Bahrein in 1889 when they aimed to excavate the numerous ancient mounds there to be found. It provides many insights into the ways of life of the inhabitants of Manamah and Moharek, and in particular it discusses coffee pots, pearling, boats, wells, springs, and the islands' history. Their excavations in which they uncovered 'objects of distinctly Phoenician origin' are discussed in chapter 2, and their visit to Rufa'a is described in chapter 3.

127 **Travels in Assyria, Media, and Persia, including a journey from Bagdad by Mount Zagros, to Hamadan, the ancient Ecbatana, researches in Ispahan and the ruins of Persepolis, and journey from thence by Shiraz and Shapoor to the sea-shore. Description of Bussorah, Bushire, Bahrein, Ormuz, and Muscat, narrative of an expedition against the pirates of the Persian Gulf, with illustrations of the voyage of Nearchus, and passage by the Arabian Sea to Bombay.**
J. S. Buckingham. London: Henry Colburn, 1829. 545p. map.
A fourth volume of the author's travels 'in the eastern World.' It provides a description of Bahrein (p. 452-58) covering such subjects as pearling, fresh water, population and mercantile activity.

128 **Ost-Arabien von Basra bis Maskat auf Grund eigener Reisen.** (East Arabia from Basra to Muscat: my journey by land.)
Von Hermann Burchardt. *Zeitschrift der Gesellschaft für Erdkunde zu Berlin,* 1906, p. 305-22.
The account of the author's journey across eastern Arabia in 1903 and 1904. He anchored off Bahrein on 19 December 1903, and was then entertained by the English Under-Political Agent at the Residence. Some details are provided of the pearl fisheries and other aspects of Bahrein's economy, before he left the islands on 27 December to continue to Hufuf and eventually Muscat.

129 **The voyage of John Huyghen van Linschoten to the east Indies.**
Edited by Arthur Coke Burnell (vol. 1), and P. A. Tiele (vol. 2).
London: Hakluyt Society, 1885. 2 vols. 21 maps.
An account of the voyage of Jan Huygen (Huyghen) van Linschoten, born around 1563 in the province of Utrecht, to the east Indies which began in 1576 and ended in 1592. Barem (Bahrain) is mentioned briefly in both volumes, where it is noted that the Captain of Ormus (Hormuz) has a factor there for the King of Portugal and that the pearls are the best of all those of the east Indies. Mention is also made of the practice of collecting fresh water from the sea bed off the Island of Barein (Bahrain).

130 **In unknown Arabia.**
R. E. Cheeseman. London: Macmillan, 1926. 447p. 3 maps.
The report of the author's journey from Bahrain, through Hufuf, to Jabrin, which began in 1923. It notes Bahrain's pearl industry, the freshwater springs, its tumuli, and some aspects of its history.

131 **The Suma Oriental of Tomé Pires an account of the East, from the Red Sea to Japan, written in Malacca and India 1512-1515 and the book of Francisco Rodrigues rutter of a voyage in the Red Sea, nautical rules, almanack and maps written and drawn in the East Indies before 1515.**
Armando Cortesão. London: Hakluyt Society, 1944. 2 vols. 31 maps. bibliog.

An account of the journey of the first official European embassy to China under the leadership of Tomé Pires, and the collection of 26 contemporary 16th-century maps by Francisco Rodrigues. It includes an English translation and the original Portuguese text. Bahrein is mentioned briefly as belonging to the kingdom of Ormuz and as having the best pearl fishing in the region.

132 **Through Turkish Arabia. A journey from the Mediterranean to Bombay by the Euphrates and Tigris valleys and the Persian Gulf.**
H. Swainson Cowper. London: W. H. Allen, 1894. 490p. 2 maps.

The record of the author's journey from the Mediterranean along the Euphrates and Tigris valleys and through the Gulf beginning in 1891. It mentions Maharak and Bahrein as one of the main pearl fisheries of the Gulf, and it also notes that fresh water was collected in leather bottles from the springs at the bottom of the sea.

133 **The book of Duarte Barbosa – an account of the countries bordering on the Indian Ocean, written in 1518 A.D.**
Translated by Mansel Longworth Dames. London: Hakluyt Society, 1918. 2 vols. 4 maps (2 in each vol.). bibliog.

A treatise on the lands, people and customs of the countries with which the Portuguese had contact around the Indian Ocean, compiled by Duarte Barbosa while he was in the service of the Portuguese government in India from 1500-1516/17. In volume 1 Beroaquem (Bahrain) is mentioned as belonging to the kingdom of Ormus as is Barem (Bahrain) where there are reported to be many merchants involved in the pearl trade.

134 **The Portuguese Asia: or, the History of the discovery and conquest of India by the Portugues; containing all their discoveries from the coast of Africk, to the farthest parts of China and Japan; all their battels by sea and land, sieges and other memorable actions; a description of those countries, and many particulars of the religion, government and customs of the natives, &c. In three tomes.**

Manuel de Faria y Sousa, translated from the Spanish by Cap. John Stevens. London: C. Brome, 1695. 3 vols. bibliog.

An extensive account of the Portuguese in Asia which covers their campaigns in the Gulf area and includes detailed descriptions of Albuquerque's conquest of Ormuz, noting that he captured a ship carrying much pearl from Baharem in 1508/9. It also notes that around 1273 King Malec Caez of Ormuz held all of the land in the region from the Island of Gerum to that of Baharem.

135 **The travels of the Abbé Carré in India and the Near East 1672 to 1674.**

Translated by Lady Fawcett, edited by Sir Charles Fawcett with the assistance of Sir Richard Burn. London: Hakluyt Society, 1947-48. 3 vols. 9 maps (3 in each vol.).

A translation of the journal written by an Abbé Carré, giving a detailed account of his travels in 1672-74 from France to India and back again to France. It provides an interesting account of Portuguese affairs in the Gulf in the latter part of the 17th century (vol. 1, chapters 3 and 4). On both of his journeys through the Gulf, in 1672 and 1674, he sailed along the Persian coast and did not actually visit Bahrain.

136 **A description of the Persian Gulf in 1756.**

Willem M. Floor. *Persica*, vol. 8 (1979), p. 163-86.

A translation of a report written in 1756 by Tido von Kniphausen and Jan van der Hulst for Jacob Mossel, the governor-general of the Dutch East India Company. It mentions the attempt by Sjeek Nassier to conquer Bahrain, and the importance of the islands of Bahrain for pearls.

137 **Narrative of a mission to India and the countries bordering on the Persian Gulf, &c. by way of Egypt and the Red Sea.**

V. Fontanier. London: Richard Bentley, 1844. 416p. map.

An account of Fontanier's mission to India beginning in 1834 in his role as vice-consul of France at Bassora. It notes tribal disputes on the Arabian shore of the Gulf, and mentions one of these in connection with the pearl fishery of Bahrain (p. 152).

Travel and Exploration

138 **A new account of the east Indies by Alexander Hamilton with numerous maps and illustrations.**
Edited by William Foster. London: Argonaut Press, 1930.
2 vols. 10 maps (5 in each vol.). bibliog.
Hamilton's account of his travels and experiences in the East 1688-1723. It was reprinted in 1744, and then republished in this new edition which includes critical notes on the text by the editor. Bareen (Bahrain) is mentioned in volume 1, where the islands are noted as belonging to the Crown of Persia and having the best pearl fishing in the world.

139 **Explorers of Arabia from the Renaissance to the end of the Victorian era.**
Zahra Freeth, H. V. F. Winstone. London: George Allen & Unwin, 1978. 308p. 11 maps. bibliog.
This survey of early exploration in Arabia briefly mentions Palgrave's stay in Bahrain in 1862/3 on the way from Hufuf to Qatar and then the Batina coast.

140 **Arabia phoenix. An account of a visit to Ibn Saud chieftain of the austere Wahhabis and powerful Arabian king.**
Gerald de Gaury. London: George G. Harrap, 1946. 169p. bibliog.
This account of the author's journey in Nejd mentions the fall of Bahrein to the Wahhabis at the beginning of the 19th century, that Abdul Aziz al Qusaibi, a pearl merchant of Bahrein, was used by Ibn Saud to obtain many of the goods that he required, and that the customs of Bahrein are usually more Persian than Arab in character.

141 **The travels of Ibn Baṭṭūta A.D. 1325-1354.**
Translated with revisions and notes from the Arabic text, edited by C. Defrémery and B. R. Sanguinetti, by H. A. R. Gibb. Cambridge, England: Cambridge University Press for the Hakluyt Society, 1960 for 1958; 1962 for 1959; 1971. 3 vols. 6 maps, 5 maps, 3 maps. bibliog.
The narrative of the travels of Muḥammad bin 'Abdallah bin Muḥammad bin Ibrāhīm bin Muḥammad bin Ibrāhīm bin Yusuf of the tribe of Luwāta and the city of Ṭanja, called Ibn Baṭṭūta, in the 14th century AD. Bahrain is principally mentioned in chapter 7, volume 2. Ibn Baṭṭūta notes that the city of al-Bahrain is 'a fine large city with gardens, trees and streams. Water is easy to get at there – one digs with one's hands [in the sand] and there it is. The city has groves of date-palms, pomegranates, and citrons, and cotton is grown there. It is exceedingly hot there and very sandy, and the sand often encroaches on some of its dwellings' (p. 409). The pearl fisheries are also mentioned.

142 **Arabia Felix: the Danish expedition of 1761-1767.**
Thorkild Hansen, translated by James McFarlane, Kathleen
McFarlane. London: Collins, 1964. 381p. 6 maps. bibliog.
The story of the expedition by von Haven, Forsskål, Niebuhr, Kramer and
Baurenfeind to Arabia. Niebuhr's comments on Bahrein are quoted in full, and
state that there was one town and about 50 villages in Bahrein, that the inhabitants
were all Shiites, and that its pearl fishery was still famous.

143 **Ben Kendim: a record of eastern travel.**
Aubrey Herbert, edited by Desmond MacCarthy. London:
Hutchinson, 1924. 380p. 6 maps.
An account of the author's travels in the Middle East in the first decade of the
20th century. It provides a brief summary of Bahrein's history before 1906, and
an account of daily life on the islands at the time of the author's visit in 1905/6.
It notes that both Arabs and Turks were jealous of the British in Bahrein.

144 **A voyage up the Persian Gulf and a journey overland from India
to England in 1817. Containing notices of Arabia Felix, Arabia
Deserta, Persia, Mesopotamia, the Garden of Eden, Babylon,
Bagdad, Koordistan, Armenia, Asia Minor, &c. &c.**
William Heude. London: Longman, Hurst, Rees, Orme & Brown,
1819. 252p.
The account of Heude's journey from Bombay to Scutari which began on 26
October 1816. It notes that Bahrein was only celebrated for its pearl fishery and
for the freshwater springs at the bottom of the sea.

145 **The penetration of Arabia: a record of the development of
western knowledge concerning the Arabian peninsula.**
David George Hogarth. London: Alston Rivers, 1905. 359p.
20 maps.
An account of exploration in Arabia mentioning Palgrave's visit to Bahrein and
the under-sea springs to be found there.

146 **Arabian adventurer. The story of Haji Williamson.**
Stanton Hope. London: Robert Hale, 1951. 335p.
A biography of W. R. Williamson, which mentions Bahrein's pearl trade and early
oil exploration on the island.

33

147 **La Mer Rouge l'Abyssinie et l'Arabie aux XVIe et XVIIe siècles et la cartographie des Portulans du monde oriental.** (The Red Sea, Abyssinia and Arabia in the 16th and 17th centuries and the Portuguese cartography of the oriental world.) Albert Kammerer. Cairo: Société Royale de Géographie d'Egypte, vol. 1, 1947; vol. 2, 1935. bibliog.

This account provides much information on the Gulf during the 16th and 17th centuries. In particular volume 1 provides details of Portuguese conquests in the region following the capture of Ormuz, and of the importance of the pearl fisheries of Bahrein. Volume 2 gives a brief history of Bahrein, and notes the 1821 attack on the islands by Antonio Correa.

148 **The unveiling of Arabia. The story of Arabian travel and discovery.** R. H. Kiernan. London, Bombay, Sydney: George G. Harrap, 1937. 360p. 13 maps. bibliog.

Mentions Palgrave's stay in Bahrein, its pearling industry and its treaty with Britain.

149 **A geographical memoir of the Persian empire, accompanied by a map.** John Macdonald Kinneir. London: John Murray, 1813. 486p. map.

An extensive account and description of the provinces of the Persian empire. Bahrein is mentioned briefly, and is described as being covered with villages and date gardens, with the town and fort of Medina containing eight or nine hundred houses. It notes that near the island of Bahrein is a bank producing the finest pearls in the world.

150 **The geographical part of the *Nuzhat-al-qulūb* composed by Ḥamd-Allāh Mustawfī of Qazwīn in 740/1340.** Translated by G. Le Strange. London: Luzac; Leiden, the Netherlands: E. J. Brill, 1919. 2 vols. (E. J. W. Gibb Memorial Series, vol. 23).

The two volumes provide a Persian text and translation of the *Nuzhat-al-qulūb* (The joy of hearts). It describes Persia and Mesopotamia in the days of Sulṭān Abu Saʿīd the Īl-Khan, the great-grandson of Hūlāgū the conqueror of Baghdād. Baḥrayn is mentioned briefly as being part of Fārs, as producing plenty of dates, and as being important for pearl diving. An anecdote of the poet Ibn Khurdādbih notes that: 'He who lives in Al-Baḥrayn his spleen enlarges, Hence he is envied for what is in his belly: though in fact he goeth hungry.'

151 **A Spaniard in the Portuguese Indies. The narrative of Martín Fernández de Figueroa.**
James B. McKenna. Harvard, Massachusetts: Harvard University Press, 1967. 288p. map. bibliog. (Harvard Studies in Romance Languages, vol. 31).

The narrative of Martín Fernández de Figueroa's travels between 1505 and 1511. It notes that the Bahrain islands are famous for their pearls.

152 **Middle East Travel.**
London: International Communications Publications, 1977- . 10 times a year.

In addition to a variety of feature articles on travel in the Middle East, this publication provides regular coverage on developments in the fields of transport, hotels, tourism, and a world round-up of travel information.

153 **A winter journey through Russia, the Caucasian Alps, and Georgia; thence across Mount Zagros, by the pass of Xenophon and the ten thousand Greeks, into Koordistan.**
R. Mignan. London: Richard Bentley, 1839. 2 vols.

Bahrain is mentioned mainly in chapter 7, volume 2, of this account of Mignan's journey from England to western India which began in 1829. Bahrain's subordination to Ormus, its pearl banks, and its palm groves are mentioned in some detail.

154 **Sultan in Oman.**
James Morris. London: Faber & Faber, 1957. 165p. 2 maps.

The story of the author's journeys in Oman in 1955. It notes that Bahrain was the centre of British administration in the region and briefly mentions the then recent strikes and disturbances there in demand for a national legislature.

155 **Description de l'Arabie d'après les observations et recherches faites dans le pays même.** (Description of Arabia based on observations and research undertaken in the country itself.)
M. [i.e. Mr.] Niebuhr. Copenhagen: Nicolas Möller, 1773. 372p. 25 maps.

Bahrein is mentioned briefly in the section on independent states around the Persian Gulf of Carsten Niebuhr's 18th-century description of Arabia. It notes that Bahrein has had a chequered political history, and that the islands are surrounded by good pearl fisheries.

156 **Description de l'Arabie faite sur des observations propres et des avis recueillis dans les lieux mêmes.** (Description of Arabia made from direct observations and from advice received in the places themselves.)
Carsten Niebuhr. Amsterdam: S. J. Baalde; Utrecht, the Netherlands: J. van Schoonhoven, 1774. 385p.

Bahrein is mentioned briefly as being under the suzerainty of the Shaikh of Abuschähhr in the section on independent states around the Persian Gulf of this translation of Niebuhr's description of Arabia.

157 **Reisebeschreibung nach Arabien und andern umliegenden Ländern.** (Travels in Arabia and other neighbouring countries.)
Carsten Niebuhr. Copenhagen: Nicolaus Möller, 1774. 2 vols.

A German publication of Niebuhr's travels, which briefly mentions Bahrein in volume 2 in connection with its political history and pearling.

158 **Travels through Arabia and other countries in the East.**
M. [i.e. Mr.] Niebuhr, translated into English by Robert Heron. Edinburgh: R. Morison & Son, 1792. 2 vols. Reprinted, Beirut: Librairie du Liban, 1970.

Bahrein is mentioned briefly in section 23, 'Of the independent Arabian states upon the sea-coast of Persia', of this account of Carsten Niebuhr's travels. It notes that the islands, the largest of which was called *Aual* by the Arabs, were famous for pearl fishing and produced an abundance of dates. Bahrein's turbulent political history is also mentioned. Volume 1 omits the last three sections of the original first volume, and volume 2 in in fact a translation of Niebuhr's *Description of Arabia* not the second volume of his *Travels*.

159 **Voyage en Arabie et en d'autres pays circonvoisins.** (Journey in Arabia and other neighbouring countries.)
C. Niebuhr. Amsterdam: S. J. Baalde; Utrecht, the Netherlands: J. van Schoonhoven, 1776, vol. 1; Amsterdam: S. J. Baalde; Utrecht: Barthelemy Wild, 1780, vol. 2.

Bahrein is mentioned briefly as being under the jurisdiction of the Shaikh of Abuschähhr in vol. 2, p. 75, of this French translation of Niebuhr's travels.

160 The voyages and travels of the ambassadors sent by Frederick Duke of Holstein to the Great Duke of Muscovy, and the King of Persia, begun in the year M.DC.XXXIII. and finish'd in M.DC.XXXIX. Containing a compleat history of Muscovy, Tartary, Persia, and other adjacent countries, with several publick transactions reaching neer the present times; in VII books. Whereto are added the travels of John Albert de Mandelslo, (a Gentleman belonging to the Embassy) from Persia, into the East Indies. Containing a particular description of Indosthan, the Mogul's Empire, the Oriental Islands, Japan, China &c. and the revolutions which happened in those countries, within these few years; in III books.
Adam Olearius, faithfully rendered into English by John Davies of Kidwelly. London: Thomas Dring & John Starkey, 1662. 424p., 287p. (in 1 vol.). 6 maps.

The fascinating 17th-century account of the travels of the Duke of Holstein's ambassadors to Muscovy and Persia. Olearius' accompanying map of Persia notes an area on the north coast of the Arabian peninsula known as Bacherin. Mandelslo's travels dating from 1638-40 describe the manner of fishing for pearls off the island of Bahram, and also note the Portuguese domination of Ormus and the Gulf. Christoph. Bathurst's map accompanying Mandelslo's travels shows the island of Bahram prominently in a central position in the southern Gulf.

161 The golden bubble: Arabian Gulf documentary.
Roderic Owen. London: Collins, 1957. 255p. map.

The story of the author's travels in the Gulf. Bahrain is described in chapters 4, 5, 8, 10, 18 and 19, and appendix 2. These provide details of the way of life on the island in the 1950s, when the author for a time lived in the old town of Muharraq and witnessed the unrest and strikes that then took place.

162 Narrative of a year's journey through central and eastern Arabia (1862-63).
William Gifford Palgrave. London, Cambridge: Macmillan, 1865. 2 vols. Reprinted, Farnborough, England: Gregg International, 1969.

Baḥreyn is described in chapter 14 of this account of Palgrave's journey in Arabia. Detailed descriptions are given of Moḥarrek and Menāmah, their inhabitants and their economy. It includes several vignettes of daily life in Baḥreyn during the mid-19th century.

Travel and Exploration

163 **Travels in Asia and Africa; including a journey from Scanderoon to Aleppo, and over the desert to Bagdad and Bussora; a voyage from Bussora to Bombay, and along the western coast of India; a voyage from Bombay to Mocha and Suez in the Red Sea; and a journey from Suez to Cairo and Rosetta in Egypt.**
Abraham Parsons. London: Longman, Hurst, Rees & Orme, 1808. 346p.

An account of the author's travels following his resignation in 1773 as Consul and Factor-Marine at Scanderoon in Turkey. Baharin (Bahrain) is described in chapter 10 where prominence is given to its role as the 'most valuable pearl fishery in the known world'.

164 **Across Arabia: from the Persian Gulf to the Red Sea.**
H. St. J. B. Philby. *Geographical Journal*, vol. 56, no. 6 (Dec. 1920), p. 446-68.

An account of the author's journey from Uqair on the Persian Gulf to Jidda on the Red Sea. It includes a mention of Sir Thomas Holdich's suggestion that the stone circles found by the author in the provinces of Kharj and Aflaj were remarkably similar to those excavated on the island of Bahrain. The discussion includes a comment by Hogarth that the evidence for calling the Bahrain mounds Phoenician is worth practically nothing.

165 **The Empty Quarter, being a description of the great South Desert of Arabia known as Rub' al Khali.**
H. St. J. B. Philby. London: Constable, 1933. 433p. 3 maps.

An account of the author's wanderings and findings in the Rub' al Khali in 1932. It includes a few references to Bahrain.

166 **The heart of Arabia: a record of travel & exploration.**
H. St. J. B. Philby. London, Bombay, Sydney: Constable, 1922. 2 vols. 2 maps.

The account of the journeys of the author in Arabia in 1917 and 1918. It includes many mentions of Bahrain, which was the point of his departure and which he described as the last outpost of civilization.

167 **Around the coasts of Arabia.**
Ameen Rihani. London: Constable, 1930. 364p.

An account of the author's journeys around the coasts of Arabia in which Bahrain is described on p. 256-304. Details are given of the country's history, economy, wars with Qatar, and relations with Britain.

168 **The travels of Pedro Teixeira with his 'Kings of Harmuz' and extracts from his 'Kings of Persia'.**
Translated and annotated by William F. Sinclair, with notes and an introduction by Donald Ferguson. London: Hakluyt Society, 2nd series, vol. 9 (1902). Reprinted, Nendeln, Liechtenstein: Kraus Reprint, 1967. cvii, 292p.

An introduction to, and translation of, the travels of Pedro Teixeira from India to Italy between 1600 and 1605. Barhen (Bahrain) is mentioned briefly in the main text, but in the appendix on the origin of the kingdom of Harmuz there is a detailed description of the island and its pearl fisheries (p. 173-77). Teixeira estimated that the known value of the yearly trade of the island in pearls was 500,000 ducats, and that the 'farm' of the land was worth more than 4,000 ducats a year to the Captain of Harmuz.

169 **Arabian sands.**
Wilfred Thesiger. London: Longman, 1959. 326p. 9 maps.

An account of the author's journeys in Abyssinia and his crossings of the Empty Quarter. It includes a description of his journey by dhow from Dibai (Dubai) to Bahrain.

170 **Desert, marsh and mountain. The world of the nomad.**
Wilfred Thesiger. London: Collins, 1979. 304p. 10 maps.

A description of the author's travels in Africa and Asia, well illustrated by his own photographs. It is divided into sections on his life prior to 1945, the deserts of the Arabian peninsula 1945-50, Persia and Kurdistan, the marshes of southern Iraq 1950-58, the mountains of Pakistan and Afghanistan, and the Yemen 1966-68. It concludes with the author's thoughts on the changes that have taken place over the last twenty years and how, through the discovery and exploitation of oil, the life of the Bedu has now disappeared from Arabia. Bahrain is briefly mentioned in the context of his journey by boom from Dubai in May 1949.

171 **Arabia Felix: across the Empty Quarter of Arabia.**
Bertram Thomas. London: Jonathan Cape, 1932. 397p. 3 maps.

This account of Thomas's crossing of the Empty Quarter briefly mentions Bahrain, noting that the name means 'two seas' in Arabic, and that the islands today known as Bahrain were in early times known as Awal.

172 **Travel in the Arab world: a special report.**
The Times (London), 1 Dec. 1982, p. I-IV.

A report on travel throughout the Arab world. The section on the Gulf mentions that Bahrain has a much more cosmopolitan and relaxed atmosphere than most of its neighbours, and that the Dilmun archaeological finds, its good facilities, and minimal restrictions make it an attractive tourist location.

Travel and Exploration

173 **Bahrain and the Persian Gulf.**
Maureen Tweedy. Ipswich, England: East Anglian Magazine, 1952. 80p. 3 maps. bibliog.

A travelogue of the Gulf as it was in the early 1950s, including several interesting contemporary photographs. Bahrain is discussed in chapter 2, where information is provided on its history during the Portuguese occupation, Persian rule, the reconquest by Arabs, slavery, purdah, education, water, oil, amenities, clothes and climate, and the ruler.

174 **Sons of Sindbad.**
Alan Villiers. London: Hodder & Stoughton, 1940. 346p. 2 maps.

The story of the author's voyages in Arab ships between Basra and Zanzibar. Bahrein is mentioned mainly in chapter 19 on the Gulf pearlers.

175 **The business traveller's handbook: vol. 4. The Middle East.**
Edited by Jane Walker. London: Michael Joseph, 1981. 286p.

After introductory sections on Muslim social customs and health information, each country is surveyed in turn. Information on Bahrain (p. 33-43) is divided into sections on geography, the economy, how to get there, entry regulations, practical information for the visitor, useful addresses, business information, business services, and Manama.

176 **Travels to the city of the Caliphs along the shores of the Persian Gulf and the Mediterranean including a voyage to the coast of Arabia and a tour on the island of Socotra.**
James Raymond Wellsted. London: Henry Colburn, 1840. Reprinted, Farnborough, England: Gregg International, 1968. 2 vols. map.

An account of the Gulf based on the travels of Lieutenant Ormsby of the Indian navy in the 1830s and the author's own knowledge of the area. It provides information on the practice of fishing for pearls in Bahrain, and notes that fresh water is found beneath the sea.

From Oqair to the ruins of Salwa.
See item no. 182.

The countries and tribes of the Persian Gulf.
See item no. 357.

Away to Eden.
See item no. 366.

Arabia through the looking glass.
See item no. 433.

Gulf Travel Trade.
See item no. 867.

Gulf Traveller.
See item no. 868.

Flora and Fauna

177 **The fishes of the Adhari Pool.**
Gerald R. Allen. *Tropical Fish Hobbyist*, vol. 26 (March 1978),
p. 89-94.

A description of fishes seen on a dive in the local freshwater spring in Bahrain
known as the Adhari Pool.

178 **Al-Areen wildlife park and reserve.**
Bahrain: Al-Areen Wildlife Park and Reserve, n.d. 22p. map.

A description of the establishment and wildlife contents of the Al-Areen wildlife
park located in the south-west of Bahrain. In addition to the traditional wildlife
of Bahrain animals from East Africa have also been introduced to Al-Areen.

179 **Biotopes of the western Arabian Gulf. Marine life and environ-
ments of Saudi Arabia.**
Phillip W. Basson, John E. Burchard Jr., John T. Hardy, Andrew
R. G. Price. Dhahran, Saudi Arabia: Aramco Department of
Loss Prevention and Environmental Affairs, 1977. 284p. bibliog.

Provides a well-illustrated handbook of the biotopes of the western Gulf. It notes
that extensive grassbeds exist in the shallows between al-Khobar and Bahrain, that
a shrimp breeding ground lies to the east of Bahrain Island, and that the logger-
head turtle *Caretta caretta* has been recorded from Bahrain.

180 **A check-list of the birds of the Arabian Gulf states.**
Graham Bundy, Effie Warr. *Sandgrouse*, no. 1 (1980), p. 4-49.

Provides some geographical notes and details of the ornithological history of the
Gulf in addition to an extensive systematic check-list of the birds to be seen in the
region.

181 **Coral fauna of the western Arabian Gulf.**
John E. Burchard. Dhahran, Saudi Arabia: Arabian American
Oil Company, Environmental Affairs Division, 1979. 129p. map.
bibliog.

Presents some of the results on marine biology of Aramco's environmental
activity. It provides a classification of coral in the western Gulf, including the sea
around Bahrain.

Flora and Fauna

182 **From Oqair to the ruins of Salwa.**
R. E. Cheeseman. *Geographical Journal*, vol. 62, no. 5
(Nov. 1923), p. 321-35.

The report of the author's visit to parts of the Gulf in 1921 in order to investigate
the movements of migratory birds. It includes a description of Bahrain, covering
its pearl and mother-of-pearl industries, its bazaar, Sheikh Isa's residence in
Maharraq Island, the freshwater springs, the ancient tumuli, and the volcanic hill
called Jabal Dukhan.

183 **Fossil mollusca from southern Persia (Iran) and Bahrein Island.**
L. R. Cox. *Memoirs of the Geological Survey of India, Palaeon-
tologia Indica*, new series, vol. 22, no. 2 (1936), 69p. + 8 plates.

An account of the molluscan fossils of southern Persia and Bahrein obtained by
officers of the Geological Survey of India between 1900 and 1930. Sixty-nine
species are described.

184 **Handbook of the birds of Europe, the Middle East and North
Africa: the birds of the western Palearctic. Volume 1: ostrich
to ducks.**
Chief editor Stanley Cramp. Oxford, London, New York:
Oxford University Press, 1977. 722p. 175 maps. bibliog.

The definitive handbook providing information on field characteristics, habitat,
distribution, population, movements, food, social patterns and behaviour, voice,
breeding, plumage, moults, and measurements of birds in the western Palearctic.
This region only includes territory as far east as Kuwait, but in view of the
limited amount of information available on the birds of Bahrain it provides a
useful guide to the avifauna of the region.

185 **Handbook of the birds of Europe, the Middle East and North
Africa: the birds of the western Palearctic. Volume 2: hawks
to bustards.**
Chief editor Stanley Cramp. Oxford, London, New York:
Oxford University Press, 1980. 695p. 155 maps. bibliog.

See above for details.

186 **Handbook of the birds of Europe, the Middle East and North
Africa: the birds of the western Palearctic. Volume 3: waders
to gulls.**
Chief editor Stanley Cramp. Oxford, London, New York:
Oxford University Press, 1983. 913p. 150 maps. bibliog.

See above for details.

187 The wild flowers of Kuwait and Bahrain.
Violet Dickson. London: George Allen & Unwin, 1955. 144p.
6 maps.

An illustrated guide to the flora of Kuwait, north-east Arabia, Dubai and Bahrain.
It includes a list of Bahrain's vascular plants by Ronald Good, and a list of marine
algae by Linda M. Newton.

188 The amphibians and reptiles of Bahrain.
Michael D. Gallagher. Bahrain: Oriental Press, 1971. 40p.
bibliog.

A description of all of the amphibians and reptiles seen and verified by the author
in Bahrain between 1969 and 1971. In 1968 only three species of lizard had been
recorded for Bahrain. This list adds eleven more lizard species, and records the
worm-lizard and four species of terrestrial snake. It is divided into sections on true
frogs, true toads, tortoises, turtles, lizards, amphisbaenians and snakes.

189 The dugong *Dugong dugon* (Sirenia) at Bahrain, Persian (Arabian)
Gulf.
M. D. Gallagher. *Journal of the Bombay Natural History
Society*, vol. 73 (1975), p. 211-12.

A report on sightings of the *Dugong dugon*, known in Bahrain as *baqarat al bahr*
(sea cow).

190 A guide to the birds of Bahrain.
Michael D. Gallagher, M. J. Strickland. Muharraq, Bahrain:
RAOC Press, 1969. 53p. map. bibliog.

A guide to what birds may be seen when and where in Bahrain. It also provides
some information on climate, migration, habitats and locations of interest to bird
watchers.

191 On the breeding birds of Bahrain.
M. D. Gallagher, T. D. Rogers. *Bonner Zoologische Beitrage*,
vol. 29 (1978), p. 5-17.

This useful report provides details of the 23 species of bird proved to breed in
Bahrain. It also includes a section on earlier ornithological studies of the islands.

192 The terrestrial mammals of Bahrain.
Michael D. Gallagher, David L. Harrison. *Journal of the Bombay
Natural History Society*, vol. 72, no. 2 (1975), p. 407-21.

A summary of 13 species of terrestrial mammal which occur in Bahrain, based
upon the identification by Harrison of specimens collected by Gallagher. It
includes a brief geographical survey of the island and notes on threats to wildlife
and conservation. The species identified are: Ethiopian hedgehog, house shrew,
naked-bellied tomb bat, trident bat, Kuhl's pipistrelle, common mongoose, Rhim
gazelle, Bahrain hare, lesser three-toed jerboa, black rat, brown rat, Sundevall's
jird, and wild cat.

Flora and Fauna

193 Mosquito notes: 1, a small collection from Bahrain Island, Persian Gulf.
G. M. Giles. *Journal of Tropical Medicine and Hygiene* (London), vol. 9 (1906), p. 130-32.
An account of ten specimens of mosquito from Bahrain.

194 The Bahrain islands and their desert flora.
R. D'O. Good. In: *Biology of deserts*. Edited by J. L. Cloudsley-Thompson. London: Institute of Biology, 1954, p. 45-55.
An account of Bahrain's climate, structure and physiography, and desert vegetation.

195 Crepuscular behaviour of wintering night herons at Bahrain.
W. A. C. Griffiths. *The Adjutant*, vol. 7 (1974), p. 14-21.
Provides information on the behaviour of night herons in Bahrain. It notes that the time the night herons land to feed at the feeding area after dusk in their winter quarters is primarily governed by the position of the sun below the horizon and that it could be a delayed reaction to a stimulus exerted on the bird by the setting sun.

196 Bahrain in winter and spring.
T. Hallam. *The Adjutant*, vol. 8 (1975/76), p. 9-16.
A description of the birds to be seen between November and May in Bahrain.

197 Wildlife in Bahrain.
Edited by T. J. Hallam, D. M. Herdson, illustrated by J. A. Downes. Bahrain: Bahrain Natural History Society, 1978. 67p. 2 maps. bibliog.
This short booklet provides a classified list of birds to be seen in Bahrain and the Hawar Islands, together with details of shore life and the Al-Areen wildlife sanctuary.

198 Wildlife in Bahrain: Bahrain Natural History Society annual reports from 1978-1979.
Edited by T. J. Hallam. Bahrain: Bahrain Natural History Society, 1980. 112p. 3 maps. bibliog.
A useful introduction to Bahrain's wildlife. It includes the following articles: 'Monthly summaries', T. J. Hallam; 'Checklist of the birds of Bahrain together with notes on species recorded during 1978 and 1979', M. Holmden and E. Hammonds; 'Some butterflies and moths of Bahrain', N. Carling; 'Al-Areen wildlife park and reserve', F. A. Izzedin; 'An introduction to the vegetation of Bahrain', K. J. Virgo; and 'Bibliography of publications relevant to the natural history of Bahrain', T. J. Hallam and D. M. Herdson.

199 **The mammals of Arabia.**
David L. Harrison. London: Ernest Benn, vol. 1, 1964; vol. 2,
1968; vol. 3, 1972. bibliog.
A comprehensive account of the mammals of Arabia. Volume 1 describes the
Insectivora (insectivores), Chiroptera (bats), and primates; volume 2 the Carnivora
(carnivores), Felidae (cats), Hyracoidea (hyraxes), and Artodactyla (even-toed
ungulates); and volume 3 the Lagomorpha (lagomorphs) and Rodentia (rodents).
For each species the following information is given: type locality, diagnosis,
external characters, cranial characters, dentition, type specimen, measurements,
distribution in the Arabian peninsula, general distribution and remarks.

200 **Mammals of the Arabian Gulf.**
David L. Harrison. London: George Allen & Unwin, 1981. 92p.
map. (Natural History of the Arabian Gulf).
A guide to the mammals of the Gulf, designed for the interested layman. Fifty
species are noted in detail as being known to occur in the Gulf, and several others
found in neighbouring parts of the Arabian peninsula are also described briefly.

201 **Birds of the Arabian Gulf.**
Michael C. Jennings. London: George Allen & Unwin, 1981.
167p. map. bibliog. (Natural History of the Arabian Gulf).
This introduction to Gulf ornithology begins with a discussion of migration
patterns and conservation issues in the region. This is followed by information on
the best places in which to observe birds in the Gulf area. The 92 species which
are known to breed in the region are then described in detail. It concludes with
a check-list of all of the birds that have been seen in recent years in the Gulf.

202 **The birds of Saudi Arabia.**
Michael C. Jennings. Whittlesford, England: M. C. Jennings,
1981. 112p. 121 maps. bibliog.
Includes a few scattered references to bird sightings in Bahrain.

203 **Sea birds of the Persian Gulf.**
Bernt Løppenthin. *Proceedings of the 10th Ornithological
Congress* (1951), p. 603-10.
A list of the seabirds observed and collected by the author in the Gulf between
17 December 1937 and 28 April 1938.

204 **Birds of Arabia.**
R. Meinertzhagen. Edinburgh: Oliver & Boyd, 1954. 624p.
35 maps. bibliog.
The first major book on the birds of Arabia. Four introductory chapters discuss
the following subjects: the geology, geography and climate, with a note on birds
and seed distribution; desert coloration; distribution and migration; systematics
and nomenclature. These are followed by a systematic list of Arabian birds.

205 **Inshore fishes of the Arabian Gulf.**
Kenneth Relyea. London: George Allen & Unwin, 1981. 149p.
map. bibliog. (Natural History of the Arabian Gulf).

This guide provides information and drawings or photographs of the fishes of inshore shallow waters of the Arabian Gulf. It also gives biological and habitat information where possible. There are indexes to both the scientific and the common names of the species.

206 **Birds of Bahrain: a provisional annotated list.**
T. D. Rogers, M. D. Gallagher. Privately circulated typescript,
1973. 37p. map.

Provides a systematic list of birds seen in Bahrain, together with some information on the habitats, climate and ornithological history of the islands. It is an updated version of *A guide to the birds of Bahrain* (q.v.), and is available through the Bahrain Natural History Society.

207 **Inland birds of Saudi Arabia.**
Jill Silsby. London: IMMEL Publishing, 1980. 160p. 2 maps.
bibliog.

This book describes and illustrates with photographs most of the birds to be found in the Arabian peninsula. Each bird is described in detail giving special attention to any distinguishing characteristic or mannerism which makes the bird readily identifiable; its habitat and status are also specified. There are several scattered references to Bahrain.

208 **The vegetation of central and eastern Arabia.**
Desmond Foster Vesey-Fitzgerald. *Journal of Ecology*, vol. 45,
no. 3 (1957), p. 779-98.

An account of the rainfall and vegetation cover of central and eastern Arabia, including the Gulf. Bahrain's vegetation is classified as consisting of coastal salt-bush associations.

209 **Common sea fishes of the Arabian Gulf and Gulf of Oman.**
A. E. White, M. A. Barwani. Dubai: Trucial States Council,
1971. 166p. 2 maps.

An illustrated list of fish caught during a fisheries survey and also found in local fishermen's catches. It does not include small reef-inhabiting fishes. Although relating directly to the eastern Arabian Gulf and the Gulf of Oman it provides a useful list of fish likely to be found in the waters around Bahrain.

210 **Over the Arabian Gulf: a view of birds and places.**
Text by Desmond E. Widgery, paintings by De Mont. Hamilton,
New Zealand: De Mont Publications, 1982. unpaged. bibliog.

A folio of paintings of 40 birds found in the Gulf, each with a short piece of explanatory text. It illustrates many of the birds found in Bahrain.

211 **The lepidoptera of Bahrain.**
E. P. Wiltshire. *Journal of the Bombay Natural History Society,*
vol. 61, no. 1 (1964), p. 119-41.

An introduction to the lepidoptera of Bahrain, giving a list of the 93 species
identified there by the author. It also includes notes on the physical features and
biotopes (vegetation) of Bahrain, together with a geographical analysis of the
ranges of the island's lepidoptera.

212 **Geobotanical foundations of the Middle East.**
Michael Zohary. Stuttgart: Gustav Fischer Verlag; Amsterdam:
Swets & Zeitlinger, 1973. 2 vols. 7 maps. bibliog.

A thorough introduction to the flora, vegetation and plant geography of the
Middle Eastern countries.

**The mollusca of the Persian Gulf, Gulf of Oman and Arabian Sea
as evidenced mainly through the collections of Mr. F. W. Townsend,
1893-1900; with descriptions of new species. Part 1.**
See item no. 109.

**The mollusca of the Persian Gulf, Gulf of Oman, and Arabian Sea
as evidenced mainly through the collections of Mr. F. W. Townsend,
1893-1906; with descriptions of new species. Part 2: Pelecypoda.**
See item no. 110.

Marine mollusca from Bahrain Island, Persian Gulf.
See item no. 118.

Seashells of the Arabian Gulf.
See item no. 119.

The Tornatinidae and Retusidae of the Arabian Gulf.
See item no. 120.

Falconry in Arabia.
See item no. 865.

The Amiri Arabian stud of Bahrain.
See item no. 869.

**A bibliography of the avifauna of the Arabian peninsula, the Levant
and Mesapotamia.**
See item no. 890.

Prehistory and Archaeology

213 A Babylonian geographical treatise on Sargon of Akkad's
     empire.
     W. F. Albright. *Journal of the American Oriental Society*,
     vol. 45 (1925), p. 193-245.
A discussion of the cuneiform geographical text published by Schroeder as no. 92
of his *Keilschrifttexte aus Assur verschiedenen Inhalts* (Leipzig, 1920). It argues
that the identification of the Babylonian Tilmun with the largest island of the
Bahrein group, formerly called Uwāl, seems to be quite certain.

214 »Der skal ikke lades sten på sten tilbage«. (The building by the
     Barbar temple)
     Harald Anderson. *Kuml* (1956), p. 175-88. In Danish with
     English summary.
An account of the excavation of the small tell by the temple at Barbar in the
spring of 1956. This building was destroyed suddenly, and the author argues that
this was the result of some enemy action.

215 **Antiquities of Bahrain.**
     Bahrain Historical and Archaeological Society with the
     Antiquities Division of the Bahrain Education Department.
     Bahrain: Oriental Press, 1971. 23p. in English, 23p. in Arabic.
     map.
Gives an account of the following sites and antiquities: Bronze Age tumuli, the
giant tumuli of Aali, Ain Umm al Sujur, the temples at Barbar, the Seleucid grave
sites, the 'Portuguese' fort at Qala'at al Bahrain, the Suq al Khamis and Rafi'a
mosques, Bilaad al Qadim, the *qanats* (underground irrigation channels), the south
of the island, the museum and legend of Dilmun, and the discovery of ancient
graves at Al-Hajjar.

216 **The ancient Indian style seals from Bahrain.**
Geoffrey Bibby, D. H. Gordon, Mortimer Wheeler. *Antiquity*,
no. 128, vol. 32 (Dec. 1958), p. 243-46.

A discussion of the five seals found in Bahrain, which Bibby argues are similar to those of the Indus Valley civilization. Gordon suggests that they should not be used to date the burial mounds on Bahrain. Wheeler cautiously considers that a safe estimate of the date of the seals would be around 2000 BC.

217 **Arabiens arkæologi.** (Arabian Gulf archaeology.)
Geoffrey Bibby. *Kuml* (1964), p. 86-111. In Danish with
English summary.

The reports of the eighth (1961-62) and ninth (1962-63) Danish Archaeological Expeditions to the Gulf, operating in Bahrain, Qatar, Kuwait and Abu Dhabi. In Bahrain in 1961-62 attention was again focused on the temple complex at Barbar and the city mound at Qala'at al-Bahrain, and new investigations were made of two of the large burial mounds south of the village of Ali. In 1962-63 work was concentrated on the tell at Qala'at al-Bahrain and the tumulus field south of Ali.

218 **Arabiens arkæologi.** (Arabian Gulf archaeology.)
Geoffrey Bibby. *Kuml* (1965), p. 133-52. In Danish with
English summary.

The report of the tenth campaign of the Danish Archaeological Expedition to Arabia in 1964. This included the initiation of a two-year programme on the city mound at Qala'at al-Bahrain, where the area investigation was extended eastwards to disclose an Islamic building level, part of the palace building, and two clay benches with associated pottery vessels which were possibly associated with the smelting of metal. In addition the paper reports on the excavations undertaken on the northern fortification wall, and a 'wild-cat' dig in the centre of the depression between the two halves of the tell which revealed Islamic building levels.

219 **Arabiens arkæologi.** (Arabian Gulf archaeology.)
Geoffrey Bibby. *Kuml* (1966), p. 75-96. In Danish with English
summary.

The report of the eleventh campaign of the Danish Archaeological expedition to the Arabian Gulf in 1965. Work was confined to Bahrain and Abu Dhabi, and in Bahrain most attention was again paid to the tell at Qala'at al-Bahrain. A small burial mound was also investigated.

Prehistory and Archaeology

220 **Bahrains oldtidshovedstad gennem 4000 år.** (The hundred-meter section.)
T. G. Bibby. *Kuml* (1957), p. 128-63. In Danish with English summary.

An account of the trench excavated at Ras al-Qala'a, which is divided into sections on the 'chain-ridge' period 2459-2304 BC, the 'Barbar' period 2303-2108 BC, the 'caramel-ware' period 1894-1165 BC, the 'glazed-bowl' period 500-0 BC, the 'Islamic-palace' period 900-1000 AD, and the Portuguese period 1500-1650 AD. It provides a chronology of the occupation of Qala'a city from its earliest occupation to the end of the Portuguese era.

221 **».. . efter Dilmun norm«.** ('. . . according to the standard of Dilmun'.)
T. Geoffrey Bibby. *Kuml* (1970), p. 345-54. In Danish with English summary.

A paper on the implications of the six stone weights found at Bahrain, which the author equates with Dilmun. These weights agree completely with the system of weights found in the cities of the Harappa civilization, and this suggests that the 'Early Dilmun' culture of Bahrain used the same system as did the Harappan culture.

222 **Fem af Bahrains hundrede tusinde gravhøje.** (Five among Bahrain's hundred thousand grave mounds.)
T. G. Bibby. *Kuml* (1954), p. 116-41. In Danish with English summary.

An account of the excavation in 1953 of five of Bahrain's tumuli.

223 **Looking for Dilmun.**
Geoffrey Bibby. London: Collins, 1970; Harmondsworth, England: Pelican, 1972. 410p. 9 maps. bibliog.

An account of the archaeological work undertaken by the Danish Archaeological Expeditions in Arabia between 1953 and 1965, in search of the ancient civilization of Dilmun. It provides many details of the discovery of Bahrain's prehistory, including the excavations of the burial mounds and the tell at Qala'at al-Bahrain.

224 **Tyrebrønden.** (The well of the bulls.)
T. G. Bibby. *Kuml* (1954), p. 154-63. In Danish with English summary.

Provides details of the investigation of the old well, known locally as Ain Umm es-Sujur, near the village of Diraz. At the commencement of the Islamic era it was the largest of the three most important wells on the island.

225 **The history and archaeology of the Gulf from the 5th century B.C. to the 7th century A.D.: a review of the evidence.**
R. Boucharlat, J-F. Salles. *Proceedings of the Seminar for Arabian Studies*, vol. 11 (1981), p. 65-94.
An overall review of the archaeological evidence relating to the Gulf with numerous mentions of Dilmun and Bahrain.

226 **Qatar archaeological report: excavations 1973.**
Edited by Beatrice de Cardi. Oxford, England: Oxford University Press for the Qatar National Museum, 1978. 218p. bibliog.
Although this book is specifically concerned with the archaeology of Qatar it also includes several references to work undertaken in neighbouring Bahrain.

227 **The Bahrain tumuli: an illustrated catalogue of two important collections.**
Elisabeth C. L. During Caspers. [Istanbul] : Nederlands Historisch-Archaeologisch Institut te Istanbul, 1980. 49p. + 42p. of plates. (Publications of the Dutch Historical and Archaeological Institute of Istanbul, no. 47).
This catalogue illustrates each of the items discovered and reported by Mrs. E. P. Jefferson and Captain R. Higham in Bahrain. The former excavated a tumulus at Hamala North in central Bahrain in 1968. The latter collected grave objects from 23 graves scattered throughout the island; these are described as unique because of the variety of fine glazed Parthian pottery included, some of which was found associated with three Roman glass vessels thus dating it to the second half of the first century AD.

228 **The bull's head from Barbar Temple II, Bahrain. A contact with Early Dynastic Sumer.**
Elisabeth C. L. During Caspers. *East and West*, new series, vol. 21, nos. 3-4 (Sept.-Dec. 1971), p. 217-24.
A description and analysis of the copper bull's head found in Barbar Temple II, Bahrain. The author argues that this bull's head is closely similar in design and technique to bull's heads from Ur and Khafajah, and that it was based on a Sumerian prototype. Its date provides a tentative Early Dynastic II-IIIB dating for Barbar Temple II.

229 **Dilmun and the date-tree.**
Elisabeth C. L. During Caspers. *East and West*, new series, vol. 23, nos. 1-2 (March-June 1973), p. 75-78.
This paper argues that at Dilmun, which was open to influences from both Sumer and the Indus civilization, some religious ceremonies were related to the veneration of the date tree, and that such ceremonies centred around the two stone structures which stood during Temples II and III periods in the centre of the courtyard and in which sacred trees had been planted.

Prehistory and Archaeology

230   A Dilmunite seal cutter's misfortune.
      Elisabeth C. L. During Caspers. *Antiquity*, no. 201, vol. 51
      (March 1977), p. 54-55.
A brief report on the discovery of a black steatite seal south-east of the well
complex at Diraz on the north coast of Bahrain. It argues for the manufacture
of such seals in Bahrain itself, and suggests that there was possibly more than one
workshop there for the production of the seals.

231   Harappan trade in the Arabian Gulf in the 3rd millenium B.C.
      E. C. L. During Caspers. *Dilmun: a Journal of Archaeology and
      History in Bahrain*, no. 5 (Dec. 1973), p. 4-6.
A brief note on the trade of the Dilmun culture based on the islands of Failaka
and Bahrain.

232   New archaeological evidence for maritime trade in the Persian
      Gulf during the Late Protoliterate period.
      Elisabeth C. L. During Caspers. *East and West*, new series,
      vol. 21, nos. 1-2 (March-June 1971), p. 21-44.
An analysis of trade in the Gulf linking finds from two cairns near Buraimi with
Late Protoliterate Mesopotamia. The paper argues that there were direct contacts
during this period between South Mesopotamia, Bahrain, and possibly India.

233   A short survey of a still topical problem: the third millenium
      Arabian Gulf trade mechanism seen in the light of the recent
      discoveries in southern Iran.
      Elisabeth C. L. During Caspers. *Acta Praehistoria et
      Archaeologica*, vol. 3 (1972), p. 35-42.
A survey of the significance and location of Dilmun, Magan and Meluhha in the
3rd millenium BC. The author argues that Dilmun must be identified with the
island of Bahrain and its mainland appendages reaching as far northwards as the
island of Failaka.

234   Statuary in the round from Dilmun.
      Elisabeth C. L. During Caspers. *Proceedings of the Seminar for
      Arabian Studies*, vol. 6 (1976), p. 58-75.
A report on the statuary discovered in archaeological excavations in Bahrain.

235 The islands of Bahrain: an illustrated guide to their heritage.
Angela Clarke. Manama: Bahrain Historical and Archaeological
Society, 1981. 286p. 32 maps. bibliog.

This book was published on the 20th anniversary of the accession of HH Shaikh
Isa bin Sulman Al-Khalifa with the aim of encouraging the study and awareness
of the history, archaeology and traditions of Bahrain and the Gulf. Part 1 describes
the topography of the Bahrain archipelago, and its resources, history and trade;
part 2 considers its archaeological sites, artifacts, architecture, ornamentation
and decoration, and traditional crafts and industries; part 3 provides a set of eight
excursions, which describe things to be seen in different parts of the country; and
part 4 comprises a chronology, glossary and site index as aids to the guide. It
includes numerous photographs of the state, and provides a useful guide for those
interested in its past history.

236 Fouilles à Umm Jidr (Bahrain). (Excavations at Umm Jidr,
Bahrain.)
Serge Cleuziou, Pierre Lombard, Jean-François Salles. Paris:
Editions ADPF, 1981. 63p. 2 maps. bibliog. In French and
English. (Recherche Sur les Grandes Civilisations, Mémoire
no. 7).

The report of the French excavations at Umm Jidr in November and December
1979. Four burial mounds were investigated, one of which was elongated and
contained several tombs. There is also a brief report on the pottery finds, bitumen-
coated baskets, stamp seals, stone beads, and a copper ring. The mounds are dated
to the 3rd millenium BC.

237 On the location of Dilmun.
P. B. Cornwall. Bulletin of American Schools of Oriental
Research, no. 103 (Oct. 1946), p. 3-11.

This paper argues that Dilmun was the island of Bahrein, based largely on an
analysis of mentions of Bahrein in cuneiform inscriptions.

238 The tumuli of Bahrein.
P. B. Cornwall. Asia and the Americas, vol. 43 (April 1943),
p. 230-34.

A report on the author's excavations of thirty tumuli in Bahrein during 1940. It
notes that similar types of tumuli are to be found on the neighbouring coast of
Saudi Arabia. The author argues that the people who built these burial mounds
were the people of Dilmun, and that they may initially have reached Bahrein
having crossed Arabia from Yemen around 1900 BC.

239 **Two letters from Dilmun.**
    P. B. Cornwall. *Journal of Cuneiform Studies*, vol. 6 (1952),
    p. 137-45.

A paper supporting the identification of Dilmun with Bahrein, based on a study of two cuneiform letters, Ni615 and 641, dating from the time of Burnaburiyaš c.1370 BC and now in the Museum of the Ancient Orient at Istanbul. It also briefly discusses the burial mounds of Bahrein. An appendix by Albrecht Goetze gives transliterations and translations of the letters.

240 **Dilmun: a Journal of Archaeology and History in Bahrain.**
    Bahrain: Bahrain Historical and Archaeological Society,
    Dec. 1971- . biannual.

Includes a variety of short archaeological and historical reports on Bahrain. The first three issues appeared as *Before Dilmun and After*; this was the newsletter of the Bahrain Historical and Archaeological Society. Several articles are reprinted from other journals and they, together with some short notes, have not therefore been included in this bibliography.

241 **The Sealand of ancient Arabia.**
    Raymond Philip Dougherty. New Haven, Connecticut: Yale
    University Press, 1932. 203p. (Yale Oriental Series).

An investigation into the country known as the Sealand, which played an important part in the history of Babylonia and Assyria. It notes that Dilmun has been connected with Bahrain, and that Bît-Yâkin, the Sealand, mentioned in the inscriptions of Sargon II, stretched as far as Dilmun.

242 **Extracts from report on the islands and antiquities of Bahrein.**
    E. L. Durand. *Journal of the Royal Asiatic Society*, new series,
    vol. 12 (1880), p. 189-201.

A description of the islands of Bahrein in the late 19th century. Aspects of their history and geography are covered, and particular detail is given to the freshwater springs, a black basalt stone with a cuneiform inscription which he found in the Madrasseh-i-Daoud in the Bilād-i-Kadīm, and the many tumuli on the islands which he suggests were Phoenician and several of which he opened.

243 **Ancient and modern man in southwestern Asia.**
    Henry Field. Coral Gables, Florida: University of Miami Press,
    1956-61. 2 vols.

An anthropological study of the Middle East. It notes that Bahrain is famous for its 50,000 tumuli concentrated in three main areas, and it mentions the work of the Danish Archaeological Expedition. The results of a survey of 45 Beharna males in the village of Jidhafs are presented. These people are seen as being the descendants of the original Shia inhabitants of the islands and possessed the following characteristics: a long, narrow head with dolichocephalic index; a narrow forehead; relatively wide face with a very narrow lower jaw; a short upper and total face; and a narrow, short nose with a leptorrhine index.

244 **Alabasterkar fra Bahrains templer.** (Alabaster vases from the Bahrain temples.)
P. V. Glob. *Kuml* (1958), p. 138-45. In Danish with English summary.

A description of the three complete alabaster vases discovered during the Danish Archaeological Expedition's first five years' work in Bahrain, and a report on the work undertaken in 1958.

245 **Arkæologiske undersøgelser i fire arabiske stater.** (Archaeological investigations in four Arab states.)
P. V. Glob. *Kuml* (1959), p. 233-39. In Danish with English summary.

A report on the excavations undertaken by the Danish Expedition in Kuwait, Bahrain, Qatar and Abu Dhabi in the spring of 1959. In Bahrain work continued on the prehistoric capital at Qala'at al-Bahrain, the temples at Barbar, and Iron Age burial mounds south of the Budaiya road.

246 **Bahrain-øen med de hundredtusinde gravehøje.** (Bahrain — island of the hundred thousand burial-mounds.)
P. V. Glob. *Kuml* (1954), p. 92-105. In Danish with English summary.

An account of the first year's work by the Danish Archaeological Bahrain-Expedition in 1953, whose main aim was to look for traces of prehistoric settlement. This revealed considerable portions of a temple complex near Barbar, and several Stone Age sites were also discovered. It discusses the possible links between Bahrain and Dilmun, and argues that the discoveries of the expedition appear to show that there existed in Bahrain an independent culture with connections to both Mesopotamia and India.

247 **Bahrains oldtidshovedstad.** (The ancient capital of Bahrain.)
P. V. Glob. *Kuml* (1954), p. 164-69. In Danish with English summary.

A brief account of the findings of a test sondage sunk in 1953 through the tell near the old Portuguese fort on the northern coast of Bahrain.

248 **Danske arkæologer i den persiske Golf.** (Danish archaeologists in the Persian Gulf.)
P. V. Glob. *Kuml* (1960), p. 208-13. In Danish with English summary.

The report of the spring 1960 excavations in Kuwait, Bahrain, Qatar and Abu Dhabi. In Bahrain the excavations of Qala'at al-Bahrain, the Barbar temple, the south-western flint sites, and the burial mounds continued.

Prehistory and Archaeology

249 **Flintpladser i Bahrains ørken.** (The flint sites of Bahrain's desert.)
P. V. Glob. *Kuml* (1954), p. 106-15. In Danish with English
summary.
An account of the surface flint sites discovered by the 1953 Danish Archaeological
Bahrain Expedition. Most of the flint objects were rough flakes and chips as well
as cores with various degrees of flaking and retouche. They therefore appear to
belong to a Middle Palaeolithic flake culture.

250 **Et nybabylonisk gravfund fra Bahrains oldtidshovedstad.** (A Neo-
Babylonian burial from Bahrain's prehistoric capital.)
P. V. Glob. *Kuml* (1956), p. 164-74. In Danish with English
summary.
The report of the third year's excavations by the Danish Archaeological Bahrain
Expedition at the beginning of 1956. It pays particular attention to the discovery
of a burial at Qala'a which included a Neo-Babylonian stamp seal.

251 **Slangeofre i Bahrains oldtidshovedstad.** (Snake sacrifices in
Bahrain's ancient capital)
P. V. Glob. *Kuml* (1957), p. 114-27. In Danish with English
summary.
The report of the discovery of snake sacrifices within the large building at Qala'at
al-Bahrain first discovered in 1954. It also mentions the excavations undertaken
within the Portuguese fort and around the city wall to the north, together with
the continued investigations of flint sites on Bahrain in the Danish Expedition's
fourth campaign.

252 **Templer ved Barbar.** (Temples at Barbar.)
P. V. Glob. *Kuml* (1954), p. 142-53. In Danish with English
summary.
The report of the first year's Danish excavations at the temple near Barbar where
a considerable number of copper and bronze objects were found.

253 **Udgravninger på Bahrain. Dansk Arkæologisk Bahrain-
Expeditions 2. udgravningskampagne.** (The Danish Archaeological
Bahrain Expedition's second excavation campaign.)
P. V. Glob. *Kuml* (1955), p. 178-93. In Danish with English
summary.
The report of the 1955 Danish Archaeological Expedition to Bahrain. Most attention was paid to the temple at Barbar, where a copper ox head was found during
extensive excavation. Work was also continued at Qala'a, the site of Bahrain's
prehistoric capital.

254 **Dentition on Bahrain, 2000 B.C.**
Karen Højgaard; *Tandlaegebladet* (1980), p. 467-75.
An account of the analysis of teeth and jaws excavated from 25 burial mounds on Bahrain.

255 **Excavations of the Arab expedition at Sar el-Jisr, Bahrain.**
Moawiyah Ibrahim. Bahrain: Ministry of Information, 1982.
224p. in English, 76p. in Arabic.
The report of the Arab expedition led by the Dean of Arts, Humanities and Social Sciences at Yarmouk University, Jordan, to Bahrain. It includes a discussion of the history of research on the Bahrain burial mounds, a general description of the Sar burial field, and then gives full details of the excavations.

256 **Bahrain Island: human skeletal material from the first millenium B.C.**
Shirley Jarman. *Bulletin of the Asia Institute*, no. 2-4 (1977), p. 19-40.
A report on the skeletal remains found at Diraz East and Ali East by the 1976 British Archaeological Expedition to Bahrain.

257 **Fouilles à Qal'at Al-Bahrein, 1ère partie, 1977-1979.** (Excavations at Qal'at Al-Bahrein, 1st part, 1977-1979.)
Monik Kervran, Arlette Nègre, Michele Pirazzoli t'Sertsevens.
Bahrain: Ministry of Information, Directorate of Archaeology and Museums, 1982. 55p. in French, 62p. in English, 84p. in Arabic.
This is the report of the 1977-79 archaeological expedition at Qal'at Al-Bahrain. It also includes details of the coins and Chinese ceramics found there.

258 **Dilmun, the land of the living.**
S. N. Kramer. *Bulletin of the American Schools of Oriental Research*, no. 96 (Dec. 1944), p. 18-28.
A paper arguing for the identification of Dilmun with Bahrain, based mainly on the evidence of Sumerian tablets.

259 **En kileskrift fra Bahrain.** (A cuneiform inscription from the island of Bahrain.)
J. Laessøe. *Kuml* (1957), p. 164-66. In Danish with English summary.
A description of the cuneiform inscription found on the inside of a sherd discovered in 1957 in Bahrain.

260 **Dilmun: gateway to immortality.**
C. C. Lamberg-Karlovsky. *Journal of Near Eastern Studies,*
vol. 41, no. 1 (Jan. 1982), p. 45-50.

This short paper argues that there is insufficient evidence of past settlement on Bahrain to account for the large number of prehistoric graves found there, and consequently that the tumuli represent an elaborate funerary cult reflected in Sumerian literature referring to Dilmun.

261 **The Arabian peninsula and prehistoric populations.**
Harold A. McClure. Miami, Florida: Field Research Projects,
1971. 92p. 3 maps. bibliog.

An outline of the palaeoclimatology, palaeography and prehistory of Arabia.

262 **Bahrein and Hemamieh.**
Ernest Mackay, Lankester Harding, Flinders Petrie. London:
British School of Archaeology in Egypt and Bernard Quaritch,
1929. 40p. + 29p. of plates.

This volume includes the results of Mackay's survey of the tumuli field at Bahrein, which he dated to around 1500 BC. It also provides photographs of some of the finds and details of the tumuli plans and pottery finds.

263 **En hellenistisk møntskat fra Bahrain.** (A Hellenistic coin hoard
from Bahrain.)
Otto Mørkholm. *Kuml* (1972), p. 183-202. In Danish with
English translation.

An account of the Hellenistic silver coin hoard discovered in Bahrain at Qala'at al-Bahrain in 1970. The author argues that the occurrence of locally minted coins testifies to the extension of Hellenistic culture to this marginal area in the latter half of the 3rd century BC.

264 **Barbartemplets ovale anlæg.** (The temple oval at Barbar.)
Peder Mortensen. *Kuml* (1956), p. 189-99. In Danish with
English summary.

An account of the excavation of the oval structure in the Barbar temple, which suggests that it is yet another indication of prehistoric cultural connections between Mesopotamia and Bahrain.

265 **Om Barbartemplets datering.** (On the date of the temple at
Barbar in Bahrain.)
Peder Mortensen. *Kuml* (1970), p. 385-98. In Danish with
English summary.

This article concludes that the first temple at Barbar was built in the beginning of the 3rd millenium and hardly later than 2700 BC. The second temple probably dates from the middle of the 3rd millenium, and the third temple dates to the period 2200-2000 BC.

266 **On the date of the temple at Barbar in Bahrain.**
Peder Mortensen. *Artibus Asiae*, vol. 33, no. 4 (1971),
p. 299-302.

A description of the findings of the Danish archaeologists working on the mound at Barbar from 1953-61. The author argues that the first temple at Barbar was built in the beginning of the third millenium, and hardly later than c.2700 BC; the second temple probably dates from the middle of the third millenium; and the third temple dated from about 2200 BC to 2000 BC.

267 **Vidt berømt for dens mange perler.** (Famed for its many pearls.)
Viggo Nielsen. *Kuml* (1958), p. 146-61. In Danish with English
summary.

An investigation of the archaeological evidence for pearl fishing in Bahrain, which suggests that small-scale pearling was present in Bahrain during the third milleniun BC.

268 **Prehistory in northeastern Arabia.**
John Oates. *Antiquity*, no. 197, vol. 50 (1976), p. 20-31.

This paper concentrates on 'Ubaid pottery sites in Saudi Arabia, but it does mention Diraz and al Markh in Bahrain.

269 **Seafaring merchants of Ur?**
J. Oates, T. E. Davidson, D. Kamilli, H. McKerrell. *Antiquity*,
no. 203, vol. 51 (Nov. 1977), p. 221-34.

An investigation of 'Ubaid pottery finds in eastern Arabia, Bahrain and Qatar, which argues that most, if not all, of the painted and plain 'Ubaid pottery found here was made in Mesopotamia. The distinctive red coarse ware found did not originate in Mesopotamia and the authors suggest that it was locally made. It concludes that significant numbers of the 'Ubaid inhabitants of Sumer travelled to this region of the Gulf, carrying pottery from home with them for their own use. It is suggested that they then stayed long enough in the region to require locally made coarse pots for cooking and other domestic purposes.

270 **'Ubaid Mesopotamia and its relation to Gulf countries.**
John Oates. In: *Qatar archaeological reports: excavations 1973*.
Edited by Beatrice de Cardi. Oxford, England: Oxford University
Press, 1978, p. 39-52.

An account of the distribution of 'Ubaid pottery sites in the Gulf, two of which have been discovered in Bahrain.

Prehistory and Archaeology

271 Remarks on seals found in the Gulf states.
Edith Porada. *Artibus Asiae*, vol. 33, no. 4 (1971), p. 331-37.
Notes that two groups of seals were made in the region of which Bahrain and Failaka were a part. The earlier group is characterized by a disk shape with a button boss pierced in one direction and divided across the other by a groove; the most common designs on these were a bull, a goat or gazelle, and a scorpion. The second later group of stamp seals has a lower wider boss with three thin parallel lines across the back and two small engraved disks with central dots in each half; these date from c.1900 BC.

272 Towards an integrated history of culture change in the Arabian Gulf area: notes on Dilmun, Makkan and the economy of ancient Sumer.
Daniel Potts. *Journal of Oman Studies*, vol. 4 (1978), p. 29-52.
A collation of the results of the various archaeological expeditions that have worked in the Gulf area. It argues that, following earlier contacts with people from Mesopotamia, Dilmun grew in importance as a trading centre during the mid-3rd millenium BC. Its florescence was then terminated in the late Old Babylonian period, possibly as a result of Indo-Aryan attacks on Makkan and Meluhha eliminating Dilmun's role as a Gulf entrepôt.

273 The sepulchral tombs of Bahrein.
F. B. Prideaux. *Indian Archaeological Survey Annual Report* (1908-09), p. 60-78.
An account of the author's archaeological investigations in Bahrein in 1906-07 in which he excavated 7 large to medium-sized tombs and 25 small tombs. It also includes a summary of the archaeological work done by Durand and the Bents in Bahrein, together with a geographical and historical introduction in which he argues that Bahrein was known as Niduk-ki (or Nituk?) in Akkadian, and Tilvun or Tilmun in Assyrian.

274 Persian coin said to have been struck at Bahrein.
H. L. Rabino. *Numismatic Chronicle* (London), series 6, vol. 7 (1947), p. 90.
A note suggesting that a coin dated 1817 in the possession of the Shah of Persia and purporting to have been struck in Bahrein is unique and was probably struck elsewhere at a later date.

275 Bronzehåndtag til et spejl fra Barbartemplet på Bahrain.
(A bronze mirror handle from the Barbar temple, Bahrain.)
M. S. Nagaraj Rao. *Kuml* (1969), p. 218-20. In Danish with English summary.
A note that the bronze mirror handle found at the Barbar temple is similar to the handle of a copper mirror from Mehi, a Kulli culture site in Baluchistan. The author argues that this is further evidence of contact between the two cultures.

276 **Notes on Capt. Durand's report upon the islands of Bahrein.**
H. Rawlinson. *Journal of the Royal Asiatic Society*, new series,
vol. 12 (1880), p. 201-27.
The author argues that a number of traits of Babylonian culture were derived
from people in the Persian Gulf. The paper includes a translation of the black
stone found by Durand, which he suggests links the islands of Bahrein with the
worship of Mercury. From an analysis of various inscriptions the author identifies
Accadian *Niduk-ki* and Assyrian *Tilvun* or *Tilmun* with Bahrein.

277 **The 'Alī cemetery: old excavations, ivory, and radiocarbon dating.**
Julian Reade, Richard Burleigh. *Journal of Oman Studies*, vol. 4
(1978), p. 75-83.
This paper draws attention to the material, including ivories, now located in the
British Museum Department of Western Asiastic Antiquities, from the Bents'
1889 excavation of Mound B in the 'Alī cemetery in Bahrain.

278 **The status of archaeology in Eastern Arabia and the Arabian Gulf.**
Michael Rice. *Asian Affairs*, vol. 8 (old series vol. 64), no. 2
(1977), p. 139-51.
An investigation into archaeological activity in eastern Arabia which began in
1878/79. In 1881 Rawlinson argued that Bahrain was the Dilmun of ancient
Sumerian records, and more recent work has tended to support this. The evidence
suggests that in the third millenium BC eastern Arabia sustained a substantial
and prosperous population which maintained considerable connections with Early
Dynastic Mesopotamia. Excavations of the *tel* near the Bahrain fort, and the
island's grave mound fields are briefly described.

279 **Excavations at Al Markh, Bahrain.**
M. Roaf. *Proceedings of the Seminar for Arabian Studies*, vol. 6
(1976), p. 146-60.
The report of the British expedition to Bahrain during the winter of 1973/4 and
the spring of 1975, which identified two phases of occupation at Al Markh.

280 **Gulf area during the first millenium.**
Jean-François Salles. *Dilmun: a Journal of Archaeology and
History in Bahrain*, no. 10 (1982), p. 4-9.
A short account of the Iron Age, the Hellenistic period, the Parthian period and
the Sasanian Age in the Gulf.

Southern Arabia.
See item no. 126.

The Bahrein islands in the Persian Gulf.
See item no. 294.

**Bahrain: protection of cultural property and development of a museum
in Bahrain.**
See item no. 856.

History

281 The United Arab Emirates: a modern history.
Muhammad Morsy Abdullah. London: Croom Helm; New York: Barnes & Noble, 1978. 365p. 8 maps. bibliog.

A mainly political analysis of the emergence of the United Arab Emirates as a federal state. Bahrain is mentioned in connection with its declaration of independence, oil concessions therein, the Persian claims to the islands, and the Political Residency at Bahrain.

282 History of eastern Arabia 1750-1800: the rise and development of Bahrain and Kuwait.
Ahmad Mustafa Abu Hakima. Beirut: Khayat, 1965. 213p. 5 maps. bibliog.

A study of the 'Utbī states of eastern Arabia in the second half of the 18th century. The Āl-Ṣabāḥ became the rulers of the first 'Utbī settlement at Kuwait in 1752. In 1766 the Āl-Khalīfa, cousins of the Āl-Ṣabāḥ, together with other 'Utbī families migrated south and established the town of Zubāra in Qatar. In 1782 the 'Utūb conquered the Bahrain islands, and by then they had become the strongest Arab maritime power in the Gulf. This book traces the nature of these developments, with Bahrain particularly being discussed in chapter 4.

283 Bahrein islands, a legal and diplomatic study of the British-Iranian controversy.
Fereydoun Adamiyat. New York: Frederick A. Praeger, 1955. 268p. bibliog.

An examination of British diplomacy in the Persian Gulf, with particular reference to Bahrein, since the beginning of the 19th century. It concludes that the British claim to title over Bahrein was not obtained by means sanctioned by international law, that the *de facto* situation of Bahrein was not in conformity with international order, that disharmony existed between the *de facto* and *de jure* status of the island, that the Persian title to the Bahrein islands is based on the rules of law and that it is supported by the facts of history and by a plethora of legal precedents.

284 A collection of treaties, engagements and sanads relating to
India and neighbouring countries, vol. XI, containing the
treaties, &c., relating to Aden and the south western coast of
Arabia, the Arab principalities in the Persian Gulf, Muscat
(Oman), Baluchistan and the North-west Frontier Province.
C. U. Aitchison. Delhi: Manager of Publications, Government
of India, 1933. rev. ed. xxi, 663, lxxxvip.

Provides an historical introduction to Bahrain (p. 190-97) in addition to full
details of treaties between Bahrain and Britain, including the 1820 Preliminary
Treaty with the Sheikhs of Bahrain, the 1856 engagement between Sheikh
Mahomed bin Khaleefa and the British government concerning the slave trade,
the 1861 Convention between Sheikh Mahomed bin Khuleefa and Captain
Felix Jones Political Resident in the Gulf, the 1868 Agreement signed by Ali bin
Khuleefa Sheikh of Bahrain, the 1880 Agreement signed by the Chief of Bahrain,
Isa bin Ali Al Khalifeh, the 1892 Exclusive Agreement, the 1898 Suppression of
Trade in Arms Agreement, the 1912 undertaking regarding the establishment of a
wireless telegraph installation at Bahrain, and the 1914 undertaking by the Shaikh
of Bahrain regarding oil.

285 Arabia unified. A portrait of Ibn Saud.
Mohammed Almana. London: Hutchinson Benham, 1980. 328p.
3 maps.

An account of the unification of Arabia by Ibn Saud during the period 1902-30,
based largely on the author's experience of nine years spent as a translator in the
Court of Ibn Saud between 1926 and 1935. It mentions the flight of the Saud
family from Riyadh to Bahrain in 1890, and the visit paid by Ibn Saud to Sheikh
Isa Ibn Ali Al Khalifa, ruler of Bahrain, in 1930.

286 British interests in the Persian Gulf.
Abdul Amir Amin. Leiden, the Netherlands: E. J. Brill, 1967.
163p. map. bibliog.

An account of British economic and political activity in the Gulf mainly during
1747-78. This is seen as being determined largely by events in India and Persia.
In 1750 Savage, the British Agent at Bandar 'Abbās, recommended that the
Agency should be removed to Bahrain, but when he was replaced by Graves in
1751 this project was dropped. It provides an interesting account of British trade
in the Gulf during the 18th century, and observes that many of the pearls from
Bahrain were exported to India.

287 Gun-running in the Gulf and other adventures.
H. H. Austin. London: John Murray, 1926. 320p.

A record of the author's experiences in attempting to stop gun running from
Arabia to Afghanistan at the beginning of the 20th century. In the fifth chapter
it describes the adventures of one Salih who took 750 rifles and 200,000 rounds
of ammunition from Matrah to the Sultan of Bahrein.

History

288 **Maritime trade and Imamate government: two principal themes in the history of Oman to 1728.**
R. D. Bathurst. In: *The Arabian peninsula: society and politics.* Edited by Derek Hopwood. London: George Allen & Unwin, 1972, p. 89-106.

An historical appraisal of the emergence of Oman prior to the 18th century. It notes that during the early 16th century the Turks were unable to capture Bahrain from the Portuguese, that in 1602 the Shah of Persia expelled the Portuguese puppet Hormuzi *malik* (king) from Bahrain, and that in 1627 the Portuguese launched a renewed attack on Bahrain.

289 **Der arabisch-persische Golf. Eine Studie zur historischen, politischen und ökonomischen Entwicklung der Golf-Region.**
(The Arabian-Persian Gulf. A study of the historical, political and economic development of the Gulf region.)
Ahmed B. al-Bayati. Munich: Verlag Ölschläger, 1978. xviii, 379, xxxvp. bibliog.

An historical and political account of the development of the Gulf states, which pays particular attention to the interests of external powers in the region's oil. Bahrain is discussed mainly in the context of Anglo-American rivalry over the early oil concessions and Iran's claims to the islands.

290 **Persian Gulf – past and present.**
Charles Belgrave. *Journal of the Royal Central Asian Society*, vol. 55, no. 1 (Feb. 1968), p. 28-35.

An account of pearls, piracy and petroleum in the Gulf. It notes the first discovery of oil in the Gulf in 1932 at Bahrain.

291 **The Portuguese in the Bahrain islands, 1521-1602.**
C. D. Belgrave. *Journal of the Royal Central Asian Society*, vol. 22 (1935), p. 617-30.

An analysis of the occupation of Bahrain by the Portuguese during the 16th century. It appears that Pero was the first Portuguese to explore the Gulf as far as Bahrain, but the island was not conquered by the Portuguese until 1521. Despite an uprising in 1522 under Shaikh Hussein bin Said, and a further rebellion in 1529, Bahrain then remained under Portuguese rule. In 1559 a powerful Turkish force attacked the islands, but this was defeated by the Portuguese. It was not until 1602 that the Portuguese were finally expelled, this time by an Iranian force.

292 **A brief survey of the history of the Bahrain islands.**
James H. D. Belgrave. *Journal of the Royal Central Asian Society*, vol. 39, no. 1 (Jan. 1952), p. 57-68.

This useful paper traces the history of Bahrain from its first mentions as Niduk-ki and Dilmun, through the early Islamic, Qarmathian, Arab and Portuguese periods, into the 18th century period of anarchy and the final emergence of the Al-Khalifah in the late 18th and 19th centuries.

293 **The past and present connection of England with the Persian Gulf.**
Thomas Jewel Bennett. *Journal of the Royal Society of Arts*, vol. 50 (13 June 1902), p. 634-52.

An analysis of Portuguese and British interests in the Gulf, related to the expansion of trade with India in the 19th century. It also notes some aspects of the suppression by the British of the slave trade and piracy.

294 **The Bahrein islands in the Persian Gulf.**
J. Theodore Bent. *Proceedings of the Royal Geographical Society*, vol. 12, no. 1 (Jan. 1890), p. 1-19.

A geographical and historical description of Bahrein, mentioning its pearl trade and aspects of daily life there in the late 19th century. It notes that classical authors assigned the original home of the Phoenicians to Bahrein and describes the author's investigations of the ancient mounds near the village of Ali which he identified as tombs.

295 **Le prodigieux destin du golfe Persique.** (The prodigious destiny of the Persian Gulf.)
J. J. Berreby. *Orient* (Paris), no. 11, vol. 3 (1959), p. 79-89.

A brief account of the history of the Gulf from the time of Alexander the Great to the age of petroleum.

296 **Progrès et évolution des principautés du Golfe persique.** (Progress and evolution of the Arab principalities of the Persian Gulf.)
Jean-Jacques Berreby. *Orient* (Paris), no. 25, vol. 7 (1963), p. 25-34.

A study of the development of the Gulf emirates which concentrates mainly on Kuwait and Bahrein. It notes Bahrein's importance as a British military base, the religious division between its Shiite and Sunni population, and the recent expansion there of social services. In conclusion it argues that Bahrein is one of the last bastions of imperialism in the region and that it is a sort of Gibraltar of the Persian Gulf.

History

297 **The affairs of Arabia 1905-1906.**
Edited by Robin Bidwell. London: Frank Cass, 1971. 2 vols.
Reprint of Foreign Office Confidential Print: Correspondence
respecting the affairs of Arabia 1905-1906.

These volumes are a collection of reports on Arabia as they arrived in Whitehall.
They include correspondence on Bahrain in connection with such subjects as civil
disorders, a protest by the Turkish ambassador against the actions of British
officers, customs, relations with the sheikh, and murders.

298 **A British official guide to the Gulf.**
Robin Bidwell. *Geographical Journal*, vol. 138, no. 2 (1972),
p. 233-35.

This is a review article on Lorimer's *Gazetteer of the Persian Gulf* (q.v.).

299 **The Islamic dynasties: a chronological and genealogical
handbook.**
Clifford Edmund Bosworth. Edinburgh: Edinburgh University
Press, 1967. 245p. (Islamic Surveys, 5).

Provides a thorough listing of all of the major Islamic dynasties. Bahrain is mentioned in chapter 4, on the Arabian peninsula, where it notes that the greatest
centre of Qarmaṭī, or Carmathian, activity was in Bahrain. This principality was
built up by Abu Sa'id at the beginning of the 10th century, and more than a
century later the Qarāmiṭa of Bahrain were still known by the general designation
of Abū-Sa'īdīs.

300 **Minaret and pipe-line: yesterday and today in the Near East.**
Margaret Bovari, translated from the German by Louisa Marie
Sieveking. London, New York, Toronto: Oxford University
Press, 1939. 422p. 16 maps.

A general history of the Near East, noting that King Sargon of Akkad sent his
ships as far as Bahrein in 2800 BC, that De Morgan thought that the inhabitants
of Bahrein (known then as Dilmun) migrated to Syria in the 2nd millenium BC
and under the name of Phoenicians expanded their seafaring skills, that it lay
within Darius's Persian empire and was then a penal settlement, and that in the
20th century Bahrein was the centre of British authority in the Gulf. It also
mentions Iran's claim to sovereignty over Bahrein, and the early development of
its oil industry.

301 **Britain and the Middle East.**
Reader Bullard. London: Hutchinson's University Library,
1951. 3rd rev. ed., 1964. 200p. 2 maps. bibliog.

A general introduction to the historical relations between Britain and the
countries of the Middle East. Bahrain is discussed in connection with the treaty
relations with Britain in the 19th century, the stationing of a division of the
Indian Army at Bahrain during the First World War, the Persian claim to Bahrain,
and the discovery of oil.

302 **The Middle East: a political and economic survey.**
Reader Bullard. London, New York, Toronto: Oxford
University Press, under the auspices of the Royal Institute of
International Affairs, 1958. 569p. 5 maps. bibliog.

Bahrain is mentioned in this general text mainly in connection with oil. It notes
that the legal status of slavery was abolished in Bahrain in 1937, and p. 131-38
provides a general introduction to the archipelago noting its history and foreign
relations, its politics, its foreign trade and finance, and its oil industry from the
granting of the first concession in 1925 to its position in the late 1950s.

303 **Britain, Iran and the Persian Gulf: some aspects of the situation
in the 1920s and 1930s.**
R. M. Burrell. In: *The Arabian peninsula: society and politics.*
Edited by Derek Hopwood. London: George Allen & Unwin,
1972, p. 160-88.

This article on Iranian interests in the Gulf notes many of the conflicts between
Britain and Iran over affairs in the region, including the establishment of a firm
British presence in Bahrain in the 1930s, the Iranian claims to Bahrain, and the
eventual transfer there of the Residency from Bushire in 1946.

304 **Britain and the Persian Gulf, 1894-1914.**
Briton Cooper Busch. Berkeley, Los Angeles: University of
California Press, 1967. 432p. 6 maps. bibliog.

This book is concerned with the reaction of Great Britain to what it deemed were
the policies of interloping powers with interests in the Gulf at the end of the 19th
and beginning of the 20th centuries. It considers four problems in detail: Anglo-
French relations in Oman concerned with the attempt by France to establish a
coal depot in 1898-99; Anglo-Ottoman conflicts on the status of Bahrain, Qatar
and Kuwait; Anglo-German relations regarding Kuwait and the terminus of the
Baghdad railway; and Anglo-Russian relations pertaining to the Gulf in general.
An introductory section provides general information on Bahrain in the 1890s
(p. 25-30), and chapter 5 is specifically concerned with Turkish-British conflicts
over Bahrain and neighbouring areas. Eight appendixes give details of trade and
the British officers associated with the Gulf in the two decades before 1914.

305 **Britain, India and the Arabs, 1914-1921.**
Briton Cooper Busch. Berkeley, Los Angeles, London: University of California Press, 1971. 522p. 5 maps. bibliog.

An investigation of the thesis that British policy in the Middle East in the era of
the First World War can only be understood by giving consideration to the
conflict between British authorities in London and British authorities in India,
as well as Anglo-French, Anglo-Arab and Anglo-Zionist relations. Bahrain is
discussed mainly in connection with Anglo-Ottoman disputes in the Gulf.

History

306 The Bahrein islands.
A. H. Charteris. *Australian Geographer,* vol. 2, no. 4 (1934), p. 7-12.

A discussion of the sovereignty controversy between Britain and Persia over Bahrein following the transfer of the oil concession for the island to the Bahrein Petroleum Company, a subsidiary of the American company Standard Oil Company of California.

307 The Arab's place in the sun.
Richard Coke. London: Thomas Butterworth, 1929. 318p. map.

An early 20th-century history of the Arabs. Bahrein is mentioned in several places, in particular in connection with the Carmathian capture of the island in 903 and its relationship with Britain in the 19th and 20th centuries.

308 Caravan: the story of the Middle East.
Carleton S. Coon. London: Jonathan Cape, 1952. 376p. 8 maps. bibliog.

A general history of the Middle East which mentions that Bahrain is believed to be the ancient Dilmun where cargoes were trans-shipped.

309 Urbanization in the Middle East.
V. F. Costello. Cambridge, London, New York, Melbourne: Cambridge University Press, 1977. 121p. 5 maps. bibliog. (Urbanization in Developing Countries).

This book aims to describe how the life of the traditional Middle Eastern city has been changed by modern physical and social urbanization. It notes the influence of British interests and the discovery of oil in Bahrein.

310 British withdrawal from the Persian Gulf.
Alvin J. Cottrell. *Military Review,* vol. 50, no. 6 (June 1970), p. 14-21.

An evaluation of the political and economic factors leading to British withdrawal from the Gulf. Some mention is made of the proposed federation of Bahrein, Qatar and the Trucial States, and the paper notes that the US naval presence in the Gulf in 1970 consisted of a seaplane tender based at Bahrein and two destroyers which made visits into the region.

311 Persia and the Persian question.
George N. Curzon. London: Longman, Green, 1892. 2 vols. 4 maps, 6 maps.

An analysis of the connection of Persia with the larger problems of Asian politics, which also presents a description of the region in the 19th century. It notes that in the mid-18th century Sheikh Nasr was master of Bahrein, Bushire and much of the Dashtistan, and that Bahrein was then an important centre of pearling. Ottoman interests in Bahrein and the practice of pearling in the 19th century are also described at some length (p. 453-58).

312 **The Persian Gulf.**
G. Dalyell of the Binns. *Journal of the Royal Central Asian Society*, vol. 25, no. 3 (July 1938), p. 349-64.

An account of the evolution of British involvement in the Gulf and of the role therein of Bahrain, which is identified as the key of the British position in the region in the 1930s.

313 **The Persian Gulf route and commerce.**
F. C. Danvers. *Imperial Asiatic Quarterly Review* (April 1888), p. 384-414.

An investigation of British commercial interests in the Gulf, through the activities of the East India Company, from the 17th to the 19th centuries. It suggests that the Phoenician settlement of Tylos was among the Bahrein islands, and it briefly mentions the capture of Bahrein by the Imaum of Muscat early in the 19th century. It also notes that the steamship trade with Bahrein began in 1869.

314 **Forty years in Kuwait.**
Violet Dickson. London: George Allen & Unwin, 1971. 335p. 5 maps.

The autobiography of the wife of Lt. Col. H. R. P. Dickson, erstwhile Political Agent of Bahrain and of Kuwait. It includes several mentions of Bahrain in the half-century following 1920.

315 **The postal agencies in eastern Arabia and the Gulf.**
Neil Donaldson. Batley, Yorkshire, England: Harry Hayes, 1975. 280p. 6 maps. bibliog. (Harry Hayes Philatelic Study, no. 14).

A handbook on the stamps and postal agencies of the Arab Gulf. The Indian and Pakistani administrations in Bahrain are described on p. 52-71, and the British administration on p. 144-63. It provides details of the various cancellations and overprinted stamps, prior to the first definitive issue of Bahrain's stamps in 1960, and concludes with a brief section on postal independence. Bahrain's recorded postal history began in 1884 when a Post Office was opened in Manama under the administration of the Bombay Circle.

316 **The Bahrein islands (750-1951): a contribution to the study of power politics in the Persian Gulf.**
Abbas Faroughy. New York: Verry, Fisher, 1951. 128p. map. bibliog.

A general description and history of Bahrein. It provides details of Bahrein's geography, geology, climate, population, towns and villages, antiquities, education, economy, pearl fishing, fishing, trade, oil, and history, paying particular attention to the 19th and 20th centuries. Appendixes provide translations of the 1880, 1892 and 1914 agreements between the Sheik of Bahrein and the British.

317 **Gun-running in the Persian Gulf.**
Lovat Fraser. *Proceedings of the Central Asian Society*, read
17 May 1911, p. 1-16.
An account of the growth in the arms trade in the countries bordering on the Gulf
in the early 20th century. Most attention is paid to the arms traffic at Muscat, but
Bahrein is also briefly mentioned. It provides a contemporary picture of the background to increased British involvement in the Gulf.

318 **Kuwait was my home.**
Zahra Freeth. London: George Allen & Unwin, 1956. 164p.
map.
An account of life in Kuwait in the mid-20th century following the exploitation
of oil, written by the daughter of Lt. Col. H. R. P. Dickson who had been appointed as British Political Agent there in 1929. Bahrain is mentioned in connection
with the establishment of British power in the region, the development of oil, the
founding of the American Mission hospital in Bahrain in 1893, and its role as the
centre of the Gulf pearl trade.

319 **The great Arab conquests.**
John Bagot Glubb. London: Hodder & Stoughton, 1963,
Quartet Books, 1980. 384p. 37 maps.
This book discusses the course of the Arab conquests of Arabia, Persia and the
Mediterranean during the 7th century AD. It mentions that in 631 AD deputations
went from Bahrain to Muhammad in Medina, and also that some resistance to
the spread of Islamic military strength after the battle of Yemama was offered in
the vicinity of Bahrain.

320 **La fin de l'empire des Carmathes du Bahraïn.** (The end of the
Carmathian empire in Bahrain.)
M. J. de Goeje. *Journal Asiatique*, 9th series, vol. 5 (1895),
p. 5-30.
An account of the collapse of Carmathian rule in Bahrain.

321 **Mémoire sur les Carmathes du Bahrain et les Fatimides.** (Memoir
on the Carmathians of Bahrain and the Fatimids.)
M. J. de Goeje. Leiden, the Netherlands: E. J. Brill, 1886.
2nd ed. 232p. (Mémoires d'Histoire et de Géographie Orientales,
no. 1).
First published in 1862, this is an analysis of the Arabic historians' accounts of
the activities of the Carmathians in the 3rd century AH and in particular their
activities in a widely defined Bahrain.

322 **The life of Sir Percy Cox.**
Philip Graves. London, Melbourne: Hutchinson, 1941. 350p.
A biography of Sir Percy Cox, who was Political Resident in the Persian Gulf
1904-13. It includes several mentions of Bahrein in connection with the Persian
claim to the island, its pearl fisheries, and relations between the British and
Sheikh Isa of Bahrein.

323 **The Omanis, sentinels of the Gulf.**
Liesl Graz. London, New York: Longman, 1982. 202p. map.
bibliog.
An introduction to the people and way of life of Oman. It briefly notes Oman's
historical connections with Bahrain, when Saif bin Sultan became master of the
islands in the 17th century and when Sayyid Said conquered them temporarily in
the 19th century.

324 **The Arab at home.**
Paul W. Harrison. London: Hutchinson, 1924. 345p. map.
A book based on the author's fourteen years' experience as the representative
in Arabia of the Trinity Reformed Church of Plainfield, New Jersey. It includes
many references to Bahrein, in particular in connection with the methods and
practices of pearl fishing, the British régime, and religion.

325 **The Trucial States.**
Donald Hawley. London: George Allen & Unwin, 1970. 379p.
5 maps. bibliog.
A mainly historical treatment of the Trucial Coast before the British withdrawal
in 1971. It discusses the tribal structure of the region in some detail, and provides
a diplomatic assessment of the relationships between British officials and the
various independent shaikhs in the area during the 19th and 20th centuries.
Although mainly concerned with the shaikhdoms now within the United Arab
Emirates, it includes many references to Bahrain.

326 **From Trucial States to United Arab Emirates: a society in**
transition.
Frauke Heard-Bey. London, New York: Longman, 1982. 522p.
9 maps. bibliog.
A thorough and detailed account of the social, political and economic changes
that have taken place in the United Arab Emirates. It refers to Bahrain in connection with the dispute with Qatar, Persian and Omani influence, the Bani Yās
tribe, its entrepôt trade, pearling, the discovery and exploitation of oil, its educational developments, negotiations over federation following the statement of
Britain's intent to withdraw from the Gulf, and the 1970 agreement with Iran.

History

327 **Bahrain is independent.**
Allan G. Hill. *Geographical Magazine*, vol. 44, no. 12 (Sept.
1972), p. 846-52.

This paper argues that many problems face Bahrain as a small independent state
and that these are mainly due to the lack of overall integrated economic planning
in the region following British withdrawal from the Gulf in 1971. It notes that the
centre of British administration in the Gulf was in Bahrain, and it suggests that
specific problems arose from the fact that it is among the world's smallest political
units, it is composed of thirty small islands, and that it is suffering from increasing
water shortages. Oil production, and in particular refining at the BAPCO (Bahrain
Petroleum Co.) refinery which was originally commissioned in 1939, is seen as
providing the main source of income through which the country has tried to
maintain its leadership in the Gulf. Details of the provision of infrastructure,
industrial expansion including the aluminium smelter, the creation of the new Isa
Town, and the provision of health services are given. The author argues that the
most profound threat facing Bahrain and the other Gulf states is the inter-state
commercial rivalry which is producing industrial plants and facilities located for
prestige rather than economic reasons.

328 **History of the Arabs from the earliest times to the present.**
Philip K. Hitti. London: Macmillan, 1951. 5th ed. 822p.
21 maps.

This historical study of the Arabs equates al-Baḥrayn with ancient Dilmun, notes
that al-Baḥrayn formed a centre of operations against Iran in the 640s, and
mentions the country's importance as a centre of the pearl trade.

329 **The origins of the Islamic state. Being a translation from the
Arabic accompanied with annotations geographic and historic
notes of the *Kitâb futûḥ al-buldân* of al-Imâm abu-l 'Abbâs
Aḥmad ibn-Jâbir al-Balâdhuri.**
Volume 1 by Philip Khûri Ḥitti, part 2 by Francis Clark
Murgotten. New York: Longman, Green; London: P. S. King &
Son, vol. 1 1916; part 2 1924. 2 vols (Columbia University
Studies in History, Economics and Public Law, vol. 68, whole no.
163 and 163A).

A translation of the 9th-century *Kitâb futûḥ al-buldân* (The book of the conquest
of the countries) of Al-Balâdhuri. Al-Bahrain is described mainly in part 1, chapter
17, which describes the delegation of al-'Alâ ibn-'Abdallâh ibn-'Imâd al-Hadrami
to the islands with the request of the prophet that the people should become
Moslem. It notes that at the time of the prophet al-Bahrain was ruled by
al-Mundhir ibn-Sâwa in the name of the Persians. Details are also given of the
islands' early Islamic history and of the apostasy of al-Ḥuṭam.

330 **Arabia.**
David George Hogarth. Oxford, England: Clarendon Press, 1922.
139p. map.
This history of Arabia notes that the term Bahrain meant anciently the whole
north-western littoral of the Persian Gulf. It also mentions the submission of
Bahrain to Muhammad, the 10th-century Carmathian occupation of Bahrain, the
country's treaties with Britain in the 19th century, and the conflicts between
Britain and Turkey over the Gulf.

331 **Farewell to Arabia.**
David Holden. London: Faber & Faber, 1966. 268p. 3 maps.
bibliog.
An account of the process of change in Arabia during the 20th century. Bahrain is
mentioned in connection with its relations with Britain, Saudi Arabia and Iran; its
oil industry; its traditional pearling and boatbuilding economy; its welfare state;
the proposed Gulf federation; the claims of the youth of the country; the 1956
riots over Suez; and the student riots there in 1965.

332 **Persian Gulf states.**
David Holden. In: *The Middle East: a handbook*. Edited by
Michael Adams. London: Anthony Blond, 1971, p. 253-62.
This provides a general introduction to the geography, history, political structure,
defence, internal preoccupations, external affairs and great power interests in the
Gulf prior to 1970.

333 **The Cambridge history of Islam.**
Edited by P. M. Holt, Ann K. S. Lambton, Bernard Lewis.
Cambridge, England: Cambridge University Press, 1970. 2 vols.
17 maps. bibliog.
Provides an account of the political, theological, philosophical, economic, scien-
tific, military and artistic background of Islam. Bahrayn is discussed mainly in
connection with the 'Abbasid Caliphate and the later influence of the Turks and
British in the Gulf region.

334 **Background of the British position in Arabia.**
Halford L. Hoskins. *Middle East Journal*, vol. 1, no. 2 (April
1947), p. 137-47.
An evaluation of the changing role of the British in Arabia, which briefly mentions
Bahrein's importance as a pearl fishery.

History

335 **Diplomacy in the Near and Middle East: a documentary record.**
J. C. Hurewitz. Princeton, New Jersey: D. van Nostrand, 1956.
2 vols.

Volume 1 of this collection of documents relating to the political development of the Middle East focuses on major international issues in the period 1535-1914. Volume 2 aims to illuminate decisive developments between 1914 and 1956. Bahrayn is included in the 1820 General Treaty for suppressing piracy and slave traffic in the Gulf, Lord Clarendon's formula of the British position on the Bahrayn islands in 1869, the 1880 agreement between Shaykh Isa bin Ali Al Khalifeh and the British, the 1892 exclusive agreement between the Shaykh of Bahrayn and Britain, and the 1913 Anglo-Ottoman draft convention on the Gulf area.

336 **The Gulf: Arabia's western approaches.**
Molly Izzard. London: John Murray, 1979. 314p. map. bibliog.

An account of the history and culture of the Gulf, which includes many personal anecdotes of the area. Bahrain is mentioned mainly in chapter 6. This describes Manama and Mohurraq, the country's economy, some aspects of its history, pearling, Bahrain's leading merchant families, social life, and the changing position of women in the country's society.

337 **Arabia, the Gulf and the West.**
J. B. Kelly. London: George Weidenfeld & Nicholson, 1980. 530p. 5 maps. bibliog.

The author argues that despite a gloss of recently acquired modernity the Gulf today is still much as it always has been, and that the resultant instability poses a major threat to Western interests in the region. Although there are mentions of the state elsewhere, Bahrain is discussed in detail on p. 178-85. The early history of the modern state, from when the Al Khalifah and Al Jalahimah in 1783 descended on Bahrain from Qatar and put the Persian garrison to flight, is recorded at some length. During the early 19th century the Persians, the rulers of Muscat, the Wahhabis of Nejd, the Egyptians and the Turks all at various times lay claim to Bahrain. However in 1861 the British forced the ruling shaikh to sign an undertaking to observe the maritime truce in perpetuity, and it is from this period that British influence on the islands became paramount. The discovery of oil in 1932 is seen as having transformed the economy, but the author argues that there is a latent, and sometimes active, threat of internal dissent hanging over the islands, deriving from the religious schism between Sunni and Shiite Muslims. This useful book also includes details of boundary agreements and Bahrain's relations with the neighbouring states of the Arabian peninsula.

338 **Britain and the Persian Gulf, 1795-1880.**
J. B. Kelly. Oxford, England: Oxford University Press, 1968.
911p. 2 maps. bibliog.
A thorough and complete survey of Britain's role in the Gulf in the 19th century.
There are numerous mentions of Bahrain on the subjects of its early history, its
conquest by the Al Khalifah, its relations with Muscat and the Wahhabis, Persian,
Egyptian and Turkish claims to the islands, its treaty relations with Britain, piracy
and the slave trade, conflicts with Qatar over Zubara, and various aspects of the
economy.

339 **Eastern Arabian frontiers.**
J. B. Kelly. London: Faber & Faber, 1964. 319p. 2 maps.
An account of the disputes between Britain and Saudi Arabia relating to frontiers
in Arabia during the 19th and 20th centuries. Bahrain is mentioned in several
places, in connection with the 1820 treaty between Britain and the Qawasim, Ibn
Saud's agreement in 1915 that Kuwait, Bahrain, Qatar and the shaikhs of the
Oman coast were in special treaty relations with Britain, and the 1951 discussions
relating to maritime frontiers between Kuwait, Bahrain and Saudi Arabia. It also
notes that in 1831 the Wahhabi Amir, Turki ibn Abdullah Al Sa'ud, forced the
Shaikh of Bahrain to resume payment of the *zakat*, alms-tax, which had been
paid to the Wahhabis twenty years earlier. This provided grounds for the Amir
Faisal's planned invasion of Bahrain in 1851, since the Shaikh of Bahrain had
ceased to pay the tax. This attempt by Faisal was stopped by the British, as was
his later attempt in 1854.

340 **The legal and historical basis of the British position in the
Persian Gulf.**
J. B. Kelly. In: *St. Antony's Papers*, vol. 4. London: Oxford
University Press, 1958, p. 119-40.
A study concentrating on the legacy of the past in its effects on British policy in
the Gulf. It notes that by 1820 all of the shaikhs of the southern Gulf, including
the Al Khalifah shaikhs of Bahrain, had been admitted to the General Treaty of
Peace with Britain. It suggests that it was not until 1839, when the Egyptian army
of Muhammad Ali Pasha arrived on the Gulf coast opposite Bahrain, that the
British government indicated that they were keen to protect Bahrain's independence. The threatened invasions of Bahrain by the Persians in 1842 and the Saudis
under Faisal ibn Turki a decade later are also mentioned. Brief details are given of
the 1861 agreement between Muhammad ibn Khalifah and the British Resident in
the Gulf, by which Britain explicitly recognised Bahrain's independence and
agreed to defend the island provided the shaikh abstained from the prosecution of
war. The 1867 attack on Dauhah and Wakrah by the shaikh of Bahrain and the
subsequent retaliation by the people of Qatar are also fully described.

History

341 **Mehemet 'Ali's expedition to the Persian Gulf 1837-1840.**
J. B. Kelly. *Middle Eastern Studies*, vol. 1, no. 4 (July 1965),
p. 350-81; vol. 2, no. 1 (Oct. 1965), p. 31-65.

An account of Mehemet 'Ali's expedition to the Gulf at the end of the 1830s. It includes details of the activities of the emissaries sent by Mehemet 'Ali to Bahrain, and his claims to the islands which were refuted by the British.

342 **The Persian claim to Bahrain.**
J. B. Kelly. *International Affairs*, vol. 33, no. 1 (Jan. 1957),
p. 51-70.

This paper traces the Persian claims to the islands of Bahrain, culminating in those of 1906, 1927 and 1955. Persian rule over the islands dated from 1602 until 1783 when the Atabi Arabs expelled the Persian garrison which had occupied them following the overthrow of the Portuguese. The paper also describes the 19th and 20th-century involvement of the British in Bahrain, which was initially aimed at ensuring the safety of her links with India, and it notes the frequent disagreements between Persia and Britain during the 19th century concerning the sovereignty of the islands.

343 **The United Arab Emirates: unity in fragmentation.**
Ali Mohammed Khalifa. Boulder, Colorado: Westview Press;
London: Croom Helm, 1979. 235p. 6 maps. bibliog.

An analysis of the development of the United Arab Emirates as a federal entity which has emerged in a primarily tribal culture. Bahrain is mentioned in connection with its contributions to the Development Fund, the negotiations over Britain's withdrawal from the Gulf and Bahrain's ultimate independence, the Iranian claims to the islands, the activities of PFLOAG (the Popular Front for the Liberation of the Occupied Arabian Gulf), and the relations between Bahrain and the USA.

344 **The Arab states and the Arab League: a documentary record.**
Muhammad Khalil. Beirut: Khayat, 1962. 2 vols.

This publication brings together a series of the more important documents covering the emergence of independent Arab states. Volume 1 is concerned with constitutional developments and volume 2 provides a record of international affairs. Bahrein is most frequently mentioned in the section on 'International affairs: Arabian peninsula', where the texts of the 1880, 1892 and 1914 agreements between Bahrein and Britain are reproduced.

345 **A short history of the Middle East from the rise of Islam to
modern times.**
George E. Kirk. London: Methuen, 1948. 301p. 14 maps.
bibliog.

Bahrain is mentioned several times in this brief history of the region, in particular in the context of the Persian, Portuguese and British occupance of the islands.

346 **Anglo-Turkish antagonism in the Persian Gulf.**
Ravinder Kumar. *Islamic Culture*, vol. 37, no. 2 (1963),
p. 100-11.

An investigation of the effects of the establishment of Turkish rule at El Hasa in
1871. The question of Bahreni rights over mainland Arabia, including Qatar, is
seen as being characteristic of the problems attendant on the new equilibrium
between Britain and Turkey in the Gulf.

347 **India and the Persian Gulf region, 1858-1907: a study in British**
imperial policy.
Ravinder Kumar. London: Asia Publishing House, 1965. 259p.
bibliog.

The Gulf is identified as a cockpit of international rivalry in the 19th century.
Bahrain is mentioned frequently in the context of Turkish, Persian and British
interests in the islands.

348 **The modernization of the Persian Gulf: the period of British**
dominance.
Robert G. Landen. In: *Middle East focus: the Persian Gulf.*
Edited by T. Cuyler Young. Princeton, New Jersey: Princeton
University Conference, 1969, p. 1-30.

A general description of the growth of British power in the Gulf, which discusses
the political origins of the modern Gulf, the establishment of British political
paramountcy, the effects of imperial collisions, and the influence of oil. It argues
that in Bahrain the Sunni Al-Khalifah were a warrior-merchant ruling class who
held the Shi'ah Baharnah, the island's indigenous agricultural population, under
tight subjugation. The growth of Bahrain as a steamer port of call just before
the First World War is also mentioned. It notes that during the 1930s, as a result
of the flooding of the world's pearl markets by Japanese cultured pearls, the
Bahrain pearling fleet dropped from 508 boats, employing 19,300 men, to 191
boats employing 7,500 men.

349 **The authority of shaykhs in the Gulf: an essay in nineteenth**
century history.
Peter Lienhardt. *Arabian Studies*, vol. 2 (1975), p. 61-75.

An investigation into the basis of the authority of shaykhs in the Gulf in the 19th
century. It notes the 1782 conquest of Bahrain by the Āl Khalīfah, and the
departure of the Āl Bin 'Alī from Bahrain in 1835.

History

350 Nadir Shah: a critical study based mainly upon contemporary sources.
Laurence Lockhart. London: Luzac, 1938. 344p. 8 maps. bibliog.

An analysis of Nadir Shah's campaigns in Turkey, India and the Gulf. It notes that in 1717 or 1718 Bahrain was captured by the Imam of Muscat, and following the Omani departure the island passed into the hands of Shaikh Jabbara of Ṭahin. In 1736 Nadir Shah's admiral, Latif Khan, recaptured Bahrain and it was then added to the province of Fars.

351 Gazetteer of the Persian Gulf, 'Omān, and Central Arabia.
J. G. Lorimer. Calcutta, India: Government Printing House, 1908-15. 2 vols. Republished Farnborough, England: Gregg International, 1970; Shannon, Ireland: Irish University Press, 1970. 2 vols.

A historical and geographical introduction to the Gulf region. Bahrain's history is discussed in volume 1, chapter 5, which covers the establishment of the 'Āl Khalīfah dynasty as shaikhs of Bahrain in 1783, the extension of Wahhabi influence over Bahrain 1803-11, the growth of Bahrain as a pirate depot, general events 1820-40, relations with Britain and Egypt 1830-40, and then the reigns of Muhammad-bin-Khalīfah 1843-68, 'Ali-bin-Khalīfah 1868-69, the interregnum of 1869, and the reign of Īsa-bin-Ali from 1869. This historical account provides abundant information on the various claims of Turkey, Persia and Britain to Bahrain. In volume 2, on the geography of the Gulf, Bahrain is described on p. 212-53, where information is given on the coastal features, hills, towns and villages, springs, geology, climate, population and tribes, agriculture, pearling, communications, industries, trade, currency, administration, class, religion, finance, military resources, and political position.

352 The Persian Gulf.
H. F. B. Lynch. *Imperial Asiatic Quarterly Review*, 3rd series, vol. 13 (April 1902), p. 225-34.

An investigation of German, Turkish and Russian attempts to violate the supremacy of the British in the Gulf at the turn of the 20th century.

353 Abu Dhabi: birth of an oil shaikhdom.
Clarence Mann. Beirut: Khayat, 1964. 153p. 4 maps. bibliog.

An historical account of the emergence of Abu Dhabi, which includes several mentions of Bahrain. In particular it notes the attacks by Musqati forces on Bahrain during the 18th century, the Amir Faisal's campaign against Bahrain in 1851, the 1861 treaty between Britain and Bahrain, the 1868 attack by the shaikh of Bahrain on Qatar, and the 1948 removal of the British Residency from Bushir to Bahrain.

354 **History of Seyd Said, Sultan of Muscat; together with an account of the countries and people on the shores of the Persian Gulf, particularly of the Wahabees.**
Shaik Mansur. London: John Booth, 1819. 174p. map.

In this account of the life and times of Seyd Said Baharem/Baarém is mentioned as being important for its pearl fisheries.

355 **The Persian Gulf in the twentieth century.**
John Marlowe. London: Cresset Press, 1962. 278p. 2 maps. bibliog.

A general introduction to the Gulf, which discusses Bahrain in the context of its domination in the past by the Portuguese and Persians, its pearl industry, the development of its oil industry, and its hostile relations with Qatar and Persia.

356 **The wells of Ibn Sa'ud.**
D. van der Meulen. London: John Murray, 1957. 270p.

A personal account of the history of Arabia and the author's time spent in the country as the former Netherlands Minister in Jedda. Bahrain's oil industry and some of its connections with Saudi Arabia are mentioned briefly.

357 **The countries and tribes of the Persian Gulf.**
S. B. Miles. London: Harrison & Sons, 1919. 2 vols. 643p.

This book is based on the notes made by Colonel Miles during his time spent in the Gulf during the second half of the 19th century. Volume 1 is divided into chapters on the history of the early colonization of the region, the Persian Gulf under Islam, the Portuguese in eastern Arabia and the Yaareba dynasty. Volume 2 has chapters on the Al-Bu Saeedi dynasty, the history of the commerce of the Persian Gulf, a description of the country and the pearl fisheries, the tribes of the Persian Gulf, eastern and south-eastern Arabia, and the history and geography of Dhofar. An appendix provides information on Colonel Miles' travels in Mesopotamia in 1879 and 1880. There are a number of mentions of Bahrain on the subjects of its history and pearl fisheries.

358 *Ḥudūd al-'ālam* **(the regions of the world): a Persian geography 372 A.H. - 982 A.D.**
Translated and explained by V. Minorsky, preface by V. V. Barthold; edited by C. E. Bosworth. London: Luzac, 1970. 2nd ed. 524p. 12 maps. (E. J. W. Gibb Memorial Series, new series, vol. 11).

A translation and commentary of the anonymous *Ḥudūd al-'ālam*. There are several mentions of Bahrayn, which is described as being a very populous region with towns, villages and prosperous places. The merchants of Bahrayn are also noted as visiting Abyssinia.

History

359 **Britain's moment in the Middle East 1914-1971.**

Elizabeth Monroe. London: Chatto & Windus, 1981. 2nd ed. 254p. 2 maps. bibliog.

An account of Britain's activities in the Middle East between the outbreak of the First World War and their final departure from the Gulf in 1971. Bahrain is mentioned mainly in the context of oil and its use as a base by the British. The riots in Bahrain that greeted the British Foreign Secretary, Selwyn Lloyd, on his visit to Bahrain in 1956 and the Persian claims to the islands are also noted. The main difference between this edition and the first, published in 1963, is the replacement of the final chapter, which now also deals with the disposal of Britain's hegemony on the coasts of Arabia.

360 **Philby of Arabia.**

Elizabeth Monroe. London, Melbourne, New York: Quartet Books, 1980. 332p. 3 maps. bibliog.

A biography of St. John Philby, which mentions Bahrain mainly in the context of the early oil concessions and the occasions when Philby travelled there.

361 **The market of Seleukia.**

James Morris. London: Faber & Faber, 1957. 337p. 7 maps.

This book is an impression of the Middle East in 1956 after the Israelis had forced the Egyptian army back to the Suez Canal. Bahrain is described on p. 244-51 where mention is made of the fact that it was the headquarters of British authority in the Gulf, and certain aspects of its social structure at that time are discussed. It also notes friction between adherents of the Sunni and Shia sects in Bahrain.

362 **The pirates of the Trucial Oman.**

H. Moyse-Bartlett. London: Macdonald, 1966. 256p. 5 maps. bibliog.

An account of the British naval and military expeditions to the Trucial Oman in the early 19th century, paying particular attention to the career of Captain T. Perronet Thompson who drafted the Treaty which laid the foundations of Britain's relationship with the sheikhdoms of the Trucial Coast. It notes the Utub control of Bahrain, Sultan Sa'id of Muscat's desires to obtain control over the Pirate Coast and Bahrain, and the British naval blockade of Manama in 1920.

363 **The Caliphate, its rise, decline, and fall, from original sources.**

William Muir, new and revised edition by T. H. Weir. Edinburgh: John Grant, 1915. 636p. 4 maps. bibliog.

An historical study, first published in 1891, of the Caliphate which mentions Bahrein in connection with the spread of Islam to the islands, its apostasy and rebellion crushed in 632-3 AD (11 AH) by Al-'Alā, the rising of Al-Khirrīt ibn Rashid which for a while also broke out in Bahrein in 658 AD (38 AH), and the later raids of the Zenji in 878 AD (256 AH).

364 **Persian Gulf studies.**
Emile A. Nakhleh. *Middle East Studies Association, Bulletin,*
vol. 11, no. 2 (1977), p. 31-43.
A report on the state of studies into the Gulf region, including a six-page bibliography.

365 **The Arabs: a narrative history from Mohammed to the present.**
Anthony Nutting. London: Hollis & Carter, 1964. 424p.
7 maps. bibliog.
A history of the emergence and expansion of Islam. It notes Khalid Ibn Walid's
conquest of Bahrein, the foundation of an independent Qarmatian state in
Bahrein in the 9th century by Said al-Hassan al-Jannabi, the Turkish conquests of
Hasa which included Bahrein in the 16th century, and Ibn Saud's unification of
Arabia in the 20th century.

366 **Away to Eden.**
Roderic Owen. London: Hutchinson, 1960. 240p. map.
The story of the author's journey from Kuwait to Afghanistan. It includes descrip-
tions of Muharraq and Bahrain islands in the late 1950s.

367 **The Ottoman Turks and the Portuguese in the Persian Gulf,
1534-1581.**
Salih Özbaran. *Journal of Asian History,* vol. 6, no. 1 (1972),
p. 45-87.
A detailed account of the Portuguese and Turkish involvement in the Gulf, paying
particular attention to Bahrayn, Basra and Hormuz. Portuguese influence was first
felt in Bahrayn in 1521 when the Portuguese forced the people of Bahrayn to pay
to Hormuz the tribute due from them. The years 1529 and 1530 saw further
Portuguese attacks on Bahrain. From 1535 the ruler of Bahrayn appears to have
shifted his allegiances from the Portuguese to the Ottomans and back again,
depending on which offered the greater advantages. It was not until 1559 that the
Ottomans made a serious attempt to establish themselves in Bahrayn, but they
were defeated by the Portuguese.

368 **British policy towards the Arabian tribes on the shores of the Persian Gulf (1864-1868).**
Dharm Pal. *Journal of Indian History*, vol. 24 (1945), p. 60-76.

This paper argues that British policy towards the Persian Gulf tribes was governed mainly by trade interests, and that its main aims were to put down piracy and to maintain peace among the Arab tribes by a judicious support of the weak but friendly Muscat state against the powerful Wahabees. It is concerned essentially with the period following the appointment of Lieutenant-Colonel Lewis Pelly as Political Resident of the Persian Gulf territories in November 1862. It describes the attack on Guttar (Qatar) by the chiefs of Bahrein and Aboothabee (Abu Dhabi) in October 1867 which the British were powerless to stop. The Guttar tribes retaliated and attacked Bahrein in June 1868, and the author notes that in the ensuing sea battle 600 craft were destroyed and upwards of 1,000 lives lost. Consequent on this battle Mahomed Bin Khuleefa, chief of Bahrein, fled and his brother Ali is noted as taking over as ruler.

369 **Remarks on the tribes, trade, and resources around the shore line of the Persian Gulf.**
Lewis Pelly. *Transactions of the Bombay Geographical Society*, vol. 17 (Jan. 1863-Dec. 1864), p. 32-112.

A collection of what the author calls 'superficial remarks, based on personal observation and hearsay, concerning the tribes, trade, and resources around the shore line of the Persian Gulf'. It provides some information on the economy of Bahrein, and in particular its pearl fisheries, and also notes that 'Bahrein once hoisted in succession Turkish, Persian and English flags. It is even added she has been known to hoist all three at once'.

370 **Arabia.**
H. St. J. B. Philby. London: Ernest Benn, 1930. 387p.

A sketch of the history of Arabia aimed at 'Members of Parliament, journalists, business men and the like'. It includes numerous mentions of Bahrain, in particular in connection with the expansion of the Wahhabi empire and the possession of the islands by the British.

371 **Arabia of the Wahhabis.**
H. St. J. B. Philby. London: Constable, 1928. 422p. map.

This volume completes the record of the author's sojourn in Arabia in 1917 and 1918 and forms the third volume of *The heart of Arabia*. It is a record of the months immediately preceding Ibn Sa'ud's first attack on Haïl, which committed him to a policy of imperial expansion. It includes several scattered mentions of Bahrain.

372 **Arabian days.**
H. St. J. B. Philby. London: Robert Hale, 1948. 336p.

The author's autobiography, in which Bahrain is mentioned in several places, principally in connection with its role as British dependency and as an oil producer.

373 **Arabian jubilee.**
H. St. J. B. Philby. London: Robert Hale, 1952. 280p.

An account of the life of Ibn Sa'ud on the day of his completion of fifty (lunar) years of absolute rule in Arabia in July 1950. Bahrain is occasionally mentioned as the seat of British authority in the area, and in connection with the oil concession obtained by Holmes on the island.

374 **Sa'udi Arabia.**
H. St. John Philby. London: Ernest Benn, 1955. 393p. map.

An history of Sa'udi Arabia up to the death of 'Abdul-'Aziz ibn Sa'ud in 1953. There are many mentions of Bahrain, particularly in connection with various Wahhabi raids on the islands. The author notes that during the 19th century the claims to various parts of mainland Arabia by the rulers of Bahrain were a constant source of trouble and unrest in the area.

375 **Oman: a history.**
Wendell Phillips. London: Longman, 1967. 246p. 2 maps.

An history of Oman, including several mentions of Bahrain. It notes that the term 'Bahrain' in mediaeval times applied to the whole mainland of eastern Arabia, and it briefly discusses the 1521 Bani Zabia insurrection against Portugal on Bahrain, Sultan Said's unsuccessful attack against Bahrain in 1828, and the country's treaty relationship with Britain.

376 **Unknown Oman.**
Wendell Phillips. London: Longman, 1966. 319p. 5 maps.
bibliog.

An account of the culture of Oman. It discusses Bahrain in connection with its joining of the Trucial League, its pearling, its archaeology and the capture of the islands by the Sassanian general at-Tabari Wahraz *circa* AD 570. A brief outline of Bahrain's history is given on p. 108-10.

377 **Essay towards the history of Arabia antecedent to the birth of Mahommed arranged from the *Tarikh Tebry*, and other authentic sources.**
David Price. London: printed for the author by Cox & Baylis, 1824. 248p.

This includes scattered references to Bahrain and is of interest as an early 19th-century history of the region. In particular it notes that in the 6th century Bahareyne was brought into the territory of Noushirvân, king of Persia.

History

378 Wahhabism and Saudi Arabia.
George Rentz. In: *The Arabian peninsula: society and politics.*
Edited by Derek Hopwood. London: George Allen & Unwin,
1972, p. 54-66.

An investigation into the foundation of Wahhabism and its relationship with the
Saudi state. It notes that for a time at the opening of the 19th century the island
of Bahrain and its rulers, the House of Khalifah, became subject to the town of
al-Dir'iyah, the ruler of which was Muhammad ibn Sa'ud.

379 Les émirats du Golfe: histoire d'un peuple. (The emirates of the
Gulf: history of a people.)
Salem al-Jabir al-Sabah. Paris: Fayard, 1980. 261p. 3 maps.
bibliog.

An historical introduction to the Gulf covering the British intervention in the
region, the traditional economy, the oil concessions, the delimitation of land
frontiers, problems associated with the sovereignty of islands, the impact of
increased oil revenues, and the independence of the various emirates from
Britain. There are frequent mentions of Bahrain, in particular in connection
with independence, the Iranian claims to the island, and the development of
its oil industry.

380 Bahrain, Qatar, and the United Arab Emirates: colonial past,
present problems, and future prospects.
Muhammad T. Sadik, William P. Snavely. Toronto, London:
Lexington Books, 1972. 255p. map. bibliog.

This study of the nine eastern Gulf states presents a summary of much useful
data relating to their history and economic development prior to the withdrawal of the British. While covering most aspects of Bahrain's economy and
history, it pays particular attention to the discovery of oil, employment,
education, its political relationships with neighbouring countries, the structure
of its government, and its past treaty relations with Britain.

381 Where time stood still: a portrait of Oman.
Duchess of St. Albans. London, Melbourne, New York:
Quartet Books, 1980. 242p. 3 maps.

A personal account of the recent changes that have taken place in Oman. It
includes several passing references to historical links between Bahrain and
Oman.

382 The Arabian peninsula.
Richard H. Sanger. Ithaca, New York: Cornell University
Press, 1954. 295p. 2 maps. bibliog.

An investigation of changes taking place in Arabia, and particularly of the role
of Americans in effecting that change. Bahrein is discussed in chapter 10,
p. 140-150, which traces its history, and describes its pearl and oil industries.

383 **Historical sketch of the Gulf in the Islamic era from the seventh to the eighteenth century A.D.**
R. B. Serjeant. In: *Qatar archaeological report: excavations 1973*. Edited by Beatrice de Cardi. Oxford, England: Oxford University Press, 1978, p. 147-63.

Notes the recapture of Bahrain in 1521 by the Portuguese leading to the construction of the fort, Qala'at 'Ajaj, on the northern shore of the island. This fort was manned by Hurmuzis, and when their governor was slain in 1602 by Bahrainis in the name of the Shah of Persia the islands came under Persian control until the end of the 17th century.

384 **Britain and the Arab states: a survey of Anglo-Arab relations, 1920-1948.**
M. V. Seton-Williams. London: Luzac, 1948. 330p. 4 maps. bibliog.

A survey of the development of political relations between Britain and the Arab states of the Middle East. Bahrain is discussed in chapter 9 on the Persian Gulf states, where a brief summary is given of the main treaties between Britain and the shaikhs of Bahrain.

385 **Arabian adventure.**
Anthony Shepherd. London: Collins, 1961. 256p. map.

An account of the author's life in the Trucial Oman Scouts between July 1957 and March 1959. It mentions his stop-over at Bahrain on his flight from England to Sharjah, and also a brief later visit he made to Bahrain.

386 **Arabian assignment.**
David Smiley, with Peter Kemp. London: Leo Cooper, 1975. 248p. map.

A record firstly of the author's life as commander of the Sultan of Muscat's armed forces during the three years following 1958, and then of his visits to Yemen. There are several mentions of his contacts with the British authorities in Bahrain.

387 **The Persian Gulf region.**
Roy E. Thoman. *Current History*, no. 353, vol. 60 (1971), p. 38-45, 50.

An examination of the historical experience, ideology, communications, antagonistic and co-operative relationships among the regional states, and the roles played by external intrusive powers in the Gulf. It includes a brief analysis of the historical claims by Iran on Bahrain, and following the United Nations decision on Bahrain's status in 1970 it suggests that the problem of the state's international status had been solved.

History

388 **The Arabs: the life-story of a people who have left their deep impress on the world.**
Bertram Thomas. London: Thomas Butterworth, 1937. 372p. 4 maps. bibliog.

This history of the Arabs notes Bahrain's importance as a centre of the pearl trade, as a potential oil producer, to Persia for a shadowy claim to suzerainty, and to Britain as an air and naval station.

389 **Historical and other information connected with the Province of Oman, Muskat, Bahrein, and other places in the Persian Gulf.**
Compiled and edited by R. Hughes Thomas. Bombay: Bombay Education Society's Press, for the Government, 1856. 687p. 6 maps. (Selections from the Records of the Bombay Government, new series, no. 24).

Provides a wide range of information on the provinces of Oman, Muskat, Bahrein and other places in the Gulf, including details of treaties, tables of events, navigation, the suppression of the slave trade, and tribal activities. It describes Bahrein's history and economy, its treaty relations with Britain prior to 1856, its tribes, its political relations with Muskat, and navigation around the islands.

390 **Arab navigation in the Indian Ocean before the coming of the Portuguese, being a translation of *Kitāb al-fawā'id fī uṣūl al-baḥr wa'l-qawā'id* of Ahmad b. Mājid al-Najdi, together with an introduction on the history of Arab navigation, notes on the navigational techniques and on the topography of the Indian Ocean, and a glossary of navigational terms.**
G. R. Tibbetts. London: Royal Asiatic Society of Great Britain and Ireland, 1971. 614p. 7 maps. bibliog. (Oriental Translation Fund, new series, vol. 42).

A translation of Ahmad ibn Mājid's *Fawā'id* (Book of the uses of the basis and rules of navigation) which was written c.1489-90, together with an extensive introduction on Arab navigation. Baḥrain is mentioned mainly in the tenth *fā'ida* (section) on islands, although there are several other scattered references to Baḥrain. Ahmad ibn Mājid observes that Baḥrain was also known as Awāl, that it had 360 villages, and that there was much sweet water on the island as well as offshore at al-Qaṣāṣīr. There were numerous pearl fisheries around the islands and 1,000 ships were involved in the pearl trade. Agriculture included the cultivation of date palms, pomegranates, figs, oranges and limes, and horses, camels, cattle, sheep and goats were kept. Baḥrain at this time was owned by Ajwad b. Zāmil b. Ḥaṣin al-'Amirī.

391 **Arabia in the fifteenth century navigational texts.**
G. R. Tibbetts. *Arabian Studies*, vol. 1 (1974), p. 86-101.

An investigation into 15th century Arabia based mainly on the navigational texts of Ahmad ibn Mājid and Sulaimān al-Mahrī (see above). It notes that very little attention was paid by the navigators to the Gulf coast of Arabia, although Baḥrain, alternatively known as Awāl, was described in the tenth *fā'idah* (section) of Ibn Mājid, where details are given of its pearl fisheries and fresh water springs. The ninth *fā'idah* also mentions Baḥrain.

392 **Heart-beguiling Araby.**
Kathryn Tidrick. Cambridge, London, New York, New Rochelle, Melbourne, Sydney: Cambridge University Press, 1981. 244p. 2 maps. bibliog.

This book is concerned with the fascination exercised upon certain Englishmen by the Arabian desert, and the development of the notion that Englishmen possessed an intuitive understanding of Arabs which gave them a right to interfere in their affairs. Palgrave's visit to Bahrein is noted briefly.

393 **Al Watheeka. (The document.)**
Bahrain: Historical Documents Centre, 1982- . half-yearly.

A journal devoted to the history of Bahrain, including articles on archaeology, coins, the British period and poetry. Most articles therein are in Arabic, but some are in English.

394 **Arabia and the Gulf: in original photographs 1880-1950.**
Andrew Wheatcroft. London, Boston, Melbourne, Henley: Kegan Paul International, 1982. 184p. map.

An illustrated historical record of Arabia and the Gulf. It is divided into six sections on deserts, the gateway of Arabia, the heart of Islam, Arabie the blest, the horn of plenty, and the Gulf. It includes photographs of the al-Khalifa family, and watermen on Bahrein Island.

395 **The origins of the Omani state.**
J. C. Wilkinson. In: *The Arabian peninsula: society and politics.* Edited by Derek Hopwood. London: George Allen & Unwin, 1972, p. 67-88.

This paper argues that the history of the state of Oman is dominated by three recurrent themes: the tribal picture, the story of the imamate, and the struggle between Omanis and foreigners for control of her coastal provinces. It mentions that the original term al-Bahrain, as used by the Arab geographers, referred to the whole area of the southern Gulf centred on the modern Hasa province, and in this context the relationship between Bahrain and Oman is frequently discussed.

History

396 **A sketch of the historical geography of the Trucial Oman down to the beginning of the sixteenth century.**
J. R. Wilkinson. *Geographical Journal*, vol. 130, no. 3 (Sept. 1964), p. 337-49.
An account of the Trucial Oman based on the works of early Arab geographers. It includes several mentions of Bahrain, and notes that the Qays Empire controlled Bahrain and Oman in the 12th century.

397 **The Persian Gulf: an historical sketch from the earliest times to the beginning of the twentieth century.**
Arnold T. Wilson. Oxford, England: Clarendon Press, 1928. 327p. map. bibliog.
A regional history of the Gulf written in the 1920s to enable local residents to learn something of the early records of the area in which they lived. It includes frequent mentions of Bahrain including discussions of its burial mounds; early history; early Arab migrations to the islands; Persian, Portuguese and British possession of the islands; its pearling and piratical economy; the arms trade; the Dutch Church Mission; and archaeological research.

398 **Saudi Arabia in the nineteenth century.**
R. Bayly Winder. London, Melbourne, Toronto: Macmillan, 1965. 312p. 7 maps. bibliog.
An account of Saudi Arabia in the nineteenth century paying particular attention to the British 'presence' in eastern Arabia, the Egyptian occupation from 1818 to 1840, the relationship between the Saudi state and the Ottoman empire, and the effects of the contacts between 'a medieval society' and 'the modern world'. It mentions the expulsion of the Wahhabis from Bahrain in 1811, the reassertion of Saudi suzerainty over the ruler of Bahrain with the payment of *zakah* (religious alms tax), the Bahraini renouncement of this sign of allegiance in 1833, the Egyptian claims to Bahrain in the late 1830s, the civil war in 1842, the war between Muhammad ibn Khalifah of Bahrain and King Faisal in 1845-46, later *zakah* tribute payments by Bahrain to Saudi Arabia, and some aspects of the country's relationships with Britain.

399 **Captain Shakespear: a portrait.**
H. V. F. Winstone. London: Jonathan Cape, 1976. 236p. 9 maps. bibliog.
An account of Shakespear's life and travels in Arabia at the beginning of the 20th century. There are several scattered mentions of Bahrain.

400 **Middle East focus: the Persian Gulf.**
Edited by T. Cuyler Young. Princeton, New Jersey: Princeton
University Conference, 1969. 220p.

Thirteen papers and numerous discussions on the Gulf forming the proceedings
of the twentieth annual Near East Conference. It is divided into four main
sections: the historical background, oil-related problems, general economic
problems, and socio-political problems. The papers by Landen, Rentz, Verrier
and Badeau mention Bahrain.

401 **Hegemony, dependence and development in the Gulf.**
Rosemarie Said Zahlan. In: *Social and economic development
in the Arab Gulf.* Edited by Tim Niblock. London: Croom Helm,
1980, p. 61-79.

Provides an historical dimension to serve as a guideline in the formulation of
strategies for the socio-economic development of the Gulf region. It considers the
context within which strategies and policies have to function, rather than the
specifics of planning. Bahrain is discussed in the context of pearling, relationships with Britain, the discovery of oil in 1932, the disputes with Qatar over
Zubarah and the Hawar Islands, the 1938 political disruptions, and the traditional
involvement with commerce.

The Persian Gulf states.
See item no. 23.

**Gazetteer of Arabia: a geographical and tribal history of the Arabian
peninsula.**
See item no. 117.

The pirate coast.
See item no. 125.

Southern Arabia.
See item no. 126.

The voyage of John Huyghen van Linschoten to the east Indies.
See item no. 129.

The travels of the Abbé Carré in India and the Near East 1672 to 1674.
See item no. 135.

**Arabia phoenix. An account of a visit to Ibn Saud chieftan of the
austere Wahhabis and powerful Arabian king.**
See item no. 140.

Ben Kendim: a record of eastern travel.
See item no. 143.

**The geographical part of the *Nuzhat-al-qulūb* composed by Ḥamd-Allāh
Mustawfī of Qazwīn in 740/1340.**
See item no. 150.

History

The islands of Bahrain: an illustrated guide to their heritage.
See item no. 235.

Dilmun: a Journal of Archaeology and History in Bahrain.
See item no. 240.

Pirates or polities? Arab societies of the Persian or Arabian Gulf, 18th century.
See item no. 437.

The Middle Eastern question or some political problems of Indian defence.
See item no. 464.

Le Golfe persique: problèmes et perspectives. (The Persian Gulf: problems and perspectives.)
See item no. 465.

The Arabian peninsula.
See item no. 496.

Oil and security in U.S. policy towards the Arabian Gulf-Indian Ocean area.
See item no. 551.

A prevalence of furies: tribes, politics, and religion in Oman and Trucial Oman.
See item no. 559.

United States policy towards the Persian Gulf
See item no. 567.

The Persian Gulf and international relations.
See item no. 571.

America and the Arabian peninsula: the first two hundred years.
See item no. 572.

Oman and Gulf security.
See item no. 580.

The U.S.S.R. and Arabia: the development of Soviet policies and attitudes towards the countries of the Arabian peninsula.
See item no. 584.

The United States and the Near East.
See item no. 598.

La question des îsles Bahrein. (The question of the Bahrein islands.)
See item no. 599.

Fishing for pearls.
See item no. 611.

Qatar, development of an oil economy.
See item no. 650.

Remarks on the pearl oyster beds in the Persian Gulf.
See item no. 661.

Memorandum respecting the pearl fisheries in the Persian Gulf.
See item no. 671.

Cargoes of the East: the ports, trade and culture of the Arabian Seas and western Indian Ocean.
See item no. 697.

Ancient trading centres of the Persian Gulf VII: Bahrein.
See item no. 703.

The rising costs of industrial construction.
See item no. 724.

British routes to India.
See item no. 794.

The Arab navigation.
See item no. 800.

The Persian Gulf submarine telegraph of 1864.
See item no. 845.

Population

402 **Arab migrations.**
Abdelwahab Bouhdiba. In: *Arab industrialisation and economic integration.* Edited by Roberto Aliboni. London: Croom Helm, 1979, p. 134-88.
An analysis of inter-Arab and Euro-Arab migration. It provides diverse information on migration into Bahrain noting the great importance of migrant workers to the state's economy.

403 **La personalité géographique des villes des Émirats du Golfe.** (The geographical personality of the towns of the Gulf emirates.)
André Bourgey. *Maghreb Machrek*, vol. 81 (1978), p. 56-62.
An analysis of the demography of the main towns of the Gulf emirates. There are several mentions of Bahrain, particularly in connection with the construction of the new Isa Town.

404 **Contemporary urban growth in the Middle East.**
John I. Clarke. In: *Change and development in the Middle East: essays in honour of W. B. Fisher.* Edited by John I. Clarke, Howard Bowen-Jones. London, New York: Methuen, 1981, p. 157-70.
This essay provides some statistical information on Bahrain's population, and notes that it had a lower urban death rate than many other countries in the Middle East in the 1970s. It was previously published in *The changing Middle Eastern city* (edited by R. I. Lawless and G. H. Blake, London: Croom Helm, 1980, p. 34-53).

405 **Populations of the Middle East and North Africa: a geographical approach.**
Edited by J. I. Clarke, W. B. Fisher. London: University of London Press, 1972. 432p.
A survey, by twelve contributors, of the characteristics of the populations of the countries within the region extending from Turkey to Iran, and from Iran to Morocco. Bahrain is mainly mentioned in the chapter by A. G. Hill.

406 **Demographic Yearbook.**
New York: United Nations, 1948- . annual.
A comprehensive collection of international demographic statistics prepared by the Statistical Office of the United Nations, covering approximately 220 countries including Bahrain.

407 **L'immigration dans la péninsule arabique.** (Immigration in the Arabian peninsula.)
Nicolas Hemsay. *Maghreb Machrek,* vol. 85 (1979), p. 55-60.
An analysis of the socio-economic impact of the extensive immigration to the Arabian peninsula resulting from the accumulation of petroleum revenue. It notes that, in contrast to some other countries in the region, only 20 per cent of Bahrein's population consists of immigrants.

408 **The Gulf states: petroleum and population growth.**
A. G. Hill. In: *Populations of the Middle East and North Africa: a geographical approach.* Edited by J. I. Clarke, W. B. Fisher.
London: University of London Press, 1972, p. 242-73.
Provides details of Bahrain's population numbers, distribution, nationality, fertility, mortality, immigration, and ethnic composition.

409 **The population situation in the ECWA region: Bahrain.**
Beirut: United Nations Economic Commission for Western Asia, 1979. 23p. map. bibliog.
Provides information on the following aspects of Bahrain's demography: data problems, size, distribution, structure, fertility, mortality, migration, growth, education, economic activity, and government policy.

Migration and labour force in the oil-producing states of the Middle East.
See item no. 410.

Migration and employment in the Arab world: construction as a key policy variable.
See item no. 821.

Nationalities and Minorities

410 Migration and labour force in the oil-producing states of the Middle East.
F. Halliday. *Development and Change*, vol. 8, no. 3 (July 1977), p. 263-91.
An analysis of the changes in the composition of the labour force of states within the Middle East resulting from the rise in oil revenues in the early 1970s. Bahrain is seen as a city state which is essentially an enclave on the shore of the Gulf and which has only acquired enough economic and political power through its oil. The paper argues, though, that Bahrain is exceptional among the city states of the Gulf in that it has diversified its economy away from oil, and that the majority of its population consists of indigenous Bahrainis.

411 The impact of Arab expatriates on social and political development in the Gulf states.
Ibrahim Ibrahim. In: *The Arab brain drain.* Edited by A. B. Zahlan. London: Ithaca Press, 1981, p. 71-81.
Notes that almost three-quarters of the working force of Kuwait, Qatar, Bahrain and the United Arab Emirates consists of expatriates.

412 World physician migration.
Alfonso Mejia. In: *The Arab brain drain.* Edited by A. B. Zahlan. London: Ithaca Press, 1981, p. 209-28.
Notes that in the early 1970s the 79 foreign physicians working in Bahrain represented 77 per cent of the total number of physicians in the country.

413 Labor markets and citizenship in Bahrayn and Qatar.
Emile A. Nakhleh. *Middle East Journal*, vol. 31, no. 2 (spring 1977), p. 143-56.
This paper argues that the long term influx of foreign nationals into Bahrayn and Qatar is full of disturbing economic, social and political consequences. It notes that labour has been a political factor in Bahrayn for over a generation, dating from the unrest of the mid-1950s and then the March 1965 general strike against the Bahrayn Petroleum Company. It provides information on Bahrayn's labour laws and gives details of the country's labour composition by country of origin.

L'immigration dans la péninsule arabique. (Immigration in the Arabian peninsula.)
See item no. 407.

Ethnic conflict: a framework of analysis and its relevance to the Gulf region.
See item no. 435.

Language

414 **A dictionary of economics and commerce: English-Arabic.**
Dictionaries Department, Librairie du Liban. Beirut: Librairie
du Liban, 1983. 392p.

A useful reference dictionary for those wishing to have a detailed knowledge of
economic and commercial terms in English and Arabic.

415 **The Muslim and Christian calendars: being tables for the
conversion of Muslim and Christian dates from the Hijra to the
year A.D. 2000.**
G. S. P. Freeman-Grenville. London: Rex Collings, 1977.
2nd ed. 87p.

Provides information on the Muslim and Christian calendars, and gives tables from
which any date and day of the week may be calculated in either calendar.

416 **Courtesies in the Gulf area: a dictionary of colloquial phrase
and usage.**
Donald Hawley. London: Stacey International, 1978. 96p.
map.

An introduction to colloquial Arabic used in the Gulf region. It includes numerous
useful phrases ranging from greetings and farewells to everyday courtesies and
formal occasions. There is a useful section on subject vocabularies referring to
agricultural terms, animals, birds, marine life, food, guns, military ranks, ships
and boats, terrain, trees and plants, and winds, and it concludes with a selection
of Omani proverbs. All phrases are written in Arabic, with transliterations and
English translations.

417 **Chihabi's dictionary of agricultural and allied terminology:
English-Arabic.**
Ahmad Sh. Al-Khatib. Beirut: Librairie du Liban, 1978. 907p.

A comprehensive dictionary covering agricultural terms. The bulk of the Arabic
material is derived from the *Dictionnaire Français-Arabe des termes agricoles,* by
Emir Moustapha El-Chihabi.

418   A new dictionary of petroleum and the oil-industry:
      English-Arabic.
      Ahmad Sh. Al-Khatib. Beirut: Librairie du Liban, 1975. 578p.
An illustrated dictionary covering all of the words likely to be of relevance to
those working in the petroleum and oil industry.

419   A new dictionary of scientific and technical terms: English-Arabic.
      Ahmed Sh. Al-Khatib. Beirut: Librairie du Liban, 1982. 5th ed.
      751p.
This dictionary provides over 60,000 terms covering about 50 branches of science
and technology. It includes over 1,500 illustrations.

420   Language and linguistic origins in Baḥrain. The Baḥārnah dialect
      of Arabic.
      Mahdi Abdalla Al-Tajir. London, Boston, Melbourne: Kegan
      Paul International, 1982. 222p. 10 maps. bibliog. (Library of
      Arabic Linguistics, Monograph no. 5).
A thorough and detailed expositon of the Baḥārnah dialect. After a description of
the ancient region of Al-Baḥrain and the geography, economy and history of its
islands, it discusses the phonology and morphology of the dialect together with its
syntactical and lexical features. It concludes with a comparative analysis of the
Baḥārnah A and B Dialects and 'Umāni and Yamāni.

The Middle East: a handbook.
See item no. 2.

Bahrain: language, customs & people.
See item no. 25.

Social Conditions

421 **The changing social scene in Bahrain.**
James Belgrave. *Middle East Forum*, vol. 38, no. 7 (July-Sept.
1962), p. 62-66.

A description of social change in Bahrain, paying particular attention to the
flowering of a middle class and the birth of a group the author describes as
'Bahrain's Angry Young Men'. It argues that the younger Bahrainis at this time
were meeting a number of frustrations in their work.

422 **Documents of the national struggle in Oman and the Arabian
Gulf.**
London: The Gulf Committee, 1974. 106p.

A series of translated documents giving an overview of the development of the
'liberation' movement in the Gulf, since the outbreak of armed struggle in Oman
in 1965. It includes mentions of the 1954-56 'major anti-imperialist movement,
under reformist leadership, in Bahrain', the 1956 'mass anti-imperialist demonstrations in Aden, Kuwait, and Bahrain', the 1965 'resurgence of opposition in March,
led by oil workers, against the ruling al-Khalifa family and British rule', and the
1972 granting of independence to Bahrain by Britain.

423 **Class struggle in the Arab Gulf.**
Fred Halliday. *New Left Review*, vol. 58 (1969), p. 31-37.

An evaluation of the potential of the Popular Front for the Liberation of the
Occupied Arab Gulf (PFLOAG) based largely on the revolution in Yemen and
Dhofar. It suggests that the attempt by Britain to create a union of Arab Emirates
on its departure from the Gulf in 1971 was doomed to failure. It predicts that the
PFLOAG will cause great damage to imperialism, and that the 'miserable neo-
colonialist plots that Britain was hatching can be defeated'.

424 **Investigations in a Shī'a village in Bahrain.**
Henny Harald Hansen. Copenhagen: National Museum of
Denmark, 1967. 208p. map. bibliog. (Publications of the National
Museum, Ethnographical Series, vol. 12).
An anthropological report on the author's research in the village of Sār undertaken
in 1960. It covers the following main subjects: the historical background, religion,
the material background, appearance and apparel, daily activities, life cycle,
veiling and seclusion, Ramaḍān, the Pilgrimage, and problems of contact. It
provides a wealth of social, economic and cultural information on Bahrain at the
beginning of the 1960s.

425 **The pattern of women's seclusion and veiling in a Shi'a village:**
field research on Bahrain, Arabian Gulf.
Henny Harald Hansen. *Folk*, vol. 3 (1961), p. 23-42.
The report of the author's field research in the village of Sâr in 1960. It gives a
detailed description of the daily life of women in the village, and notes that its
people were extremely strict in keeping up the seclusion and veiling of women.
Despite this the author observed that within certain parts of the house neither veil
nor seclusion seemed to exist.

426 **Problems of contact and change. Field research in a Muslim**
village in the island of Bahrain.
Henny Harald Hansen. *Jahrbuch des Museums für Völkerkunde*
zu Leipzig, vol. 23 (1966), p. 82-94.
After a brief introduction, noting that the ruling family of Bahrain is Arab and
Sunni, whereas the village population calling itself *baharna* is Shi'a, this paper
summarises the two months of research undertaken by the author in the village
of Sār in 1960. It provides a useful description of traditional lifestyles in Bahrain
and the ways in which these have been changed by the development of the oil
industry.

427 **Social change in the Gulf states and Oman.**
Frauke Heard-Bey. *Asian Affairs*, vol. 59 (new series vol. 3),
no. 3 (Oct. 1972), p. 309-16.
A study of the repercussions of the discovery and exploitation of oil on social,
economic and political patterns in the Gulf. It notes Bahrain's traditional
importance as a merchant community, and also that the country has recently
been producing more graduates for white collar jobs than it needs.

Social Conditions

428 **The new Arab social order: a study of the social impact of oil wealth.**
Saad Eddin Ibrahim. Boulder, Colorado: Westview Press; London: Croom Helm, 1982. 208p. map. bibliog. (Westview's Special Studies on the Middle East).

This book challenges the commonly accepted view of the impact of manpower movements across the Arab 'wealth divide', and looks at the new social formations, class structures, value systems and social cleavages that have been emerging in both rich and poor Arab countries. Bahrain is mentioned briefly in a section on the well-to-do Arab states, and the author argues that, of all the small oil-exporting countries of the Gulf, Bahrain has evolved a relatively more balanced overall development.

429 **Journey into chaos.**
Paul Johnson. London: MacGibbon & Kee, 1958. 178p. map.

An account of the author's experiences in the Middle East. Bahrein is mentioned briefly in connection with the oil industry, and it notes that educational standards were higher in the 1950s in Bahrein than elsewhere in the Gulf.

430 **How they lived – 2: the dying customs of Bahrain. Series 1 – the marriage ceremony.**
Mohamed Ali Khalfan. *Dilmun: a Journal of Archaeology and History in Bahrain*, no. 5 (Dec. 1973), p. 14-15.

A short account of the traditional marriage ceremony in Bahrain.

431 **Tribe and state in Bahrain: the transformation of social and political authority in an Arab state.**
Fuad I. Khuri. Chicago, London: University of Chicago Press, 1980. 289p. map. bibliog. (Publications of the Center for Middle Eastern Studies, no. 14).

A comprehensive analysis of the development of political authority in Bahrain. It focuses on two general themes: the changing authority system with regards to colonial rule and socio-economic transformations, and the impact of these forces on the processes of interaction between tribe, peasantry, and urban society. It concludes that the dissolution of parliament in 1975 was intended to restrict the increasing power of the opposition. The author argues that in Bahrain tribalism emerged as a socio-political force opposing other forces with comparable vested interests. It provides much information on the effects of colonial intervention and the development of the oil industry on the social and political structures of Bahrain.

432 **Social classes and tensions in Bahrain.**
Fahim I. Qubain. *Middle East Journal*, vol. 9, no. 3 (Summer 1955), p. 269-80.

An examination of the tensions expressed in the Sunni-Shi'i riots in September 1953, the July 1954 Shi'i demonstration and attack on a police post, and the December 1954 general strike in support of demands made to the government for already promised reforms.

433 **Arabia through the looking glass.**
Jonathan Raban. London: Collins, 1979. 348p.

The story of the author's travels in Bahrain, Qatar, the United Arab Emirates, Yemen, Egypt and Jordan. Life in Manama, the British Club, the Game Park, and conversations with people living in Bahrain are included.

434 **The mode of production in the Arab Gulf before the discovery of oil.**
Mohamed G. Rumaihi. In: *Social and economic development in the Arab Gulf.* Edited by Tim Niblock. London: Croom Helm, 1980, p. 49-60.

This article argues that the social relations existing in the Gulf today are heavily influenced by the mode of production in the area before the discovery of oil. It provides some information on pearling in the Gulf, and notes its decline from the 1920s when the Bahraini pearling fleet consisted of some 500 ships to the situation in the 1950 census where no one was recorded in Bahrain as being employed in the pearl industry.

435 **Ethnic conflict: a framework of analysis and its relevance to the Gulf region.**
Abdul Aziz Said. In: *Conflict and cooperation in the Persian Gulf.* Edited by Mohammed Mughisuddin. New York, London: Praeger Publishers, 1977, p. 103-15.

A study of ethnic consciousness and the politics of disassociation in the Gulf. It notes that Bahrain is a successor to colonial territory and that it is inhabited by a colourful mixture of peoples.

436 **Social and political change in the Third World: some peculiarities of oil producing principalities of the Persian Gulf.**
Frank Stoakes. In: *The Arabian peninsula: society and politics.* Edited by Derek Hopwood. London: George Allen & Unwin, 1972, p. 189-215.

Briefly notes that the British presence in Bahrain has evoked animosity among certain sectors of the indigenous population.

Social Conditions

437 **Pirates or polities? Arab societies of the Persian or Arabian Gulf, 18th century.**
Louise E. Sweet. *Ethnohistory*, vol. 11 (1964), p. 262-80.

This paper investigates the nature and potential scale of integration of Arab societies in the Gulf during the 18th century. It notes that the Europeans were not impressed by the seacraft and lack of military forces at Bahrain in the mid-18th century, but that as the century progressed the maritime Arabs conspicuously increased the sizes of their ships, fleets and the scale of their raids. Bahrain's pearl industry and its role as a centre of commerce are also mentioned, as is the conflict between the 'Utub alliance of Kuwait, Bahrain and Qatar, and the Jowasim of the Trucial States. It argues that the Sunni Arab seafaring lineages were a controlling élite class or caste in coastally focused polities and settlements with mixed ethnic or sectarian population.

438 **The changing status of the Bahraini woman.**
Ali Hassan Taki. Bahrain: Oriental Press, 1974. 52p.

This booklet discusses the status of women and its relation to economic and social development in Bahrain. Following a general introduction, the second chapter considers the Arab Muslim woman and her inhibitions. The third chapter pays particular attention to the women of Bahrain and argues that, although the emancipation of women in Bahrain took place much later than in many other Arab countries, it has progressed very rapidly. Particular attention is paid to chastity requirements, early marriage, dowry, polygamy, divorce, access to social services, and civil rights.

439 **Center-periphery interaction patterns: the case of Arab visits, 1946-1975.**
W. R. Thompson. *International Organization*, vol. 35, no. 2 (Spring 1981), p. 355-73.

Bahrain is one of a number of countries in the Middle East to be used as examples of a theoretical model of center-periphery interaction patterns.

440 **Progresso culturale nelle isole el-Bahrein.** (Cultural progress in the island of Bahrein.)
L. Veccia Vaglieri. *Oriente Moderno*, vol. 15, no. 12 (1935), p. 656.

A brief note on socio-economic change in Bahrein.

441 **Leading the Saudis into temptation.**
    Peter Wilsher. *Sunday Times* (London), 21 November 1982,
    p. 18.

A discussion of the future significance of the causeway joining Al Aziziyah in Saudi Arabia to Al Jasrah in Bahrein, the foundation stone of which had been recently laid by King Fahd of Saudi Arabia. It highlights the potential conflicts between morality and economics that the causeway will produce, suggesting four possible future scenarios: its use only by heavy goods trucks; permits only being given to a limited number of Saudi cars; a Saudi demand for temperance before it allows its people to travel abroad; and the possibility of Bahrein becoming a free-for-all similar to Hong Kong.

Bahrain: language, customs & people.
See item no. 25.

Al-Bahrain islands.
See item no. 27.

The Middle East: a social geography.
See item no. 106.

Farewell to Arabia.
See item no. 331.

The market of Seleukia.
See item no. 361.

The Arabian peninsula: society and politics.
See item no. 477.

Bahrain: political development in a modernizing society.
See item no. 488.

Bahrain: social and political change since the First World War.
See item no. 491.

Arab states of the Persian Gulf.
See item no. 728.

Social Services, Health and Welfare

442 **Bahrain: a model for the Gulf.**
People, vol. 6, no. 4 (1979), p. 24-25.
A brief report on the progress of family planning in Bahrain. It notes that 85 per cent of births currently take place in hospitals, and that the small Family Planning Association has persuaded the Ministry of Health to open family life centres in each of the ten health centres which provide general health services throughout the state.

443 **Middle East Health.**
Sutton, Surrey: IPC Middle East Publishing, 1976- . 11 times a year.
A trade journal for those working in the provision of medical and hospital supplies in the Middle East. It contains a number of interesting articles on health care in Bahrain.

444 **State of Bahrain health services.**
Bahrain: Ministry of Health, n.d. [1977/78]. 31p.
Provides a summary of the work achieved by the Ministry of Health prior to the mid-1970s together with its plans for the future. After an introduction discussing government, industry, shipping, commerce, communications and education, it describes the health services in detail with sections on the Medical Centre, primary health care, public health services, health manpower development, the College of Health Sciences and Yusuf Kanoo School of Continuing Education, and it concludes with a section on career opportunities in the Ministry of Health.

445 **The golden milestone. Reminiscences of pioneer days fifty years ago in Arabia.**
Samuel M. Zwemer, James Cantine. New York: Fleming H. Revell, 1938. 157p.
An account of Christian missionary work in Arabia. Chapter 10 described the origins and opening of the mission and hospital in Bahrain.

The Middle East: a handbook.
See item no. 2.

Bahrain: from dhow to discoteque.
See item no. 15.

Progrès et évolution des principautés du Golfe persique. (Progress and evolution of the Arab principalities of the Persian Gulf.)
See item no. 296.

Politics

446 Oil, power and politics: conflict in Arabia, the Red Sea and the Gulf.
Mordechai Abir. London: Frank Cass, 1974. 221p. 3 maps. bibliog.

An analysis of conflicting political forces in Arabia, both at the local level and in the wider contexts of the Arab-Israeli conflict and East-West rivalry. Bahrain is mentioned in the context of British withdrawal from the Gulf, Iran's claims to the islands, the 1970 referendum on their future, and the 1971 renewal of the US basing agreement in Bahrain. It argues that Bahrain seems to be the most vulnerable of the new Gulf states.

447 Persian Gulf oil in Middle East and international conflicts.
Mordechai Abir. Jerusalem: Leonard Davis Institute for International Relations, Hebrew University of Jerusalem, 1976. 35p. 2 maps. (Jerusalem Papers on Peace Problems, no. 20).

This publication argues that the Gulf oil producers hold in their hands the key to the region's, and possibly the world's, peace, stability and balance of power. It has sections on Gulf oil and power politics, Saudi Arabia and inter-Arab relations, and tensions between Arab and non-Arab countries, and it pays particular attention to the influence of the Arab-Israeli conflict on oil policy. It notes that in 1971 Iran relinquished its claim to Bahrayn.

448 The development of the Gulf states.
Ahmad Mustafa Abu-Hakima. In: *The Arabian peninsula: society and politics.* Edited by Derek Hopwood. London: George Allen & Unwin, 1972, p. 31-53.

An investigation primarily into the political development of the Gulf states, which concentrates on Kuwait. It includes a section on the Shaikhdom of Bahrain, the Al Khalifah who were rulers of Bahrain from 1782, early government and involvements, Britain and Bahrain, modern Bahrain 1935-68, oil and development, councils and committees in Bahrain, and the role of Bahrain in Arabian Gulf politics.

449 **Politics in the Gulf.**
M. S. Agwani. New Delhi: Vikas Publishing House, 1978. 199p.
bibliog.

An analysis of the political conflicts in the Gulf resulting from its significance as an oil producer. Information is provided on the constitutional development of Bahrain, the anti-British riots, the Iranian claims to the islands, the development of the oil industry, and the state's path to individual independence in 1971.

450 **The Persian Gulf and Indian Ocean in international politics.**
Edited by Abbas Amirie. Tehran: Institute for International Political and Economic Studies, 1975. 417p.

Thirteen papers and discussions given at a conference held in Tehran in March 1975 on the role of the Gulf and the Indian Ocean in international politics. The papers by John C. Campbell, R. M. Burrell, Amir Taheri, Jahangir Amuzegar, and Thomas Stauffer all mention Bahrain.

451 **Arab states of the lower Gulf: people, politics, petroleum.**
John Duke Anthony. Washington, DC: Middle East Institute, 1975. 273p. map. bibliog. (James Terry Duce Memorial Series, vol. 3).

An attempt to provide insights and information on the political functioning of societies in the Gulf at a key point in their history as they emerge onto the international stage in an area of great strategic significance. Bahrayn is discussed extensively in chapter 2. It is described as the lower Gulf's most advanced state socially and economically as well as politically. Information is given on the country's government, social and political structure, non-élites, and regional relations.

452 **The Persian Gulf in regional and international politics: the Arab side of the Gulf.**
John Duke Anthony. In: *The security of the Persian Gulf.* Edited by Hossein Amirsadeghi. London: Croom Helm, 1981, p. 170-96.

An analysis of the local and regional aims of the Arab governments of the Gulf in terms of the nature of political interaction among the states, the contest between conservative and radical régimes in the area, and the connection between these states and the Arab-Israeli conflict. Among territorial disputes still outstanding in the region, it notes that between Qatar and Bahrain over the Hawar Islands and Zabarah as being of importance. It also mentions the settlement of the maritime boundary between Bahrain and Saudi Arabia, the political wrangling between Bahrain and Qatar over independence in 1971, Bahrain's relationships with Iraq and South Yemen, Iran's old claim to the islands of Bahrain relinquished in 1970, the role of Jordanian officers in Bahrain's army, and the use of oil prices as a weapon against countries supporting Israel.

Politics

453 **The Middle East in world politics.**
Edited by Mohammed Ayoob. London: Croom Helm, in association with the Australian Institute of International Affairs, Canberra, 1981. 217p.

Papers and discussion resulting from a symposium on the Middle East held in March 1980 at the Australian Institute of International Affairs. The papers by Rony Gabbay, Mohammed Ayoob, and Stuart Harris mention Bahrain.

454 **Oil, Arabism and Islam: the Persian Gulf in world politics.**
Mohammed Ayoob. In: *The Middle East in world politics.* Edited by Mohammed Ayoob. London: Croom Helm, 1981, p. 118-35.

An evaluation of the changing political influence of the oil-producing countries of the Gulf. It argues that the linkages between Bahrain, together with the other countries of the Gulf, and the remainder of the Middle East became stronger during the 1970s.

455 **Bahrain.**
In: *Political handbook of the world 1981.* Edited by Arthur S. Banks, William Overstreet. New York: McGraw-Hill, 1981, p. 72-73.

Provides basic information on the State of Bahrain and includes sections on the political background, constitution and government, foreign relations, political parties, legislature, the cabinet, news media, and intergovernmental representation.

456 **Recent developments in the Persian Gulf.**
H. G. Balfour-Paul. *Journal of the Royal Central Asian Society,* vol. 56, no. 1 (Feb. 1969), p. 12-19.

An account of political changes and international relations in Bahrain, Qatar and the Trucial States between 1961 and 1968.

457 **Offshore politics and resources in the Middle East.**
Gerald H. Blake. In: *Change and development in the Middle East: essays in honour of W. B. Fisher.* Edited by John I. Clarke, Howard Bowen-Jones. London, New York: Methuen, 1981, p. 113-29.

A summary of the nature of offshore sovereignty and a consideration of the complex problems associated with offshore boundary delimitation. It notes that Bahrain has a commercial fishery specializing in the processing of Gulf shrimps and prawns for export.

458 **Yesterday and tomorrow in the Persian Gulf.**
William Brewer. *Middle East Journal*, vol. 23, no. 2 (Spring
1969), p. 149-58.

An assessment of the political future of the Gulf following the announcement on
16 January 1968 by the government of the United Kingdom that its troops would
be withdrawn from the area by the end of 1971. It records some details of the
first tentative meetings by the rulers of Baḥrayn, Qatar and the Trucial States, and
their agreement to establish the Federation of Arab Emirates.

459 **Britain and the Gulf – don't go just yet please!: the wisdom of
withdrawal reconsidered.**
Neville Brown. *New Middle East*, no. 24 (Sept. 1970), p. 43-46.

An evaluation of the political future of the Gulf states following the announcement of 16 January 1968 that Britain would withdraw from the area by the end
of 1971. In March 1968 the Federation of the Emirates of the Arab Gulf, including
Bahrein, Qatar and the seven Trucial States, was formed, and the paper argues
that this federation was extremely unstable. One source of conflict is identified as
the emnity between the 'worldly and nonchalant Bahreini establishment' and the
régime in Qatar, which is seen as retaining 'manifold traces of its puritanical
Wahhabi origins'. The author suggests that the most serious threat to the survival
of the federation was the attitude of Bahrein and the desire of its inhabitants for
full national independence for the state.

460 **The Persian Gulf.**
R. M. Burrell. Washington, DC: Center for Strategic and Inter-
national Studies, Georgetown University; New York: Library
Press, 1972. 81p. map. (Washington Papers, no. 1).

This publication analyses the course of events following the British withdrawal
from the Gulf, outlines the current major issues on both the Iranian and Arabian
shores of the Gulf, and indicates some of the factors which the author believes
to be of continuing importance in the region. Bahrein is discussed mainly in
chapter 3, where accounts are given of the settlement of the Iranian claim to the
islands as a result of the United Nations mission to Bahrein in March 1970 and the
consequent referendum; of the foundation of the United Arab Emirates, which
Qatar and Bahrein did not join; and of the political and economic unrest which
began early in March 1972 in the form of a strike by members of the airport
labour force, and which spread to the docks, shipyards and aluminium processing
plant, against the employment of non-Arabs in Bahrein and the United States-
Bahrein naval treaty.

Politics

461 **Policies of the Arab littoral states in the Persian Gulf region.**
R. M. Burrell. In: *The Persian Gulf and Indian Ocean in international politics.* Edited by Abbas Amirie. Tehran: Institute for International Political and Economic Studies, 1975, p. 227-48.

This paper analyses the threats to political stability in the Arab states around the Gulf as potential threats to global trade and communications. Much attention is paid to the war in Dhofar and the activities of the PFLOAG (Popular Front for the Liberation of the Occupied Arab Gulf) and PFLO (Popular Front for the Liberation of Oman), but political unrest in Bahrain is also discussed. The strikes in Bahrain in 1972, 1973 and 1974 over wage rates, the employment of non-Arabs, and the existence of the US naval base at Jufair are mentioned at some length.

462 **Politics and participation where Britannia once ruled.**
R. M. Burrell. *New Middle East*, no. 51 (Dec. 1972), p. 32-36.

A review of the first twelve months of independence in the Gulf following British withdrawal in 1971 and an assessment of the future political and economic prospects of the region. It includes discussion of the March 1972 decision by OAPEC to choose Bahrein as the site for its drydock scheme, the use by the USA of naval facilities in Bahrein, and the March 1972 sporadic riots in Bahrein over low wages, the employment of non-Arabs, and the US presence on the islands.

463 **Problems and prospects in the Gulf: an uncertain future.**
R. M. Burrell. *Round Table* (London), 1972, p. 209-19.

An evaluation of the politics of the Gulf in the wake of Britain's withdrawal in December 1971. Particular attention is paid to the growth of Iranian power in the region, and the paper notes that following the 1970 agreement between Britain and Iran over Bahrein's future the Iranian government made every effort to improve relations with Bahrein. The proposed federation of the nine Gulf emirates including Bahrein is also discussed.

464 **The Middle Eastern question or some political problems of Indian defence.**
Valentine Chirol. London: John Murray, 1903. 512p. 2 maps. bibliog.

This analysis of early British interests in the Middle East notes the 1895 attempt by 'pirate dhows' under Turkish influence to seize Bahrein, which was then the centre of pearl fishing in the Gulf. This was thwarted through the action of a British gunboat.

465 **Le Golfe persique: problèmes et perspectives.** (The Persian Gulf:
problems and perspectives.)
Mohammad-Reza Djalili. Paris: Dalloz; Tehran: Libraire
Larousse Internationale, 1978. 252p. map. bibliog.

A mainly political analysis of the Gulf states divided into four sections on
geographical and historical background, the coastal states, the economic and
military situation, and relations of the external powers of the USA, the USSR,
Great Britain and France with the Gulf. Bahrein is specifically discussed in
chapter 7, where some details are given of its history, independence, economy
and politics.

466 **Persian Gulf – contrasts and similarities.**
Mohammed Reza Djalili, Dietrich Kapelier. *Aussenpolitik*
(English edition), vol. 29 (1978), p. 228-34.

Provides details on so-called facts concerning the Gulf, including sections on the
territories, populations, political systems, military capability, foreign policy, and
economic situations and prospects of countries in the region, and also on what
these imply in terms of the Gulf as an oil regulator, unequal chances for the
future, unequal power distribution, external interests and potential sources of
upheaval. Among other scattered mentions of Bahrain it notes that the state had
already reached the stage of diminishing oil production by the late 1970s and also
that it has had some success in developing a service sector, particularly in the
financial field.

467 **Persian Gulf countries at the cross-roads.**
G. Dymov. *International Affairs* (Moscow), no. 3 (March 1973),
p. 53-59.

An analysis of the collapse of *Pax Britannica* in the Gulf and its replacement by
US interests. It argues that 'British imperialism stubbornly resisted the national
liberation movement before it gave in'. It also notes the US-Bahrain agreement
permitting US military forces to use the old Jufair naval base on Bahrain, and
further argues that this was part of an attempt by the US to set up a broad
military-political alliance in the Gulf. It concludes by suggesting that the future
of the Gulf emirates will largely depend on their success in shaking off the yokes
of the imperialist oil magnates who are seeking to reverse the tide of history.

468 **Arabia: when Britain goes.**
Fabian Research Bureau. London: Fabian Society, 1967. 28p.
map. (Fabian Research Series, no. 259).

An investigation of the effects of British withdrawal from the south of Arabia by
1968, divided into sections on the various states of Arabia, oil and defence.
Bahrain is briefly mentioned in a subsection on the states of the lower Gulf, and
it argues that since the island already had well developed public services it could
well claim to stand on its own feet both politically and economically. Standard
Oil of California's and Texaco's interests in Bahrain Oil are also mentioned.

Politics

469 Israel and the Middle East.

Rony Gabbay. In: *The Middle East in world politics.* Edited by Mohammed Ayoob. London: Croom Helm, 1981, p. 40-74.

Bahrain is used as an example of a 'midget state', which emerged in the early 1970s as an independent entity, in the context of a discussion of how a shift in ideological and political thinking during the 1960s enabled local distinctive entities to opt for full independence rather than being swallowed in the name of unity.

470 Arabia without sultans.

Fred Halliday. Harmondsworth, England: Penguin, 1974. Reprinted with postscript, 1979. 528p. 16 maps.

An analysis of what the author sees as the subjugation of Arabia to imperialism and the emergence of a revolutionary resistance to this domination. Bahrain is discussed in chapters 12 and 13, where it is noted that the Exclusive Agreement of 1892 with Bahrain formed the model for the treaties with other tribal leaders in the area. Conflicts between the population of Bahrain and the British administration, and the formation of the National Liberation Movement are noted on p. 440-47.

471 The Gulf between two revolutions: 1958-1979.

Fred Halliday. In: *Social and economic development in the Arab Gulf.* Edited by Tim Niblock. London: Croom Helm, 1980, p. 210-38.

An analysis of recent political change in the Gulf. It suggests that in Bahrain, where some of the Shia population has evinced sympathy for Ayatollah Khomeini, the future position of the ruling Khalifa family is uncertain.

472 Iran: dictatorship and development;

Fred Halliday. Harmondsworth, England: Penguin, 1979. 348p. 4 maps. bibliog.

A book analysing the divided and politically troubled nature of Iran prior to the fall of the Shah. It notes that in 1970 the Shah abandoned Iran's claim to Bahrain.

473 The Gulf states and Oman in transition.

Frauke Heard-Bey. *Asian Affairs*, vol. 59 (new series vol. 3), no. 1 (Feb. 1972), p. 14-22.

An evaluation of the transformation of the political landscape of the Gulf states following Britain's withdrawal in 1971. It notes Bahrain's declaration of independence on 14 August 1971, and it argues that Bahrain has outgrown its traditional form of government with its political reality being for some time out of tune with its constitutional condition.

474 **Federation and the future of the Gulf.**

Nicholas Herbert. *Mid East*, vol. 8, no. 6 (1968), p. 10-14.

This paper on the future political prospects of the Arab Gulf states, following the 1968 announcement of British withdrawal from the region, notes that during the late 1960s Iran was reasserting its longstanding claim to Bahrein and was describing the Federation of Arab Emirates as illegal because it included Bahrein. The author also suggests that Bahrein was likely to be more influential in the region than its diminishing importance as an oil producer would suggest.

475 **The Annual Register: a Record of World Events.**

Currently edited by H. V. Hodson. London: Longman, 1758- . annual.

A summary of events throughout the world. All recent issues have included a section on the Arab states of the Gulf which includes Bahrein.

476 **The Persian Gulf after the British Raj.**

David Holden. *Foreign Affairs*, vol. 49, no. 4 (1971), p. 721-35.

An evaluation of the politics of the Gulf at the time of the British withdrawal in 1971. It notes that Bahrein then had by far the largest and most sophisticated population of the nine states which were to become independent from Britain, and it argues that within the Gulf as a whole a number of sources of instability existed, which the author saw as being likely to lead to a period of fairly radical readjustment.

477 **The Arabian peninsula: society and politics.**

Edited by Derek Hopwood. London: George Allen & Unwin, 1972. 320p.

Papers presented to the joint seminar on the Arabian peninsula organised in spring 1969 by the Centre of Middle Eastern Studies at the School of Oriental and African Studies, University of London, and the Middle East Centre of St. Antony's College, Oxford. The papers by Ahmad Mustafa Abu-Hakima, George Rentz, J. C. Wilkinson, R. D. Bathurst, J. B. Kelly, R. M. Burrell, Frank Stoakes, Edith Penrose, and Yusif A. Sayigh mention Bahrain.

478 **The Persian Gulf: prospects for stability.**

J. C. Hurewitz. New York: Foreign Policy Association, 1974. 64p. 2 maps. (Headline Series, no. 220).

This study analyses the political side-effects of what was seen in the early 1970s as an emerging oil crisis. Details are given of the British loss of influence in the area and the subsequent state of balanced instability that prevailed. One chapter investigates Soviet interests in the Gulf, and another specific US policies relating to the area.

Politics

479   **Jail for 73 convicted of Bahrain Muslim plot.**
The Times (London), 24 May 1982, p. 4.

Gives details of the trial of 73 persons accused of plotting to overthrow the
monarchy in December 1981. The defendants included 11 Saudi Arabians, one
Kuwaiti and one Omani, with the rest being Bahrain nationals. Three defendants
received life imprisonment, 60 were sentenced to 15 years, and 10 to 7 years. The
Bahrain authorities claimed that the accused had plotted to overthrow the government and to proclaim an Iranian-style Islamic republic.

480   **The future in Arabia.**
John B. Kelly. *International Affairs* (London), vol. 42, no. 4
(Oct. 1966), p. 619-40.

An evaluation of the political future of countries in the Arabian peninsula. It
argues that Bahrain was confronted by the dual problem of maintaining her
independence and her internal stability, and that the potential for insurrection
in Bahrain was higher than for many of the other countries of the Gulf.

481   **Oil politics in the Persian Gulf region.**
M. A. Saleem Khan. *India Quarterly*, vol. 30 (1974), p. 25-41.

A study of oil politics in the Gulf in terms of the energy crisis and the use of oil as
a political weapon.

482   **Stabilité et instabilité dans le golfe Arabo-Persique.** (Stability and
instability in the Arab-Persian Gulf.)
Wilfred Knapp. *Maghreb Machrek*, no. 77 (July-Sept. 1977),
p. 69-74.

An analysis of political life in the Gulf states. It notes that Bahrein has had a long
history of relative prosperity, but that there have recently been religious troubles
and labour agitation.

483   **Gulf union.**
David Ledger. *Middle East International*, no. 9 (Dec. 1971),
p. 6-7, 44.

Written soon after the full independence of Bahrain, Qatar and the United Arab
Emirates, this short paper argues that the Gulf's future was bound to be stormy.
The solution of the Iranian claim to Bahrain, and negotiations over the planned
federation of the Gulf states are mentioned briefly. It argues that at independence
Bahrain was one of the most advanced states of the Gulf, but that there was likely
to be internal pressure for reform in the state's government.

484 **Politics in the Persian Gulf.**
A. R. Lindt. *Journal of the Royal Central Asian Society*, vol. 26, no. 4 (Oct. 1939), p. 619-33.

An account of politics in the Gulf at the outbreak of the Second World War. It notes that, since the abandonment of the naval stations on the Iranian coast, Bahrain had become the most important Royal Navy and Royal Air Force base in the Gulf.

485 **Political geography of Trucial Oman and Qatar.**
Alexander Melamid. *Geographical Review*, vol. 43, no. 2 (April 1953), p. 194-206.

An evaluation of the effects of the oil industry on the native population of the south-east shores of the Gulf, and the resultant needs to introduce national boundaries. It notes that the 1820 agreement between the states of the Trucial Coast and Britain was, in the case of Qatar, signed for by the sheikh of Bahrein.

486 **The Middle East.**
London: IC Publications. May-June 1974- . monthly.

This journal covers a wide range of political and economic issues, and also includes useful book reviews.

487 **Middle East Newsletters: Gulf States, Iraq, Iran, Kuwait, Bahrain, Qatar, United Arab Emirates, Oman.**
London: IC Publications, 1 Dec. 1980- . fortnightly.

Formerly *Middle East Newsletter*. Includes sections on politics and defence; economy and trade; oil, energy and minerals; and banking, finance and aid.

488 **Bahrain: political development in a modernizing society.**
Emile A. Nakhleh. Lexington, Massachusetts; Toronto: London: Lexington Books, 1976. 191p. bibliog.

A thorough analysis of the changing political structure of Bahrain. It covers the following main themes: the influence of education on Bahrain's political development; communications and political socialization; the role of labour and foreign policy in political development; the Constitutional Assembly and the first national election.

489 **I saw for myself: the aftermath of Suez.**
Anthony Nutting. London: Hollis & Carter, 1958. 103p.

An account of the impressions gained by the former Minister of State for Foreign Affairs 1954-56 during his visit to North Africa and the Middle East in 1957. It argues that Bahrain was in an explosive state and that it was 'hardly democratic by any standard'. It discusses the riots that occurred in Bahrain following the Suez crisis, and it suggests that the ruler was a spent force who refused to think ahead. It also suggests that the best future for Bahrain lay in a federation with Qatar and the Trucial sheikhdoms.

Politics

490 **Political and economic integration in the Arab states of the Gulf.**
Roger P. Nye. *Journal of South Asian and Middle Eastern Studies*, vol. 2, no. 1 (fall 1978), p. 3-21.
An account of the different methods by which the Arab states of the Gulf have sought political and economic integration. It argues that nationalism, the manpower problem, the fragility of traditional régimes, and tribalism are all factors hindering this aim.

491 **Bahrain: social and political change since the First World War.**
M. G. Rumaihi. Epping, England: Bowker, in association with the Centre for Middle Eastern and Islamic Studies of the University of Durham, 1976. 258p. bibliog.
A thorough analysis of social and political change between the end of the First World War and the departure of the British in 1971. The study is divided into four parts. Part 1 investigates the historical tribal and demographic background to Bahrain and its people. Part 2 looks at economic and social change, concentrating on traditional activities, such as the pearl fisheries and agriculture, commerce and industry, and the social impact of modern industry. Part 3 assesses the impact of education on social change, and part 4 investigates political change and conflict, noting the growth of political awareness in the 1930s and the development of conflict in the 1950s.

492 **L'Arabie à l'âge du petrole.** (Arabia in the oil age.)
Édouard Sablier. *Table Ronde*, vol. 126 (June 1958), p. 145-60.
An investigation into the politics of Arabia, written soon after the beginnings of major oil developments in the area.

493 **Conflict and cooperation in the Gulf.**
K. R. Singh. *International Studies* (Delhi), vol. 15, no. 4 (1976), p. 487-508.
A study of the regional politics of the Gulf following the withdrawal of the British, who had been the dominant political force, in 1971. It briefly mentions the evacuation of the British strategic base at Bahrain, the 1970 solution of the dispute between Iran and Britain over Bahrain, the 1958 offshore boundary agreement between Bahrain and Saudi Arabia, the continuing disputes between Qatar and Bahrain over the Huwar Islands, and the Bahraini request for the USA to withdraw its military presence from the island by the middle of 1977. Much of the paper is devoted to a study of the tensions between Iran and Iraq.

494 **The geopolitical significance of Persian Gulf oil.**
Thomas Stauffer. In: *The Persian Gulf and Indian Ocean in
international politics.* Edited by Abbas Amirie. Tehran: Institute
for International Political and Economic Studies, 1975, p. 347-58.

An investigation of three main issues: the significance of Persian Gulf oil to the
West, the effect of oil surpluses on political balances in the area, and whether or
not industrial development in the region will ever be significant on a global scale.
The aluminium smelter at Bahrain is mentioned briefly.

495 **Der Persisch/Arabische Golf – Wirtschaftsraum und Krisenherd.**
(The Persian/Arabian Gulf – centre of economic development
and political crises.)
Udo Steinbach. *Geographische Rundschau,* vol. 32, no. 12
(Dec. 1980), p. 514-22.

This paper argues that in the Gulf there are considerable conflicts resulting from
the inequality of the territories and their populations, the different historical
experiences and contrasting ideological orientations, and from the reciprocal land
claims. It suggests that the instability of the Gulf, evident in the open hostility
between Iraq and Iran, has led to the possibility of the involvement of the superpowers and thus an escalation of tension in the area. There are several mentions of
Bahrain mainly in connection with its oil industry and revenue.

496 **The Arabian peninsula.**
Louise E. Sweet. In: *The central Middle East: a handbook of
anthropology and published research on the Nile valley, the
Arab Levant, southern Mesopotamia, the Arabian peninsula,
and Israel.* Edited by Louise E. Sweet. New Haven, Connecticut:
Human Relations Area Files, 1971, p. 199-266.

Bahrain is noted as being more complex in political structure than the other
countries of the Gulf, and it is argued that the state has developed as a stratified
conquest chiefdom since the 18th century. The importance of pearl fishing, boat-
building and commerce in the traditional economy is also mentioned.

497 **The decision to withdraw from the Gulf.**
D. C. Watt. *Political Quarterly,* vol. 39, no. 3 (July-Sept. 1968),
p. 310-21.

A discussion of the confusion following the decision by the British government to
withdraw from the Gulf by 1971. It argues that this provides an outstanding illus-
tration of all that was then wrong with the British official decision-making process.

498 **Iran since the revolution.**
S. Zabih. London: Croom Helm, 1982. 240p.

An account of internal political activity in Iran following the overthrow of the
Pahlavi dynasty in 1978. It notes that Iran is now susceptible to reckless political
moves, such as the renouncement of the 1969 Bahrain Settlement.

117

Politics

499 **The origins of the United Arab Emirates. A political and social history of the Trucial States.**
Rosemarie Said Zahlan. London: Macmillan, 1978. 278p. map. bibliog.

A thorough account of the political development of the United Arab Emirates, which mentions Bahrain in connection with the country's relations with Britain, planned federation on Britain's departure from the area in 1971, the Iranian claim to the islands, its oil industry, and the choice of Bahrain by the RAF as its main centre for the air route down the Gulf.

The United Arab Emirates: a modern history.
See item no. 281.

Der arabisch-persische Golf. Eine Studie zur historischen, politischen und ökonomischen Entwicklung der Golf-Region. (The Arabian-Persian Gulf. A study of the historical, political and economic development of the Gulf region.)
See item no. 289.

The Middle East: a political and economic survey.
See item no. 302.

British withdrawal from the Persian Gulf.
See item no. 310.

Arabia, the Gulf and the West.
See item no. 337.

Documents of the national struggle in Oman and the Arabian Gulf.
See item no. 422.

Tribe and state in Bahrain: the transformation of social and political authority in an Arab state.
See item no. 431.

Ethnic conflict: a framework of analysis and its relevance to the Gulf region.
See item no. 435.

Political participation and the constitutional experiments in the Arab Gulf: Bahrain and Qatar.
See item no. 515.

Bahrain, pearl of the Gulf.
See item no. 517.

Inter-Arab social and political relationships.
See item no. 525.

Defending the Gulf: a survey.
See item no. 540.

Constitution and Legal System

500 **The Arabian Gulf states: their legal and political status and their international problems.**
Husain M. Albaharna. Beirut: Librairie du Liban, 1975. 2nd rev. ed. 428p. 9 maps. bibliog.
A revised and updated version of the author's *The legal status of the Arabian Gulf states* (q.v.). Five monographs at the end of the book contain the post-1968 developments. The first of these monographs is specifically concerned with the settlement of the Bahrain-Iran dispute, and Bahrain is also mentioned in connection with territorial disputes following the independence of the Arab Gulf states in 1971.

501 **The fact-finding mission of the United Nations Secretary General and the settlement of the Bahrain-Iran dispute, May 1970.**
Husain Al-Baharna. *International and Comparative Law Quarterly*, vol. 22 (1970), p. 541-52.
An analysis of the rival claims by Britain and Iran to Bahrain, and a description of the United Nations fact-finding mission which led to Iran relinquishing its claims to the islands in 1970. The mission was led by Mr. Winspeare, the Personal Representative of the UN Secretary General, and it spent 20 days in Bahrain, reaching the conclusion that the Bahrainis were virtually unanimous in wanting a fully independent and sovereign Arab state.

502 **The legal status of the Arabian Gulf states: a study of their treaty relations and their international problems.**
Husain Muhammad Albaharna. Manchester, England: Manchester University Press; Dobbs Ferry, New York: Oceana Publications, 1968. 351p. 4 maps. bibliog.
A comprehensive examination of the international legal problems of the Arabian Gulf. There are many mentions of Bahrain in connection with British, Turkish and Persian interests in the islands, the Zubarah dispute, and boundary delimitations necessitated by the discovery of oil. Details are given of the following treaties of which Bahrain was a signatory: Draft Treaty of Friendship (Britain) 1816, Treaty of Peace 1820, agreement concerning suppression of slave trade 1856, Friendly Convention 1861, agreements with Britain 1880 and 1892, subsidiary agreements with Britain 1898, and Offshore Boundary Agreement with Saudi Arabia 1958.

120

503 **Legal development in Arabia. A selection of articles and addresses on the Arabian Gulf.**
W. M. Ballantyne. London: Graham & Trotman, 1980. 125p.

A collection of the author's writings on law in the Gulf, dating from the period 1957-79. It provides information on Bahrain's agency, charter companies, civil law, company law, common law, contracts law, corporation tax, Council of Ministers, criminal procedure code, exempt companies regulation, income tax, investment, banking licence, judges, judicature law, patents, designs and trademarks law, penal code, *shari'a* (Islamic) law, workmen's compensation law, and aspects of its oil production. Bahrain's constitution, published on 6 December 1973, states that the Islamic *shari'a* is the principal source for legislation.

504 **Le golf persique et les isles de Bahrein.** (The Persian Gulf and the islands of Bahrein.)
M. Malek Esmaili (Azizollah). Paris: Domat-Montchrestien, 1936. 285p. map. bibliog.

An analysis of the claims of Iran and Britain to the islands of Bahrein, which is divided into two parts: the first includes a geographical and historical description of the Gulf, and the second investigates the Anglo-Iranian dispute. It argues that the Iranian claim to Bahrein is older and more secure than that of the British, and indeed that the 1882 accord between Captain Bruce and the Prince Governor of Chiraz acknowledged the Shah of Iran's title to Bahrein. It concludes that Iran had sovereignty over the islands of Bahrein in 1783 and that this sovereignty has not been lost since then.

505 **The Middle Eastern states and the Law of the Sea.**
Ali A. El-Hakim. Manchester, England: Manchester University Press, 1979. 293p. 17 maps. bibliog.

An investigation of the significance of the Law of the Sea for Middle Eastern states. Part One considers general practices and policies relating to the Law of the Sea, and then part 2 concentrates on specific regional issues with chapter 3 concentrating on legal problems of offshore boundaries in the Arabian Gulf. Within this chapter details are given of the Bahrain-Saudi Arabia Boundary Agreement of 1958, the 1970 agreement over the continental shelf between Bahrain and Iran, and the continuing dispute over the sovereignty of the Hawar Islands and the offshore boundary between Bahrain and Qatar.

506 **The modernization of labor and labor law in the Arab Gulf states.**
Enid Hill. Cairo: American University in Cairo, 1979. 113p. 2 maps. bibliog. (Cairo Papers in Social Science, monograph 2).

This paper explores the anomaly by which the creation of labour law has generally preceded the modernization of the legal systems in the Gulf.

Constitution and Legal System

507 **Iran's claim to the sovereignty of Bahrayn.**
Majid Khadduri. *American Journal of International Law*,
vol. 45, no. 4 (Oct. 1951), p. 631-47.

An account of Iran's claim to the islands of Bahrayn, following the passing of the
Oil Nationalization Act by both houses of the Iranian Parliament in March 1951.
It provides details of Iran's historical and contemporary claims, the British
protection of the islands, and the juridical status of Bahrayn.

508 **The labour law for the private sector, Amiri decree law no. 23 of 1976.**
Bahrain: Ministry of Labour and Social Affairs, 1976. 43p.

A translation of the labour law with 170 articles divided into twenty chapters.

509 **Administrative and legal development in Arabia: the Persian Gulf principalities.**
Herbert J. Liebesny. *Middle East Journal*, vol. 10, no. 1 (winter 1956), p. 33-42.

This paper argues that administrative and legal developments in Arabia came
about due to the British desire to make the route to India secure and to prevent
the establishment of a strategic position by another power which might threaten
their approaches to India. It notes that the highest British official in the Gulf
was the Political Resident based in Bahrein, which was the most modernized of all
the principalities, and it provides some details of the political administration of
the country.

510 **British jurisdiction in the states of the Persian Gulf.**
Herbert J. Liebesny. *Middle East Journal*, vol. 3, no. 3 (July 1949), p. 330-32.

A note concerning the set of Orders in Council enacted in 1949 by Great Britain
for the principalities in the Persian Gulf, dealing with British criminal and civil
jurisdiction over British subjects and over other non-Muslim foreigners. These
Orders in Council were introduced as a result of the granting of independence to
India in 1947, prior to which Indian Codes were the foundation of law applied to
these territories. Three new courts were established as a result of the 1949 Orders:
the Court of the Political Agent, the Chief Court, and the Full Court. In Bahrein
two further courts existed, with members selected jointly by the Political Agent
and the Sheikh of Bahrein. These were the Majlis al-Urf, a local civil court
composed of four members, and the Salifah Court dealing with local diving and
marine matters.

511 **Legislation on the sea-bed and territorial waters of the Persian Gulf.**
Herbert J. Liebesny. *Middle East Journal*, vol. 4, no. 1 (Jan. 1950), p. 94-98.

This paper notes that Bahrein issued a proclamation concerning its sea bed, as did
Kuwait, Qatar, and the sheikhdoms of the Trucial Coast, a few days after the
Saudi Arabian sea bed proclamation of 28 May 1949.

512 Iran, Saudi Arabia and the Law of the Sea: political interaction
and legal development in the Persian Gulf.
Charles G. MacDonald. Westport, Connecticut; London:
Greenwood Press, 1980. 226p. 8 maps. bibliog.
A study focusing on the approaches of Iran and Saudi Arabia to the Law of the
Sea in the Gulf as a study of the development of the Law of the Sea in general.
Particular attention is paid to the relationship between specific claims and
treaties and the underlying political interests that influenced these developments.
Bahrain is specifically discussed in the context of its pearl fisheries, Iran's claim
to the archipelago, and the Saudi Arabian and Iranian offshore boundary agree-
ments with Bahrain.

513 Part 1. The Higher Council for Vocational Training: Amiri decree
no. 20 of 1975. Amiri decree no. 1 of 1978; Part 2. The Higher
Council for Labour Services: Amiri decree no. 11 of 1976; Part
3. Subsidiary legislation enacted under the provisions of the
Labour Law for the private sector. Amiri decree law no. 23 of
1976; Part 4. (i) Organisation and functions of the Ministry of
Labour and Social Affairs (ii) Organisation and functions of the
Directorate of Planning and Technical Services.
[Ministry of Labour and Social Affairs]. Bahrain: Ministry of
Labour and Social Affairs, n.d. [1978/79]. 112p.
A translation of the official Arabic texts of a number of important laws of
Bahrain relating to labour and social affairs.

514 The settlement of the Bahrain question: a study in Anglo-Iranian-
United Nations diplomacy.
Hooshang Moghtader. *Pakistan Horizon*, vol. 26, no. 2 (2nd
quarter 1973), p. 16-29.
An account of the processes by which the United Nations approved the findings
of its fact-finding mission to Bahrain in 1970, and as a result of which the Anglo-
Iranian conflict over the islands was resolved. It provides details of the historical
claims by both parties to Bahrain.

515 Political participation and the constitutional experiments in the
Arab Gulf: Bahrain and Qatar.
Emile A. Nakhleh. In: *Social and economic development in the
Arab Gulf*. Edited by Tim Niblock. London: Croom Helm, 1980,
p. 161-76.
This article argues that evolutionary change in the Gulf can only come about
peacefully through a process of internal political reform, that to function
effectively and to endure peacefully such participation must be institutionalized,
and that the people must have a clearly defined and systematic method of influencing decision making. In a discussion of Bahrain's experience it notes that the
Emir of Bahrain dissolved the one-and-a-half year old Bahrain National Assembly
in June 1975 as a result of the breakdown of co-operation between the ruling
family and the Assembly.

Constitution and Legal System

516 **The legal framework for oil concessions in the Arab world.**
Simon G. Siksek. Beirut: Middle East Research and Publishing
Center, 1960. 140p. bibliog. (Middle East Oil Monographs, no. 2).
An examination of the general legal principles that governed oil concession contracts in the Arab world. It aims to present an objective analysis of the fundamen-
tal legal problems that faced the parties to oil concession contracts. Although
only concerned with the period before 1960, it provides a useful framework in
which to view the early oil developments in the Gulf.

The Middle East: a handbook.
See item no. 2.

Personal column.
See item no. 16.

A British official guide to the Gulf.
See item no. 298.

The Arab states and the Arab League: a documentary record.
See item no. 344.

**The authority of shaykhs in the Gulf: an essay in nineteenth century
history.**
See item no. 349.

Politics in the Gulf.
See item no. 449.

Bahrain.
See item no. 455.

The Gulf states and Oman in transition.
See item no. 473.

Bahrain: political development in a modernizing society.
See item no. 488.

The Persian Gulf and American policy.
See item no. 579.

Administration and Local Government

517 **Bahrain, pearl of the Gulf.**
James H. Belgrave. *Journal of the Royal Central Asian Society,*
vol. 47, no. 2 (April 1960), p. 117-26.
This paper provides a summary of political developments in Bahrain during the 1950s. In passing it notes that Bahrain was the site of the Garden of Eden in the Babylonian and Sumerian versions of that place, and it briefly discusses the finds of the Danish Archaeological Expedition to Bahrain between 1953 and 1960. It elaborates on the appearance in 1954 of the organization entitled the Higher Executive Committee, the later establishment of the Labour Law Advisory Committee, the emergence of the Committee of National Union, and the ruler's Administrative Council. Following demonstrations after the Suez crisis in the autumn of 1956 the members of the Committee of National Union were arrested, and thus the first political party in the Gulf came to an end.

518 **The Persian Gulf Gazette.**
London: HM Stationery Office, vol. 1, no. 1 (Oct. 1953)
-vol. 20, no. 1 (May 1972); supplements no. 1-58
(Oct. 1953-Aug. 1968).
This gazette contains notices of appointments and of all Orders in Council, Regulations, Rules and other instruments affecting the exercise of British jurisdiction in Bahrain, Kuwait, Qatar, the Trucial States, and Muscat and Oman.

Administration and Local Government

519 **The records of the British Residency and Agencies in the Persian Gulf.**
Penelope Tuson. London: India Office Library and Records, Foreign and Commonwealth Office, 1979. 201p. map. bibliog.

This reference book to the records of the British administration in the Gulf between 1763 and 1948 also includes introductions to the administration of each Agency. The records of the Political Agency at Bahrain 1900-47 and the Political Agent's Court there 1913-48 are detailed on p. 43-127, and cover such topics as Agency buildings and political administration, arms, banks, cinemas, currency, customs, defence, education, food, hospitals, passports, the pearl industry, the Persian claims to the islands, police, press, relations with other countries, shipping, slavery, trade, the Waqf (religious endowments) Department and water supply. In the 1820s the Bombay Government had appointed a Native Agent at Bahrain who was expected to report regularly to the Resident at Bushire, and in 1900 the employment of a European officer at Bahrain was sanctioned following increasing Turkish influence in the region. From 1904 this post was increased in status to that of a Political Agency. British courts were established in the islands as a result of the Bahrain Order in Council of 1913, but this was not actually brought into force until 1919.

Foreign Relations

520 **American domestic and foreign policy and the Arab-Israeli conflict.**
James E. Akins. In: *Oil and security in the Arabian Gulf.*
Edited by Abdul Majid Farid. London: Croom Helm, 1981,
p. 86-95.
This paper analyses how US policy towards the Arab-Israeli conflict has been influenced by US oil requirements. It notes that Christian missionaries in Bahrain were of great assistance indirectly to the US by creating a favourable attitude among the Arabs about America and Americans.

521 **The security of the Persian Gulf.**
Edited by Hossein Amirsadeghi. London: Croom Helm, 1981.
294p. 2 maps. bibliog.
A volume of papers on the Gulf in the wake of the Iranian revolution. The editor believes that the Khomeini régime in Iran will eventually collapse, and argues that if Soviet backed extremists gain the upper hand, the likelihood of an East-West confrontation over the Gulf's energy resources will be greatly increased. Bahrain is mentioned in the papers by John C. Campbell, Geoffrey Kemp, Shahram Chubin, Richard Haass, John Duke Anthony, and Edmund Ghareeb.

522 **Persian Gulf oil and the world economy.**
Jahangir Amuzegar. In: *The Persian Gulf and Indian Ocean in international politics.* Edited by Abbas Amirie. Tehran: Institute for International Political and Economic Studies, 1975, p. 321-45.
A general analysis of the interdependence between the Gulf oil-producing states and the oil-importing countries of the West. Bahrain is seen as one of a group of countries where the potential for non-oil development is strictly limited due to a paucity of cultivable land and other non-oil raw material.

523 **The Persian Gulf as a regional subsystem.**
William D. Anderson. In: *Conflict and cooperation in the Persian Gulf.* Edited by Muhammed Mughisuddin. New York, London: Praeger Publishers, 1977, p. 1-12.
A preliminary sketch for applying the regional subsystem approach to the Persian Gulf. There are several passing references to Bahrain.

524 **The Union of Arab Amirates.**
John D. Anthony. *Middle East Journal*, vol. 26, no. 3
(summer 1972), p. 271-87.

An account of the creation of the Union of Arab Amirates, which came into being
on 2 December 1971. It describes the early discussions on federation, which
included the countries of Bahrayn and Qatar, following the 1968 announcement
of British withdrawal from the Gulf by 1971.

525 **Inter-Arab social and political relationships.**
John S. Badeau. In: *Middle East focus: the Persian Gulf.*
Edited by T. Cuyler Young. Princeton, New Jersey: Princeton
University Conference, 1969, p. 194-202.

A discussion of the potential for political co-operation in the Gulf, which notes
the foundation of the Federation of Arabian Gulf Emirates in March 1969, with
the ruler of Bahrain as its chief.

526 **Contemporary Gulf.**
Edited by Surendra Bhutani. New Delhi: Academic Press, 1980.
148p.

A collection of papers from a two-day seminar on security in the Gulf organized
by the Arab Cultural Centre in New Delhi in October 1979. Bahrain is mentioned
in connection with its relations with Britain, Iran and Oman.

527 **U.S. supports admission of Bahrain to the United Nations.**
George Bush. *Department of State Bulletin,* no. 1,681, vol. 65
(Oct. 1971), p. 294-95.

The statement by the US Representative to the United Nations on 18 August
1971 supporting Bahrain's application for membership.

528 **The Gulf region in the global setting.**
John C. Campbell. In: *The security of the Persian Gulf.* Edited
by Hossein Amirsadeghi. London: Croom Helm, 1981, p. 1-25.

This paper notes that following British withdrawal there was potential for trouble
in Bahrain because of the newness of its independence, possible political instability
and the danger of being squeezed by Arab-Iranian rivalry.

529 **The superpowers in the Persian Gulf region.**
John C. Campbell. In: *The Persian Gulf and Indian Ocean in
international politics.* Edited by Abbas Amirie. Tehran: Institute
for International Political and Economic Studies, 1975, p. 39-59.

A discussion of the role of the USA and the USSR in the Gulf. It notes that
following Britain's withdrawal from the Gulf a small US naval force of two destroyers and a tender was based at Bahrain.

530 The international politics of the Persian Gulf.
Shahram Chubin. *British Journal of International Studies,* vol. 2,
no. 3 (Oct. 1976), p. 216-31.
An analysis of the political relations between the countries of the Gulf and the
superpowers. It notes that Bahrayn's arms purchases increased twofold between
1972 and 1975.

531 Security in the Gulf.
Shahram Chubin, Robert Litwak, Avi Plascov. Farnborough,
England: Gower for the International Institute for Strategic
Studies, 1982. 90, 105, 183, 180p.
The publication in one volume of four separate collections of papers on security
in the Gulf, produced by the International Institute for Strategic Studies. For
individual details see the four separate entries for *Security in the Persian Gulf*...

532 Security in the Persian Gulf 1: domestic political factors.
Edited by Shahram Chubin. Farnborough, England: Gower for
the International Institute for Strategic Studies, 1981. 90p.
A collection of four papers on various aspects of Gulf security: 'Political institutions in Saudi Arabia, Kuwait and Bahrain', by Arnold Hottinger; 'Transformation
amidst tradition: the U.A.E. in transition', by John Duke Anthony; 'Economic
problems of Arabian peninsula oil states', by Michael Field; and 'Population,
migration and development in the Gulf states', by Allan G. Hill. It provides much
information on Bahrain, particularly in connection with its constitutional development, economic diversification, immigrant labour, infrastructural development,
oil production, religious division, and social structure.

533 Security in the Persian Gulf 4: the role of outside powers.
Shahram Chubin. Farnborough, England: Gower for the
International Institute for Strategic Studies, 1982. 180p.
An investigation into the role of the superpowers, the potential for regional
co-operation, and the problems associated with arms transfer in the Gulf region.
Bahrain is mentioned mainly in connection with the US naval force MIDEASTFOR
which is based there.

534 The Soviet Union and the Persian Gulf.
Shahram Chubin. In: *The security of the Persian Gulf.* Edited
by Hossein Amirsadeghi. London: Croom Helm, 1981, p. 43-56.
An investigation of Soviet interests in the Gulf which briefly notes that in Bahrain,
as in Kuwait, the pressing concerns are those of national integration and societal
cohesion.

Foreign Relations

535 **Conflict in the Persian Gulf.**
Alvin J. Cottrell. *Military Review*, vol. 51, no. 2 (Feb. 1971),
p. 33-41.

This paper argues that hopes for stability in the Gulf following British withdrawal in 1971 rested on the possibility of collaboration between Iran and Saudi Arabia. It identifies two main factions within the Federation of Arab Emirates: Abu Dhabi backed by Bahrein, and Dubai and Qatar whose ruling houses are linked by marriage. The uncertainty that persisted as late as 1971 over whether Britain would in fact withdraw, following the elections of the Edward Heath Conservative government, is clearly evident, and the author suggests that many of the revolutionary elements in the Gulf were biding their time until the British forces actually left the region. The ruling family of Bahrein is seen as being the most likely to be overthrown by revolutionaries.

536 **Iran, the Arabs and the Persian Gulf.**
Alvin J. Cottrell. *Orbis,* vol. 17, no. 3 (1973), p. 978-88.

An evaluation of the regional influence of Iran, which is seen as the strongest local power in the Gulf following the British withdrawal. It notes that in 1970 Iran gave up its long-standing claim on Bahrain, and it argues that Bahrain, together with the other Arab Gulf states, needs a respite from strife and conflict in order to permit the resolution of remaining threats to its security. It suggests that strikes and riots in Bahrain, such as those that flared in March 1972, will become more widespread when the state's limited oil resources are exhausted.

537 **Military forces in the Persian Gulf.**
Alvin J. Cottrell, Frank Bray. Beverley Hills, California;
London: Sage Publications for the Center for Strategic and
International Studies, Georgetown University, 1978. 72p. map.
bibliog. (Washington Papers, vol. 6, 60).

A guide to the balance of indigenous forces in the Gulf, and an examination of historical political and social concerns that have led to leaders of the countries in the area improving their defence positions. Bahrain is discussed specifically on p. 59-60, where details are given of Britain's military facilities there prior to 1971, the brief American use of facilities there, and the size of the country's armed forces in 1978. It notes that in 1978 the defence force consisted of 2,300 men organized into one infantry batallion and one armoured car squadron, using Saladin armoured cars.

538 **Combat fleets of the world 1982/83: their ships, aircraft and armament.**
Edited by Jean Labayle Couhat, English edition prepared by A. D. Baker. London, Melbourne: Arms and Armour Press, 1982. 873p. + addenda.

Bahrain's naval fleet is described on p. 27-28. In 1982 it consisted of two TNC 45-class guided-missile boats, two FPB 38-class patrol boats, two 32-ton patrol craft, three 6.3-ton patrol craft, one tracker-class patrol craft, two Spear-class patrol craft, three 27-foot patrol craft, one 50-foot patrol craft, one 15-ton patrol craft, one Loadmaster-class landing craft, ten wooden motor dhows for logistic and patrol duties, and one utility hovercraft.

539 **Border and territorial disputes.**
Edited by Alan J. Day. Harlow, England: Longman, 1982. 406p. 44 maps. bibliog.

An account of border and territorial disputes throughout the world. Bahrain's disputes with Iran and Qatar are described by Henry W. Degenhardt on p. 209-13.

540 **Defending the Gulf: a survey.**
The Economist, 6 June 1981, special report. 38p.

An investigation into the geopolitics of the Gulf in the light of the establishment of the US Rapid Deployment Force and the Gulf Co-operation Council.

541 **An atlas of territorial and border disputes.**
David Downing. London: New English Library, 1980. 121p. 52 maps. bibliog.

Iran's claim to the islands of Bahrain is discussed on p. 48 of this book describing the territorial disputes that the author considers to be most likely to disturb local or international peace during the 1980s. It notes that Bahrain was under British protection from 1820 to 1971, and that in 1968 the referendum held in Bahrain under the auspices of the United Nations revealed that the islands' inhabitants preferred independence, or a continued British presence, to incorporation into Iran. Although the Shah of Iran then dropped the matter, the 1979 Iranian Shia revolution is seen as sparking chords among the Shia majority of Bahrain, who are ruled by a Sunni élite.

542 **The Middle East and North Africa: the challenge to Western security.**
Peter Duignan, L. H. Gann. Stanford, California: Hoover Institution Press, 1981. 141p. 8 maps. bibliog.

An investigation of the Middle East from the standpoint of American vital interests. Following an overview of Islam and the political, economic and social problems of the region, it presents a summary of the main trouble spots. It argues that, unlike the other Gulf states, Bahrain and Kuwait are stable. In the case of Bahrain this stability is seen as resulting from its role as a trading depot and purveyor of mercantile and banking services, in addition to its oil revenues. One source of potential conflict, though, is seen as Iran's desire that Bahrain should become an 'Islamic state'.

Foreign Relations

543 **Where soldiers fear to tread.**
Ranulph Fiennes. London, Sydney, Auckland, Toronto:
Hodder & Stoughton, 1975. 256p. map.

An account of the war in Dhofar between the Sultan of Oman's Arab army,
commanded by British officers, and the Qara communist guerrillas. Bahrein is
mentioned in several places as the airport from which supplies were sent to
Dhofar and to which severely wounded British officers were sent for treatment.

544 **Soviet policy toward the Middle East since 1970.**
Robert O. Freedman. New York: Praeger Publishers, 1978.
2nd ed. 373p. bibliog.

This book is mainly concerned with relations between the Soviet Union and
Egypt, and the Arab-Israeli conflict. It notes that while the Soviet Union
supported the Popular Front for the Liberation of Oman and the Arab Gulf it
also welcomed good relations with the conservative governments of the Gulf
states, such as Bahrain, following their independence in 1971. Bahrain is also
mentioned in the context of the government's order to the US to remove its naval
installations there at the time of the October War, and the final departure of the
US from the naval installation in July 1977.

545 **Iraq: emergent Gulf power.**
Edmund Ghareeb. In: *The security of the Persian Gulf.* Edited
by Hossein Amirsadeghi. London: Croom Helm, 1981,
p. 197-230.

An evaluation of Iraq's influence in the Gulf, which notes that Iraq supported the
creation of a federation including the seven Trucial Emirates, Qatar and Bahrain,
that the Shah of Iran cancelled a visit to Bahrain in March 1968 as a protest
against the Saudi reception of the Amir of Bahrain as head of state, and that
Iraqi-Iranian hostilities were partly influenced by Iran's claim to Bahrain and
other islands in the Gulf.

546 **Resolution of the Bahrain dispute.**
E. Gordon. *American Journal of International Law,* vol. 65,
no. 3 (July 1971), p. 560-68.

An analysis of the resolution of the dispute between the United Kingdom and
Iran over the sovereignty of Bahrain, achieved through the offices of the Secretary
General of the United Nations. Following the Shah of Iran's statement in January
1969 that he would not use force to reunite his country with Bahrain, a United
Nations fact-finding mission spent three weeks in Bahrain in 1970 investigating
the opinions of the Bahraini population as to their future. On 11th May 1970 the
mission's report was unanimously endorsed by the Council, accepting that
'the overwhelming majority of the people of Bahrain wish to gain recognition of
their identity in a fully independent and sovereign state'. Following the Council's
endorsement of this report's findings, Iran formally renounced her claim on
Bahrain.

547 **Gulf states: a special supplement.**
International Herald Tribune, July 1981. 4p.
A report on the Gulf Co-operation Council established in May 1981 by Bahrain, Kuwait, Oman, Qatar, Saudi Arabia and the United Arab Emirates.

548 **The Gulf war.**
In: *Oil and security in the Arabian Gulf.* Edited by Abdul Majid Farid. London: Croom Helm, 1981, p. 141-52.
A summary of the views and debate presented in the round table discussion about the Iran-Iraq war held at the Arab Research Centre in December 1980. It notes that in 1840 Iranians attempted to occupy Bahrain, and that following the overthrow of the Shah Iraqi forces have blocked renewed claims by Iranian Ayatollahs and Mullahs on Bahrain.

549 **Saudi Arabia and Iran: the twin pillars in revolutionary times.**
Richard Haass. In: *The security of the Persian Gulf.* Edited by Hossein Amirsadeghi. London: Croom Helm, 1981, p. 151-69.
An investigation of the relationships between Iran and Saudi Arabia viewed in the context of multiple domestic, regional and international threats to their stability. It notes that during the 1970s Iran gave up its claim to Bahrain.

550 **The Iranian revolution in international affairs: programme and practice.**
Fred Halliday. In: *Oil and security in the Persian Gulf.* Edited by Abdul Majid Farid. London: Croom Helm, 1981, p. 18-35.
This paper argues that while the Iranian revolution did not have the effects foreseen by many people it nevertheless set in motion processes that have affected much of the Middle East. It notes that the Shah had abandoned his claim to Bahrain in 1970, and that Ayatollah Rouhani after the revolution called for the return of Bahrain to Iran, although this call was never endorsed by any government official.

551 **Oil and security in U.S. policy towards the Arabian Gulf-Indian Ocean area.**
Robert J. Hanks. In: *Oil and security in the Arabian Gulf.* Edited by Abdul Majid Farid. London: Croom Helm, 1981, p. 36-56.
An historical assessment of changing US policy towards the Gulf, by a former commander of the US Middle East Force in Bahrain. It notes that the conflict between Bahrain and Qatar over the ownership of adjacent islands encompasses the potential for armed conflict which could endanger the flow of oil from the Gulf.

552 **The Persian Gulf states and their boundary problems.**
Rupert Hay. *Geographical Journal,* vol. 120, no. 4 (Dec. 1954),
p. 433-45.

This paper is a brief geographical description of the ten shaikhdoms of the Gulf
and Muscat, paying specific attention to the problems to which their boundaries
give rise. It notes that determining sea-bed boundaries in the case of an archipelago
like Bahrain is a particularly difficult process.

553 **Inside the Middle East.**
Dilip Hiro. London: Routledge & Kegan Paul, 1982. 471p.
bibliog.

A political and economic survey of what are termed the 'core' countries of the
Middle East. It is divided into five parts: part 1, an historical survey, begins with
an introduction establishing Islam and the Arabic language as the unifying factors
of the Arab world; part 2 outlines the socio-economic context in which each of
the Arab countries exists today; part 3 considers Israel's domestic politics and
foreign relations; part 4 studies the Arabs and the superpowers; and part 5
presents an analysis of future prospects for the region. Bahrain is discussed in the
context of banking, its relations with Britain, its constitution and elections, the
Iranian claims to the archipelago, its relations with Qatar, Saudi Arabia and the
USA, its parliament, and the religious structure of its population.

554 **Ferment on the Persian Gulf.**
Arnold Hottinger. *Swiss Review of World Affairs,* vol. 20, no. 2
(Feb. 1971), p. 12-16.

An evaluation of the antagonism between Iran and the Arabian Gulf states early
in 1971. It includes some discussion of the desire by Britain to form a federation
of the nine Gulf states including Bahrain.

555 **Britain and the Gulf.**
Douglas Hurd. In: *Oil and security in the Arabian Gulf.* Edited
by Abdul Majid Farid. London: Croom Helm, 1981, p. 99-102.

This paper argues that the interests of the Gulf states coincide with those of the
West in general and of Britain in particular. It notes that Bahrain, Qatar and the
UAE have all joined the Arab League and the United Nations following their
independence from Britain.

556 **The Persian Gulf after Iran's revolution.**
J. C. Hurewitz. New York: Foreign Policy Association, 1979.
64p. 2 maps. bibliog. (Headline Series, no. 244).

This pamphlet traces the political emergence of the states of the Gulf and in
particular the potential for change following Iran's 1979 revolution. The departure
of British power in 1971 is seen as having led to a situation of balanced instability
in the Gulf, and the fall of the Shah of Iran as having led to a power vacuum.

557 **The Persian Gulf: British withdrawal and Western security.**
J. C. Hurewitz. *Annals of the American Academy of Political and Social Science,* no. 401 (May 1972), p. 106-15.

An essentially cautious evaluation of the likely outcome of British withdrawal from the Gulf, which notes the considerable importance of this region as an oil supplier to the Western world. It is written largely as a review of previous British activity in the region, and notes Bahrain's importance as a centre of British influence.

558 **Oil prospects in the Gulf: the E.E.C. and the Gulf.**
Michel Jobert. In: *Oil and security in the Arabian Gulf.* Edited by Abdul Majid Farid. London: Croom Helm, 1981, p. 107-21.

An examination of the reasons for and conditions of a European policy towards the Gulf, in the light of future prospects for the oil industry in the region. It notes that Bahrain is a US port-of-call, which is paralleled by the Soviet one at Basra.

559 **A prevalence of furies: tribes, politics, and religion in Oman and Trucial Oman.**
J. B. Kelly. In: *The Arabian peninsula: society and politics.* Edited by Derek Hopwood. London: George Allen & Unwin, 1972, p. 107-44.

This analysis of political intrigue in Oman briefly notes that most of the Al Bu Sa'id princes were primarily interested in affairs abroad in Bahrain, Bander Abbas and East Africa rather than their obligations at home.

560 **Sovereignty and jurisdiction in eastern Arabia.**
John B. Kelly. *International Affairs* (London), vol. 34, no. 1 (Jan. 1958), p. 16-24.

This paper mentions the territorial dispute between Bahrain and Qatar over the ruined town of Zubara in the context of a number of territorial disputes in the eastern Arabian peninsula.

561 **The strategic balance and the control of the Persian Gulf.**
Geoffrey Kemp. In: *The security of the Persian Gulf.* Edited by Hossein Amirsadeghi. London: Croom Helm, 1981, p. 26-42.

This essay argues that the major threat to Western interests in the Gulf is the potential for Soviet control and that unless a coherent and well orchestrated Western policy towards the area is implemented Soviet interference is likely to increase. It notes that Iran has given up its historic claim to Bahrain.

562 **The Persian Gulf: arms race or arms control.**
Edward M. Kennedy. *Foreign Affairs,* vol. 54, no. 1 (Oct. 1975), p. 14-35.

A study of US arms sales to the Gulf. It notes the presence of a miniscule US naval Middle East Force stationed at Bahrain.

563 **Revolution in the Gulf.**

Helen Lackner. *Race*, vol. 15 (1974), p. 515-27.

Although specifically concerned with revolution in Oman, this paper argues that the rulers of all of the Gulf states only retain power with imperialist support and by building up massive military strength. It notes the occupation of the Bahrein base by the US Navy following the British withdrawal from the region in 1971.

564 **The struggle for the Middle East: the Soviet Union and the Middle East 1958-68.**

Walter Laqueur. London: Routledge & Kegan Paul, 1969. 360p. bibliog.

A review of Soviet policy in the Middle East during the 1960s which briefly notes that the Soviet Union supported Iran's claims to Bahrain. It also mentions the activities of 'liberation fronts' in Bahrain, and the state's oil industry.

565 **International relations of Arabia: the dependent areas.**

Herbert J. Liebesny. *Middle East Journal*, vol. 1, no. 2 (April 1947), p. 148-68.

This account of the international relations of countries in the Arabian peninsula pays particular attention to their relations with the United States of America. It provides details of the British administration of Bahrein, which was the seat of the Political Resident, the Political Agent for Bahrein, the Assistant Political Agent, the Political Officer for the Trucial Coast, and the Publicity Officer in the Persian Gulf. It gives some information on the country's oil industry, and notes that Iran has repeatedly challenged Bahrein's position as an independent sheikhdom under British protection.

566 **Security in the Persian Gulf 2: sources of inter-state conflict.**

Robert Litwak. Farnborough, England: Gower for the International Institute for Strategic Studies, 1981. 105p. 3 maps.

An examination of both the traditional and novel sources of inter-state conflict which threaten the stability of the Gulf area. Bahrain is discussed mainly in the context of the Iranian claims to the islands and the continental shelf agreements between Bahrain and both Saudi Arabia and Iran. The dispute with Qatar over the Hawar Islands is also discussed.

567 **United States policy towards the Persian Gulf.**

David E. Long. *Current History*, no. 402 (Feb. 1975), p. 69-73, 85.

An account of the historical relationships between Britain and the Gulf, the implications of British withdrawal, and the evolution of United States policy in the region. Bahrain's independence on 19 August 1971, the dropping of Iran's claim to Bahrain in the spring of 1970, the lease by the United States of the naval installations on Bahrain, its subsequent termination following the October 1973 Arab-Israeli war, and the eventual reversal of this decision in the summer of 1974 are all mentioned.

568 **Britain in the Persian Gulf: mistaken timing over Aden.**
William Luce. *Round Table,* no. 227 (July 1967), p. 277-83.
A study of the factors behind Britain's continued presence in the Gulf despite her withdrawal from India, set against the contradictory forces tending towards unity and disunity between nations in the area. It notes that in Bahrain, where the population still firmly adhered to tradition and gradualism, education has widened mental horizons and loosened the ties of tribal loyalty. It concludes that the 1968 decision by the British government to withdraw all of its forces from south Aabia was damaging because it encouraged an intensification of the contest between revolutionaries and traditionalists in Arabia, and also because it weakened the power of the British to influence the future course of events in the region.

569 **Britain's withdrawal.**
William Luce. *Survival,* vol. 11, no. 6 (June 1969), p. 186-92.
An investigation of the ramifications of British withdrawal from the Gulf. It argues that prior to 1948 British interests in the region arose largely due to her interests in India, but that after this date the presence of oil in the region became the dominant factor. It notes that in 1969 Iran was hostile to the inclusion of Bahrain in the proposed federation of Arab Gulf Emirates and suggests that without Bahrain there would probably be no federation at all.

570 **Soviet policy in the Persian Gulf.**
R. D. McLaurin. In: *Conflict and cooperation in the Persian Gulf.* Edited by Mohammed Mughisuddin. New York, London: Praeger, 1977, p. 116-39.
An analysis of Soviet policy in the Gulf considering, first, the historic and actual regional framework in which Soviet policy must operate; second, the interests of the Soviet Union in the Gulf; third, Soviet objectives in the area; and finally, actual Soviet policy and activities in the Gulf. It briefly discusses the 'Jufair Agreement', an exchange of notes between the US chargé d'affaires and the government of Bahrain through which the United States was granted the right to use Bahrain as the base for the US Navy's Middle East Force. As a result Bahrain, though following a policy of public non-alignment, has been the butt of many Soviet attacks on Western imperialism in the Gulf.

571 **The Persian Gulf and international relations.**
A. T. Mahan. *National Review,* vol. 40 (Sept. 1902), p. 27-45.
A general evaluation of the interests of Great Britain, Russia and Germany in the Gulf at the beginning of the 20th century.

572 **America and the Arabian peninsula: the first two hundred years.**
Joseph J. Malone. *Middle East Journal,* vol. 30, no. 3 (Summer 1976), p. 406-24.
An account of American relations with Arabia, noting, in connection with Bahrayn, the work of the Arabian Mission and the exploitation of the country's oil resources.

573 **Arab-Persian rivalry in the Persian Gulf.**
John Marlowe. *Royal Central Asian Journal*, vol. 51 (1964),
p. 23-31.
An investigation of Arab-Persian conflicts of interest in the Gulf, which briefly
mentions the Persian claim to Bahrain.

574 **The Military Balance.**
London: International Institute for Strategic Studies, 1963-.
annual.
An annual summary of the military forces of the world, recently including
Bahrain. In 1983 Bahrain's army is recorded as having a personnel of 2,300
strong, its navy 300, and its air force 100.

575 **British bases in the Middle East: assets or liabilities?**
Elizabeth Monroe. *International Affairs* (London), vol. 42,
no. 1 (Jan. 1966), p. 24-34.
A critical evaluation of the validity of the British military bases in Cyprus, Libya,
Aden and Bahrain in the mid-1960s.

576 **The changing balance of power in the Persian Gulf.**
Elizabeth Monroe. New York: American Universities Field
Staff, 1972. 79p. 2 maps. bibliog.
The report of an international seminar at the Center for Mediterranean Studies in
Rome in the summer of 1972. It begins with a summary of the political and social
background of the area, before discussing oil, internal problems, and the Soviet
and Chinese 'problems'. There are many scattered references to Bahrain.

577 **Conflict and cooperation in the Persian Gulf.**
Edited by Mohammed Mughisuddin. New York, London:
Praeger, 1977. 192p. (Praeger Special Studies in International
Politics and Government).
An investigation of three levels of cooperation and conflict in the Gulf: the
domestic, the subsystemic, and the systemic. Bahrain is mentioned in the papers
by William D. Anderson, R. D. McLaurin, and Abdul Aziz Said.

578 **Arab-American relations in the Persian Gulf.**
Emile A. Nakhleh. Washington, DC: American Enterprise
Institute for Public Policy Research, 1975. 82p. 2 maps.
(Foreign Affairs Study, no. 17).
An examination of the political and ideological nature of the Arab regimes of the
Gulf, the religious/tribal foundations of these regimes and the oil-generated
affluence of their ruling families, the diplomatic and military activities of regional
and other powers, and the new economic structure of the Gulf. It concludes with
a long-range projection of American international relations in the region and the
various options available to US policy makers. There are numerous scattered
mentions of Bahrain.

579   The Persian Gulf and American policy.
Emile A. Nakhleh.   New York: Praeger, 1982. 151p. bibliog.
An evaluation of the relationships between the Gulf states and the policy of the
USA. Bahrain is discussed particularly in the context of its experiments with a
Constitutional Assembly, and the Gulf Co-operation Council.

580   **Oman and Gulf security.**
B. K. Narayan.   New Delhi: Lancers Publishers, 1979. 192p.
map. bibliog.
A study of the history, manners, customs and economic problems of Oman and
the Gulf countries, depicting the challenges thrown up consequent to the discovery
of oil and the new affluence it has brought about. The author argues that the
Islamic tradition and culture that binds these countries together will emerge as a
stabilising influence in this conflict-prone area. There are numerous scattered
references to Bahrein.

581   **Iraq: the contemporary state.**
Edited by Tim Niblock.   London: Croom Helm, 1982. 283p.
2 maps.
A collection of 16 papers on Iraq, most of which were presented to a symposium
at Exeter University in July 1981 on 'Iraq: the contemporary state'. Bahrain is
considered briefly among the Arab states of the lower Gulf in the chapter by Tim
Niblock on 'Iraqi policies towards the Arab states of the Gulf, 1958-1981', and
that by Naomi Sakr on 'Economic relations between Iraq and other Arab Gulf
states'.

582   **The clouded lense: Persian Gulf security and U.S. policy.**
James H. Noyes.   Stanford, California: Hoover Institution
Press, 1982. 2nd ed. 168p. map. bibliog.
A study of the transition of the Gulf states from being objects of strong colonial
influence to complete independence, and the role played by the USA in this
transition. It includes many references to Bahrain, in particular about Iran's claim
to the islands, political relations with Qatar, the 1956 riots, its past role as the
headquarters of the British Gulf Command, the activities of the US MIDEASTFOR
and the naval facilities in Bahrain, and the political role of the indigenous labour
force.

583   **Moscow and the Persian Gulf countries, 1967-1970.**
Stephen Page.   *Mizan*, vol. 13, no. 2 (1971), p. 72-88.
An investigation of the cautious line pursued by the USSR towards the Gulf between 1967 and 1970. Most attention is paid to Soviet attitudes to Saudi Arabia
and Kuwait, but the Soviet scepticism in 1968 of the planned British withdrawal
from Bahrain and the remainder of the southern Gulf states is also discussed at
some length.

584 **The U.S.S.R. and Arabia: the development of Soviet policies and attitudes towards the countries of the Arabian peninsula.**
Stephen Page. London: Central Asian Research Centre, 1971. 152p. map. bibliog.

An historical analysis of Soviet interests in Arabia. It observes that in 1953 the Soviet Union generally supported Iran's claim to Bahrain, and that later Soviet commentators were seeing the evolution of Bahrain as the emergence of a national liberation movement struggling against the repression of the Sheikh, the oil monopolies and the British colonialists. It also notes that the disturbances in Bahrain in 1965 were closely followed by the Soviets.

585 **Foreign policies of the Persian Gulf states, part 1.**
Don Peretz. *New Outlook,* (Jan.-Feb. 1977), p. 27-31.

An introduction to foreign policy in the states surrounding the Gulf which concentrates mainly on the role of Iran.

586 **Security in the Persian Gulf 3: modernization, political development and stability.**
Avi Plascov. Farnborough, England: Gower for the International Institute for Strategic Studies, 1982. 183p.

This study aims to assess the nature and magnitude of potential domestic sources of conflict and the conditions under which they might become salient, contributing to the acceleration of various political trends inducing instability in the Gulf. It provides much information on recent political change in Bahrain, particularly concerning labour relations and disputes, the Shi'ah community and unrest following the Iranian revolution, and the social and political consequences of rapid urbanization and industrialization.

587 **The American answer.**
Robert Pranger. In: *Oil and security in the Arabian Gulf.* Edited by Abdul Majid Farid. London: Croom Helm, 1981, p. 82-85.

This short article suggests that the Middle East has never been seen by the United States after the Second World War as a major theatre of military operations. It argues that, contrary to Soviet press reports, the small flotilla in the Gulf making up the US Mid-East Force, which is based in Bahrain, is not armed with nuclear missiles.

588 **A view from the Rimland: an appraisal of Soviet interests and involvement in the Gulf.**
Melvyn Pryer. Durham, England: Centre for Middle Eastern and Islamic Studies, University of Durham, 1981. 98p. 5 maps. bibliog. (Occasional Papers Series, no. 8).

A political geography of Soviet interests in the Gulf. It notes that Soviet military assistance and training were offered to the PFLOAG (Popular Front for the Liberation of the Occupied Arab Gulf) in the early 1970s.

589 **The Persian Gulf and the Strait of Hormuz.**
R. K. Ramazani. Alphen aan den Rijn, Netherlands: Sijthoff &
Noordhoff, 1979. 180p. 2 maps. (International Straits of the
World, vol. 3).

A study of the potential for conflict or co-operation over the Strait of Hormuz,
through which passes much of the world's oil. There are several scattered mentions
of Bahrain, mainly in connection with Iran's claims to the archipelago and the
dispute with Qatar over the Hawar Islands.

590 **The Persian Gulf: Iran's role.**
Rouhollah K. Ramazani. Charlottesville, Virginia: University
Press of Virginia, 1972. 157p. 2 maps. bibliog.

A study of Iran's role, as that of the most prominent regional element, in the
Gulf, set against the interests of the superpowers. The Iranian claims on Bahrain
are discussed at length on p. 45-56. It notes that Iran asserted its claim to Bahrain
on two occasions following the Second World War: in 1951 when Iran wanted its
Oil Nationalization Laws also to apply to the Bahrain Petroleum Company, and in
1957 when the Iranian Council of Ministers approved a bill indicating the continuation of Iran's claim. At Bahrain's indpendence in 1971 Iran made clear its
preference for an independent sovereign Bahrain outside the framework of an
Arab federation.

591 **Security in the Persian Gulf.**
Rouhollah K. Ramazani. *Foreign Affairs,* vol. 57, no. 4
(spring 1979), p. 821-35.

This paper investigates the question of who should maintain the future security of
the Persian Gulf. In particular it studies the possible role of the USA. It argues
that a comprehensive economic and security partnership between a group of
OECD countries would provide the best solution to the problem of peacemaking
in the Persian Gulf.

592 **Arabs, oil and history: the story of the Middle East.**
Kermit Roosevelt. New York: Harper & Row, 1949; reissued
Port Washington, New York: Kennikat Press, 1969. 271p.

An analysis of the emergence of the Middle East as a theatre in which the 'Big
Powers' acted out their interests. It notes that most of the early production of
oil in Saudi Arabia was taken to Bahrain by barge for refining.

593 **Oil and security in the Gulf: an Arab point of view.**
Mohammed El-Rumaihi. In: *Oil and security in the Arabian
Gulf.* Edited by Abdul Majid Farid. London: Croom Helm,
1981, p. 134-37.

This short article notes that nobody seems to care what are the ambitions and
goals of the people of the Gulf. It argues that security in the smaller states of the
Gulf, such as Bahrain, can only be achieved if the area is left free from foreign
interference.

Foreign Relations

594 **A proposito delle rivendicazioni Persiane sul Baḥrein.** (Concerning the Persian claims on Baḥrein.)
Gianroberto Scarcia. *Oriente Moderno*, no. 38 (Jan. 1958), p. 1-18.
An account of Anglo-Persian conflict over Baḥrein.

595 **The Middle East in China's foreign policy 1949-1977.**
Yitzhak Schichor. Cambridge, London, New York, Melbourne: Cambridge University Press, 1979. 268p. bibliog.
This book provides a comprehensive analysis of China's Middle East policy. It notes that in 1975 Kuwait, Bahrain and Qatar absorbed 28 per cent of China's exports to the region, and also that Bahrain does not maintain diplomatic relations with the People's Republic of China.

596 **Middle Eastern oil and the Western world: prospects and problems.**
Sam H. Schurr, Paul T. Homam, with Joel Darmstadter, Helmut Frank, John J. Schanz Jr., Thomas R. Stauffer, Henry Steele. New York: American Elsevier, 1971. 206p. 3 maps. (Middle East: Economic and Political Problems and Prospects).
An investigation of the symbiotic relationship between the Middle East oil-producing countries and the consuming countries of the West. Details are given of Bahrain's membership of OAPEC, its oil production, and its oil revenues.

597 **Moscow and the Persian Gulf: an analysis of Soviet ambitions and potential.**
O. M. Smolansky. *Orbis*, vol. 14, no. 1 (1970), p. 92-108.
This paper argues that the short term policy of the USSR will be aimed at a gradual erosion of Western interests in the Gulf. It briefly describes the negotiations over the creation of the planned federation of Gulf emirates which would have included Bahrain.

598 **The United States and the Near East.**
E. A. Speiser. Cambridge, Massachusetts: Harvard University Press, 1950. 283p. 2 maps. bibliog. (American Foreign Policy Library).
A brief analysis of the history and politics of the Near East prior to 1950. Bahrayn is mentioned in the context of its political links with Britain and its role as an oil producer.

599 **La question des îsles Bahrein.** (The question of the Bahrein islands.)
Gholam-Reza Tadjbakhche. Paris: Pédone, 1960. 389p. 3 maps. bibliog.

An investigation supporting the Iranian claims to Bahrein, which is divided into three parts. The first considers the country's geography, political history, and global importance; the second is concerned with the political and diplomatic affairs of Bahrein; and the third is about the legal status of the islands. It argues that the convention of 31 May 1861 was a unilateral act by Britain and thus null and void; that the Persians have never ceased their claims to the islands; and that in 1869 the British recognized Persian rights to the islands. It includes three appendices of documents relating to the legal status of the islands.

600 **Policies of Iran in the Persian Gulf region.**
Amir Taheri. In: *The Persian Gulf and Indian Ocean in international politics.* Edited by Abbas Amirie. Tehran: Institute for International Political and Economic Studies, 1975, p. 259-78.

This paper on Iran's political activity in a widely defined Gulf region briefly notes that Bahrain became independent from the British with Iran's agreement and that Iran has negotiated a continental shelf agreement with Bahrain.

601 **The dispute between Persia and Great Britain over Bahrayn (1927-1934).**
Arnold J. Toynbee. *Survey of International Affairs,* (1934), p. 221-24.

A brief account of the disputes between Britain and Persia over the islands of Bahrayn.

602 **The U.K. and Arabia: a commemorative issue to mark the visit of H.M. Queen Elizabeth II.**
Middle East Economic Digest, special report, February 1979. 52p.

A survey of past and present relations between the United Kingdom and the Arabian peninsula, in which most attention is paid to banking and the construction industry. It includes a summary of British trade with the Middle East 1974-78, and a list of recent contracts with individual countries including Bahrain.

603 **The British withdrawal from the Gulf and its consequences.**
Anthony Verrier. In: *Middle East focus: the Persian Gulf.*
Edited by T. Cuyler Young. Princeton, New Jersey: Princeton
University Conference, 1969, p. 134-49.

An evaluation of the role of the British in the Gulf, which concludes that the consequences of their withdrawal are incalculable. Bahrain is mentioned as one of the states which might have formed a federation, and the British garrison there, together with its important anchorage, are also noted briefly.

604 **Qatar: progressive puritans.**
M. Wall. *The Economist*, vol. 235 (6 June 1970), supplement.
p. xxii-xxvii.

This note in a special report on the Arabian peninsula observes the conflict of natures between Bahrain and Qatar.

605 **The Arabs, the Heath government and the future of the Gulf.**
D. C. Watt. *New Middle East*, no. 30 (1971), p. 25-27.

A study of the attitudes of Arab states, particularly Egypt, to the political manoeuvres behind Britain's planned withdrawal from the Gulf, and the emergence of a federation of the smaller Gulf states, following the succession to power of the Edward Heath Conservative government in Britain in June 1970.

606 **U.K. & the Gulf 1971-1981: a MEED special report.**
Edited by John Whelan. *Middle East Economic Digest*, Dec.
1981. 64p.

An investigation of the changed political and economic relationships between Britain and the Gulf since Britain withdrew from the region in 1971. A concluding statistical section provides details of Bahrain's imports and exports 1971-1981.

607 **The changed balance of power in the Persian Gulf.**
Denis Wright. *Asian Affairs*, vol. 60, no. 3 (Oct. 1973),
p. 255-62.

An account of the British position in the Gulf and the effects of British withdrawal in 1971. It notes that Bahrain and Qatar opted for separate independence in 1971 rather than choosing to join the Union of Arab Emirates.

608 **In the direction of the Persian Gulf. The Soviet Union and the Persian Gulf.**
A. Yodfat, M. Abir. London; Totowa, New Jersey: Frank Cass, 1977. 167p. 3 maps. bibliog.

An analysis of the Soviet Union's interest in the countries of the Gulf, set against the background of its relations with the Arab world and the complexities of power politics. Its emphasis is on relatively recent developments and the 19th century is covered only briefly. Particular attention is paid to the Soviet Union's interest in the oil produced in the Gulf. Bahrayn is mentioned in connection with the British attempts to form a federation of the nine sheikhdoms of the southern Gulf, which were described by the USSR as intended 'to maintain the feudal regimes' against Arab 'national liberation movements'. Following Bahrayn's indpendence from the proposed federation Soviet analyses have seen the state as being higher in the capitalist stage than Saudi Arabia, Qatar and the United Arab Emirates, since it has a proletariat and an emerging class conflict. Iran's claims to Bahrayn are also mentioned.

609 **The Gulf in the 1980s.**
Valerie Yorke. London: Royal Institute of International Affairs, 1980. 80p. map. (Chatham House Papers, no. 6).

An investigation of the consequences of the 1979 Iranian revolution for the countries of the Gulf, which suggests that there is a possibility of an adventurist Iran pushing territorial claims against Bahrain. Bahrain's political and economic structures are discussed specifically on p. 21-22. Other chapters refer to sources of instability in the region, the role of the USA, Arab policies in connection with politics and oil, and Western policy choices towards the region. It investigates the external pressures on the Gulf from the Soviet Union, the Arab-Israeli conflict, Iran and Iraq, together with what is seen by the Gulf régimes as the ambiguous role of the USA.

610 **The creation of Qatar.**
Rosemarie Said Zahlan. London: Croom Helm; New York: Barnes & Noble, 1979. 160p. 2 maps. bibliog.

A description and identification of the processes and forces that contribute to change and continuity in Qatari society. It includes numerous mentions of the relationships between Qatar and Bahrain. Chapter 2 is concerned with the Al-Khalifah settlement of Bahrain in the period 1766-1820, and other main mentions of Bahrain are in connection with the 1867 attack on Qatar, the Zubara and Hawar Islands territorial disputes between Bahrain and Qatar, the anti-Qatar feelings of people in Bahrain, civil disturbances in Bahrain during the 1840s, relationships with Britain, oil exploitation, and recent economic changes.

The United Arab Emirates: a modern history.
See item no. 281.

Bahrein islands, a legal and diplomatic study of the British-Iranian controversy.
See item no. 283.

Foreign Relations

A collection of treaties, engagements and sanads relating to India and neighbouring countries, vol. XI, containing the treaties, &c., relating to Aden and the south Western coast of Arabia, the Arab principalities in the Persian Gulf, Muscat (Oman), Baluchistan and the North-west Frontier Province.
See item no. 284.

Der arabisch-persische Golf. Eine Studie zur historischen, politischen und ökonomischen Entwicklung der Golf-Region. (The Arabian-Persian Gulf. A study of the historical, political and economic development of the Gulf region.)
See item no. 289.

The past and present connection of England with the Persian Gulf.
See item no. 293.

Minaret and pipe-line: yesterday and today in the Near East.
See item no. 300.

Britain and the Middle East.
See item no. 301.

Britain, Iran and the Persian Gulf: some aspects of the situation in the 1920s and 1930s.
See item no. 303.

Britain and the Persian Gulf, 1894-1914.
See item no. 304.

Britain, India and the Arabs, 1914-1921.
See item no. 305.

The Bahrein islands.
See item no. 306.

Farewell to Arabia.
See item no. 331.

Persian Gulf states.
See item no. 332.

Diplomacy in the Near and Middle East: a documentary record.
See item no. 335.

Eastern Arabian frontiers.
See item no. 339.

The Persian claim to Bahrain.
See item no. 342.

The United Arab Emirates: unity in fragmentation.
See item no. 343.

The Persian Gulf in the twentieth century.
See item no. 355.

Les émirats du Golfe: histoire d'un peuple. (The emirates of the Gulf: history of a people.)
See item no. 379.

The Arabian peninsula.
See item no. 382.

Britain and the Arab states: a survey of Anglo-Arab relations, 1920-1948.
See item no. 384.

The Persian Gulf region.
See item no. 387.

Saudi Arabia in the nineteenth century.
See item no. 398.

Oil, power and politics: conflict in Arabia, the Red Sea and the Gulf.
See item no. 446.

Persian Gulf oil in Middle East and international conflicts.
See item no. 447.

The Persian Gulf in regional and international politics: the Arab side of the Gulf.
See item no. 452.

Bahrain.
See item no. 455.

Problems and prospects in the Gulf: an uncertain future.
See item no. 463.

Arabia without sultans.
See item no. 470.

Iran: dictatorship and development.
See item no. 472.

Jail for 73 convicted of Bahrain Muslim plot.
See item no. 479.

Gulf union.
See item no. 483.

Bahrain: political development in a modernizing society.
See item no. 488.

Conflict and cooperation in the Gulf.
See item no. 493.

Der Persisch/Arabische Golf — Wirtschaftsraum und Krisenherd. (The Persian/Arabian Gulf: centre of economic development and political crisis.)
See item no. 495.

Foreign Relations

The decision to withdraw from the Gulf.
See item no. 497.

Iran since the revolution.
See item no. 498.

The origins of the United Arab Emirates. A political and social history of the Trucial States.
See item no. 499.

The Arabian Gulf states: their legal and political status and their international problems.
See item no. 500.

The fact-finding mission of the United Nations Secretary General and the settlement of the Bahrain-Iran dispute, May 1970.
See item no. 501.

The legal status of the Arabian Gulf states: a study of their treaty relations and their international problems.
See item no. 502.

Le golfe persique et les isles de Bahrein. (The Persian Gulf and the islands of Bahrein.)
See item no. 504.

The Middle Eastern states and the Law of the Sea.
See item no. 505.

Iran's claim to the sovereignty of Bahrayn.
See item no. 507.

Iran, Saudi Arabia and the Law of the Sea: political interaction and legal development in the Persian Gulf.
See item no. 512.

The settlement of the Bahrain question: a study in Anglo-Iranian-United Nations diplomacy.
See item no. 514.

Oil policies of the Gulf countries.
See item no. 725.

Claims to the oil resources in the Persian Gulf: will the world economy be controlled by the Gulf in the future?
See item no. 746.

Middle East oil and changing political constellations.
See item no. 751.

Economy

611 **Fishing for pearls.**
Samy H. Abboud. *Middle East Forum*, vol. 38, no. 7 (July-Sept. 1962), p. 68-72.
A descriptive account of pearl fishing with the Bahraini fleet in the 1950s. It observes that, although in the past Bahrain's pearl fleet numbered 700-800 boats, by the 1950s only 50 sailed in search of pearls.

612 **Arab industrialisation and economic integration.**
Edited by Roberto Aliboni. London: Croom Helm, 1979. 196p.
The results of a research project on 'Development and stability in the Mediterranean' which the Istituto Affari Internazionali of Rome started in December 1973. All of the three papers, by Z. Y. Hershlag, Samir A. Makdisi and Abdelwahab Bouhdiba, mention Bahrain.

613 **The Arab Economist.**
Beirut: Centre for Economic, Financial and Social Research and Documentation. 1969- . monthly.
A monthly publication of approximately 50 pages, which includes a business round-up, general economic reports, a financial report, a discussion on oil affairs, and a section on documentation on the Arab world.

614 **Middle East economies in the 1970s: a comparative approach.**
Hossein Askari, John Thomas Cummings. New York: Praeger, 1976. 581p. bibliog. (Praeger Special Studies in International Economics and Development).
A comprehensive account of oil, agriculture, industry, manpower, trade and the role of governments in economic development in the Middle East. Bahrain is mentioned in detail in connection with education, expatriates, industry, oil, and trade. It includes an extensive bibliography, and concludes that it is not in the long-term interests of the Middle Eastern oil states to pursue a policy of confrontation with the industrialized countries of the world.

Economy

615 **Bahrain.**
London: Grindlays Bank Group, Economics Department, Jan.
1982. unpaged. map.
A useful summary account of Bahrain's economic background, recent economic
developments, planning and development, offshore banks and commercial
companies, foreign trade and payments. and economic outlook. It is regularly
updated.

616 **Bahrain: all set for another boom.**
Arab Economist, no. 137, vol. 13 (Feb. 1981), p. 23-28.
An analysis of Bahrain's economic potential which argues that after a period of
consolidation, the state is now set for a period of expansion similar to that of the
post-1973 boom. It reports on the '10,000 scheme' launched in May 1980 to train
1,000 Bahrainis a year for the next 10 years, and it provides a summary of progress
in recent years, covering banking, the aluminium rolling mill, the ASRY shipbuilding yard, and the BAPCO refinery. It notes that the success of the Mina
Sulman industrial development area has led to the beginning of a new development area at North Sitra, and it argues that the final big boost to Bahrain's manufacturing industry will come with the construction of the iron and steel pelletization plant. The article also reports briefly on the four-year development programme being prepared by the Bahrain Ministry of Finance and Economy.

617 **Bahrain and Qatar.**
London: British Overseas Trade Board, 1977. 96p. 3 maps.
bibliog. (Hints to Businessmen).
Details on Bahrain for businessmen are provided in the first part of this booklet
(p. 8-41). Sections cover general information, travel, hotels and restaurants,
post and telecommunications, economic factors, import and exchange control
regulations, and methods of doing business. It is now a little out of date.

618 **Bahrain business directory.**
Manama: Arab Communications, 1981/82. 3rd ed. 441p.
A thorough source of references for all aspects of Bahrain's economy. It includes
sections on basic information, history, the state, communications, development
and industry, banking and finance, trade, the economy, welfare, labour, costs of
living, traditional crafts and industries, leisure, and the government, and it provides
details of all of the relevant labour and commercial laws as well as a list of
businesses in Bahrain.

619 **Bahrain: business information.**
London: Standard Chartered Bank, Nov. 1982. 23p.
An introduction to Bahrain for businessmen, providing details on background
information, establishing a business in Bahrain, trading with Bahrain, and banking.
It concludes with a section on useful ministry, embassy and airline addresses in
Bahrain. It is regularly updated.

620 **Bahrain: an economic report.**
London: National Westminster Bank, International Banking
Division, April 1983. unpaged. 2 maps.

A brief report on politics, the domestic economy, development, economic sectors,
offshore banking activities, the external economy, and future prospects of
Bahrain. It also provides a few economic statistics.

621 **Bahrain: Financial Times survey.**
Financial Times, 5 June 1979, p. I-X.

An account of Bahrain's economy, banking, ASRY drydock, aluminium industry,
causeway project with Saudi Arabia, air transport, telecommunications, quality of
life, and the expatriate community.

622 **Bahrain: Financial Times survey.**
Financial Times, 4 Nov. 1980, p. I-XII.

Gives details on Bahrain's politics, economy, causeway project, telephone system,
oil and gas industry, offshore banking units, domestic banks, insurance, expatriate
life, airport services, aluminium industry, drydock, agriculture and fishing.

623 **Bahrain: Financial Times survey.**
Financial Times, 2 June 1981, p. I-XII.

Provides information on Bahrain's role in regional integration in the Gulf, its
economy, oil and gas industries, industry, causeway with Saudi Arabia, manpower,
banking, public works, agriculture and fisheries, social welfare, education, aviation,
travel industry, and business environment.

624 **Bahrain: foundations are laid for an oil-less future.**
Middle East Economic Digest, vol. 17, no. 11 (16 March 1973),
p. 289-91.

An account of Bahrain's plans for its economy when oil revenues are depleted,
based on analysis of the budget for 1973/74.

625 **Bahrain: Lloyds Bank Group economic report 1982.**
London: Lloyds Bank, Overseas Department, Sept. 1982. 22p.
map.

A useful and thorough summary of Bahrain's economy, with main sections on
basic data, its land and people, domestic economy, structure of production, and
external trading and financial position. Within the section on the structure of
production information is provided on energy sources, power and water, agriculture and fishing, manufacturing, housing and construction, transport and tourism,
banking and finance, and other services. It is regularly updated.

Economy

626 **Bahrain: poised for growth after recent shutdown.**
Arab Economist, no. 144, vol. 13 (Sept. 1981), p. 19-22.
A report on recent economic changes in Bahrain, which discusses the oil sector, new administrative developments, the natural gas decline, aluminium developments, the control of inflation, the expansion of construction, the balance in foreign trade, and the increase in money supply.

627 **Bahrain, Qatar, United Arab Emirates and the Sultanate of Oman: the businessman's guide.**
London: Standard Chartered Bank, 1979. 60p. map.
After a general introduction for businessmen to the region as a whole, each country is discussed in detail, with Bahrain being analysed on p. 20-27. Information is provided on the state's geography and population, government, economic development, trade, immigration requirements, import documentation, labour force, public utilities, requirements for establishing a business, taxation and tariffs, transport and telecommunications, and general information, and it concludes with a list of useful addresses.

628 **Bahrain: a rewarding diversity.**
Arab Economist, supplement, no. 77, vol. 7 (June 1975). 42p.
An economic review of Bahrain, concentrating on its advanced services sector, the 1975 budget, industrial development, the Alba aluminium smelter, changes in the agricultural sector, and Bahrain's drydock. An appendix includes various economic statistics relating to the early 1970s.

629 **Bahrain: a special report.**
The Times (London), 16 Dec. 1976, p. I-VIII.
This report considers the island's economic future with a particular look at off-shore banking in the mid-1970s. It has sections on the oil industry, banking, tourist sites, water, agriculture, fishing, communications, the property market, industry, employment, and education.

630 **Bahrain: a special report.**
The Times (London), 16 Dec. 1977, p. I-VIII.
This includes an introduction to the 35 islands making Bahrain, and reports on the political scene, port and drydock development, other industries, archaeology, property prospects, oil, tourism, finance, desert spots, and facts of living in Al-Manama.

631 **Arab Business Yearbook 1980/81.**
Edited by Simon M. A. Barrow. London: Graham & Trotman,
1980. 661p.

The first part of this publication provides pan-Arab data on transportation, telecommunications, banking, oil, OPEC, OAPEC, population, construction and
taxation. The second part is a country-by-country guide for businessmen, with
Bahrein being surveyed on p. 180-203. Here information is provided on government institutions, business travel data, times and dates, the economy, finance,
foreign investment, import regulations, development plans and oil. Some statistics
relating to the budget and trade are given.

632 **Pearl diving in Bahrain.**
C. Dalrymple Belgrave. *Journal of the Royal Central Asian
Society,* vol. 21, no. 3 (July 1934), p. 450-52.

A brief account of the nature and extent of the pearl diving economy in Bahrain.
It comments that the economic depression of Europe and America combined with
the increased export of cultured pearls from Japan had caused a slump in the
pearl market. It also notes that, following the accession of Shaikh Hamad bin Isa
al Khalifah to the throne in 1923, thorough reforms of the diving system were
initiated leading to improvements in the position of the Bahrain pearl divers.

633 **The changing Middle Eastern city.**
Edited by G. H. Blake, R. I. Lawless. London: Croom Helm;
New York: Barnes & Noble, 1980. 273p. 28 maps.

In this book on recent urban change in the Middle East the papers by Peter Beaumont, J. I. Clarke, and J. S. Birks and C. A. Sinclair mention Bahrain.

634 **The pearl fisheries of the Persian Gulf.**
Richard Le Baron Bowen. *Middle East Journal,* vol. 5, no. 2
(spring 1951), p. 161-80.

An account of the pearl fisheries of the Gulf from earliest times to the 1950s. It
discusses the pearling fleets, diving techniques, marketing of the pearls, and the
economic relationships between divers and the *nakhodas,* or captains, of the
pearling boats.

635 **Major companies of the Arab world 1980/81.**
Edited by Giselle C. Bricault. London: Graham & Trotman,
1980. 5th ed. 731p.

A list of the major industrial and commercial companies of the Arab world
arranged by country. Bahrain's companies are mentioned alphabetically on
p. 17-49.

Economy

636 **Bahrain.**
British Bank of the Middle East. [London: British Bank of the Middle East], April 1981. 2nd ed. 27p. 3 maps. (Business Profile Series).

A useful introduction to the economy of Bahrain, which is divided into five main sections: introduction, economy, facts and figures, business information, and information for visitors and residents. Within the section on the economy it provides some details on oil production, oil refining, gas production, aluminium production, development projects, infrastructure, banking, telecommunications, and tourism. The appendix gives a list of useful telephone numbers and addresses. It is regularly updated.

637 **Bahraini strategy for prosperity.**
Denys Brunsden. *Geographical Magazine* (London), vol. 52, no. 5 (Feb. 1980), p. 349-55.

This article asserts that Bahrain's 'strategic position and the presence of fresh water springs, reasonably fertile soils, abundant vegetation and safe anchorages have determined that the islands would have a long and chequered history as a trading nation, coveted island stronghold, administrative and service centre'. It notes that traditional income was derived from trade, pearl fishing, agriculture, white donkeys, fishing, pottery, weaving, gutch and lime manufacture, and some other minor industries, but that the economy has been totally transformed since the first oil well was sunk in 1932.

638 **The United Arab Emirates: an economic and social survey.**
K. G. Fenelon. London, New York: Longman, 1976. 2nd ed. 164p. 3 maps. bibliog.

A survey of recent changes in the United Arab Emirates. It notes that Bahrain seems to have been the cradle of boat-building in the Gulf, that the British Residency was moved from Bushire to Bahrain in 1946, and that Bahrain provided many school teachers during the early expansion of education in the United Arab Emirates.

639 **The oil states.**
W. B. Fisher. London: Batsford Academic and Educational, 1980. 71p. 6 maps. (Today's World Series).

A brief introduction to the oil states of the Middle East, aimed primarily at schoolchildren. Bahrain's oil industry, the development of Isa Town, which is described as the first 'new town' in the Middle East, and the country's aluminium plant are mentioned.

640 **Focus on Bahrain: proceedings of a one-day conference held on 17 June 1981 by the Arab-British Chamber of Commerce.**
London: Arab-British Chamber of Commerce, 1981. 33p. map.

Provides information on Bahrain in the following fields: the economy, telecommunications, its aluminium industry, exempt companies, banking and export finance, offshore banking units, and statistics. It concludes with a short section on essential information for businessmen.

641 **Economic issues in the Middle East.**
Stuart Harris. In: *The Middle East in world politics*. Edited by Mohammed Ayoob. London: Croom Helm, 1981, p. 175-202.

This paper concentrates on those economic issues which have important relationships with political issues in the Middle East and with significant implications for the international economic system. It notes that Bahrein has developed as a regional financial centre, and that the offshore market in Saudi currency that had been built up in Bahrein was stopped because of its disruptive effect on domestic financial management of the Saudi economy.

642 **Gold rush economics: development planning in the Persian/ Arabian Gulf.**
Jared E. Hazleton. *Studies in Comparative International Development*, vol. 13, no. 2 (1978), p. 3-22.

An evaluation of the options open to the countries of the Gulf, including Bahrain, for the use of their greatly increased oil revenues following the price rises of 1973. The paper argues that the gold rush atmosphere may fail to provide a viable base for meeting long-term economic and social needs.

643 **A golden dream. The miracle of Kuwait.**
Ralph Hewins. London: W. H. Allen, 1963. 318p. 2 maps.

An account of the emergence of Kuwait and its oil history, which includes scattered references to Bahrain.

644 **The Arabs and the West.**
Clare Hollingworth. London: Methuen, 1952. 285p. 8 maps. bibliog.

Provides an account of events leading up to, and the aftermath of, the Palestine War. Bahrain is mentioned in the context of its role as an oil-producing country, and is discussed in detail on p. 244-47, where it is described as 'the strategic centre for Britain's position in the Gulf'. It notes that Bahrain Petroleum Company's refinery treated more Saudi Arabian oil than it did oil from the Ahwali wells in Bahrain and that although it is owned by Standard Oil Company of California and the Texas Oil Company 90 per cent of its European staff are British. The role played by C. Dalrymple Belgrave, who is described as 'virtually Prime Minister', is seen as being crucial to the prosperity of the country. It also notes the rationing scheme introduced for foodstuffs, and the Persian claims to the islands.

Economy

645 Oil revenues in the Gulf emirates. Patterns of allocation and impact on economic development.
Ali Khalifa Al-Kuwari. Epping, England: Bowker, in association with the Centre for Middle Eastern and Islamic Studies of the University of Durham, 1978. 218p. map. bibliog.

An analysis of the efficiency with which oil revenues have been utilized in the Gulf, with the aim of providing a better understanding for the future use of petroleum resources. Chapter 4 is specifically about Bahrain and considers its public revenue, expenditure and reserve, and the allocation of the state's oil revenue in the period 1947-70.

646 Urbanization in the Gulf.
Lord Llewelyn-Davies. In: *Engineering and development in the Gulf.* Bahrain Society of Engineers. London: Graham & Trotman, 1977, p. 1-13.

This paper identifies three main themes in the present expansion of Gulf cities: the drive for national identity, change and improvement; the evaluation of aspirations and resources; and the problems associated with social and economic change. The development of the new town of Isa Town is noted.

647 Arab economic co-operation.
Samir A. Makdisi. In: *Arab industrialisation and economic integration.* Edited by Roberto Aliboni. London: Croom Helm, 1979, p. 90-133.

This study has four aims: to portray the current status of Arab economic co-operation; to assess some of the major factors which govern the effectiveness of Arab economic co-operation and explain its present limitations; to analyse the potential gains from a closer and more effective Arab economic co-operation; and to examine some of the implications of an assumed close Arab economic co-operation to the world economy. It notes that Bahrain maintains a liberal exchange system with no restrictions being imposed on international economic transactions. As in Oman and the UAE the dollar rate of Bahrain's national currency is fixed, and as a result the value of these three countries' national currencies *vis-à-vis* one another is also fixed.

648 Economic development and regional cooperation: Kuwait.
Ragaei El Mallakh. Chicago, London: University of Chicago Press, 1968. 265p. bibliog.

This analysis of Kuwait's economic development includes mentions of Bahrain's oil production and trading relations between Bahrain and Kuwait.

649 **The economic development of the United Arab Emirates.**
Ragaei El Mallakh. London: Croom Helm, 1981. 215p. map.
bibliog.

An account of recent economic change in the United Arab Emirates with individual chapters on current perspectives, economic development policies, social infrastructure, economic infrastructure, oil, foreign trade, the financial sector, and business and investment. Bahrain is mentioned in several places in connection with aid given by it to the Trucial States, Britain's withdrawal from the area, its role in shipbuilding and repair work, and trade relationships between the two states.

650 **Qatar, development of an oil economy.**
Ragaei El Mallakh. London: Croom Helm, 1979. 183p. map.
bibliog.

A study of the economic underpinning of Qatar's growth and future development. There are frequent mentions of Bahrain, mainly in the context of historical and economic links between the two states.

651 **Saudi Arabia: rush to development. Profile of an energy economy and investment.**
Ragaei El Mallakh. London, Canberra: Croom Helm, 1982.
472p. 7 maps. bibliog.

An investigation of the recent rapid changes in the economic structure of Saudi Arabia. Bahrain is mentioned briefly in the context of joint Arab investment and the Saudi Development Fund.

652 **The Middle East: a political and economic survey.**
Edited by Peter Mansfield. London, New York, Toronto,
Melbourne: Oxford University Press, 1980. 5th ed. 579p. map.
bibliog.

After a general introduction on the region as a whole, its history, politics, faiths, sects and minorities, Arab political movements, and economic and social affairs, each part of the region is discussed in detail. Bahrain is described on p. 174-77 of the chapter on Arabia, where mention is made of its population, government, recent history and the economy.

653 **The Arab world: a guide to business, economic and industrial information sources.**
Joseph O. Mekeirle. Dallas, Texas: Inter-Crescent Publishing,
1980. 492p.

After a general introduction and lists on bibliographies and reference works on the Arab world as a whole, each country is then treated separately. Information on Bahrain (p. 141-47) is divided into sections on general introductory books; economy; business; industry; directories, guides and yearbooks; company information sources; periodicals; and periodical articles divided into sub-sections on economics, and business and industry. It has an author, organization and subject index, together with a source directory.

Economy

654 **Eastern Arabia, Kuwait, Bahrain.**
Alexander Melamid. In: *The Middle East.* Edited by Alice
Taylor. Newton Abbot, England: David & Charles in co-operation
with the American Geographical Society, 1972, p. 125-38.
This chapter notes that the exploitation of oil resources has brought rapid change
to Bahrain and has altered it from being a pearl producer to a modernized country
with an oil refinery and planned aluminium smelter.

655 **Middle East Economic Digest.**
London: Middle East Economic Digest, March 1957- . weekly.
A comprehensive weekly account of economic events in the Middle East, with
both regional comments and sections on individual countries, including Bahrain.
It provides details of contracts, and there is also an annual review of Middle
Eastern events published in December.

656 **Middle East International.**
London: Middle East International, April 1971- . fortnightly.
A fortnightly publication of approximately fifteen pages covering current
economic and political issues, and including book reviews and translations of relevant documents.

657 **Dilemmas of non-oil economic development in the Arab Gulf.**
Tim Niblock. London: Arab Research Centre, 1980. 18p.
(Arab Papers: Research Paper Series, 1).
A study of the recent economic development of Bahrain, Kuwait, Oman, Qatar,
Saudi Arabia and the United Arab Emirates, concentrating on the dilemmas
caused by the distribution of natural resources, reliance on migrant labour, the
political requirement, the necessity for co-ordination and integration, and inter-
national investment strategies.

658 **The prospects for integration in the Arab Gulf.**
Tim Niblock. In: *Social and economic development in the Arab
Gulf.* Edited by Tim Niblock. London: Croom Helm, 1980,
p. 187-209.
A paper supporting the argument that economic integration is essential for the
satisfactory development of the Gulf states. It discusses the attempts at federation
between the Trucial States, Qatar and Bahrain in the period 1968-72, and analyses
social and economic co-ordination in 1972-79.

659 **Social and economic development in the Arab Gulf.**
Edited by Tim Niblock. London: Croom Helm, 1980. 242p.
5 maps.

A selection of papers presented to the inaugural conference of the Centre for Arab Gulf Studies at the University of Exeter, England, 9-13 July 1979. Those by Mohamed G. Rumaihi, Rosemarie Said Zahlan, Keith McLachlan, John Townsend, J. S. Birks and C. A. Sinclair, Emile A. Nakhleh, Tim Niblock, and Fred Halliday mention Bahrain.

660 **Gulf states and Oman.**
Christine Osborne. London: Croom Helm, 1977. 208p. 5 maps.
bibliog.

A journalistic account of recent socio-economic change in the Gulf. Chapter 1 is about Bahrain and briefly describes the following subjects: pearling, oil and the economy, business opportunities, social life, hotels and housing, and local life and tourism. Two concluding chapters are concerned with the changing lifestyle of the bedouin and the 'emerging women of the Gulf'.

661 **Remarks on the pearl oyster beds in the Persian Gulf.**
Lewis Pelly. *Transactions of the Bombay Geographical Society,*
vol. 18 (Jan. 1865-Dec. 1867), p. 32-36.

This account of pearling in the 19th century by Her Britannic Majesty's Political Resident, Persian Gulf, records that the richest pearl banks were those of Bahrein. It also notes that some 1,500 fishing boats may have belonged to Bahrein, and that all of the pearl beds were held to be the property of the Arabs in common. The best pearls were sent to the Bombay market.

662 **Quarterly Economic Review of the Arabian Peninsula:**
Shaikhdoms and Republics.
London: Economist Intelligence Unit, first quarter 1971-first
quarter 1978. quarterly.

A quarterly review providing useful information on the economies of the countries of the Arabian peninsula. It has been replaced by the *Quarterly Economic Review of Bahrain, Qatar, Oman, the Yemens* (see below) and two other publications on the UAE and Kuwait.

663 **Quarterly Economic Review of Bahrain, Qatar, Oman, the**
Yemens.
London: Economist Intelligence Unit, second quarter 1978- .
quarterly.

Provides a quarterly review and outlook of the economy of Bahrain. An annual supplement is also published.

Economy

664 Quarterly Economic Review of Oil in the Middle East.
London: Economist Intelligence Unit, first quarter 1960- last quarter 1980. quarterly.

A review of oil developments in the Middle East. It has been succeeded by the *Quarterly Energy Review: Energy in the Middle East* (see below).

665 Quarterly Energy Review: Energy in the Middle East.
London: the Economist Intelligence Unit, first quarter 1981-. quarterly.

A detailed publication primarily concerned with the economics of oil in the Middle East. An annual supplement is also produced.

666 Rim of prosperity. The Gulf: a survey.
The Economist, special report (13 Dec. 1980). 84p.

An economic and political survey of the Gulf, paying particular attention to oil and the effects of the Iran-Iraq war of 1980-81. It notes that Bahrain has more Shia than Sunni Moslems, and that the police had violently to break up a demonstration in April 1980 when Bahrain's Shias demonstrated at the arrest in Iraq of the Shia prelate Ayatollah Bakr Sadr. There is a special section on the 'Ten Thousand' scheme which plans to train 10,000 Bahraini nationals for promotion during the 1980s to key positions currently held by expatriates, and shorter reports mention Aluminium Bahrain and the archaeological investigations into Dilmun.

667 An urban profile of the Middle East.
Hugh Roberts. London: Croom Helm, 1979. 239p. 54 maps.

Includes some statistics on the rates of urbanization in Bahrain in a wider discussion of the changes that have taken place in Middle Eastern cities in recent decades.

668 Problems and prospects of development in the Arabian peninsula.
Yusif A. Sayigh. In: *The Arabian peninsula: society and politics.* Edited by Derek Hopwood. London: George Allen & Unwin, 1972, p. 286-309.

This paper argues that the problems of development in Arabia are closely connected with the underlying contrasts between states in the peninsula. It includes many scattered references to Bahrain's economic structure.

669 Wirtschaftsmacht Arabische Erdölförderländer: Die globale
      wirtschaftliche Bedeutung und finanzpolitische Rolle der
      arabischen Golfstaaten und ihre internen Entwicklungsprobleme.
      (The economic powers of the Arabian oil producing countries:
      the global economic importance and fiscal role of the Arabian
      Gulf states and their internal development problems.)
      Fred Scholz. *Geographische Rundschau*, vol. 32, no. 12 (Dec.
      1980), p. 527-42.

This paper is concerned with the importance of the Arab oil producing countries
for the international economic and monetary system. It argues that, despite the
enormous wealth of the Gulf countries, they are still all developing countries as
far as their internal structure and external dependence are concerned.

670 Saudi Arabia with an account of the development of its natural
      resources.
      K. S. Twitchell. Princeton, New Jersey: Princeton University
      Press, 1947. 192p. map.

An introduction to the social, economic and political structures of Saudi Arabia
in the mid-20th century. Bahrain's pearl fishery, freshwater springs, and oil
industry are mentioned.

671 Memorandum respecting the pearl fisheries in the Persian Gulf.
      D. Wilson. *Journal of the Royal Geographical Society*, vol. 3
      (1833), p. 283-86.

This article by the late Resident in the Persian Gulf pays particular attention to
Bahrein's pearl fisheries, the ways in which the pearls were obtained, and the
economic returns available from pearl fishing in the early 19th century.

672 The economies of the Middle East.
      Rodney Wilson. London: Macmillan, 1979. 209p.

A country-by-country account of the economies of the Middle East, concentrating
on those aspects of development that the author considers to be crucial for the
future shape of the region's economic activity. Bahrain is discussed in chapter 5
on the Gulf, which notes that the state has a more modest per capita GNP
($2,410) than the other countries of the region due to the fact that it is not a
major producer of crude oil. It notes that farming in Bahrain is declining due to
a lowering of the water table and rising salinity due to an excessive number of
wells being drilled. Details are also given of Bahrain's oil refinery, the largest in
the Gulf with 250,000 barrels per day being produced, and of the OAPEC financed
dry dock project in Bahrain.

Economy

673 **Kuwait: prospect and reality.**
H. V. F. Winstone, Zahra Freeth. London: George Allen &
Unwin, 1972. 232p. 9 maps. bibliog.
An account of the political and economic emergence of Kuwait. The first chapter
provides a description of the archaeological work undertaken in Bahrain and
Kuwait, linking the two to ancient Dilmun.

674 **Issues in development: the Arab Gulf states.**
Edited by May Ziwar-Daftari. London: MD Research and
Services, 1980. 224p. 3 maps.
A collection of economic analyses of the Gulf grouped into three parts: bottle-
necks, case studies, and viewpoints. Its objective is to raise questions and instigate
future investigations in economic and social matters. The papers by Henry T.
Azzam, H. Bowen-Jones, Rodney J. A. Wilson, Alan E. Moore, Jawad Hashim and
Louis Turner all discuss Bahrain.

**Der arabisch-persische Golf. Eine Studie zur historischen, politischen
und ökonomischen Entwicklung der Golf-Region.** (The Arabian-Persian
Gulf. A study of the historical, political and economic development of
the Gulf region.)
See item no. 289.

The Middle East: a political and economic survey.
See item no. 302.

Bahrain is independent.
See item no. 327.

**Bahrain, Qatar, and the United Arab Emirates: colonial past, present
problems, and future prospects.**
See item no. 380.

The Middle East.
See item no. 486.

**Middle East Newsletters: Gulf States, Iraq, Iran, Kuwait, Bahrain,
Qatar, United Arab Emirates, Oman.**
See item no. 487.

Political and economic integration in the Arab states of the Gulf.
See item no. 490.

Inside the Middle East.
See item no. 553.

Iraq: the contemporary state.
See item no. 581.

Bahrain Monetary Agency Annual Report.
See item no. 677.

162

Finance and Banking

675 **The external economic and monetary positions of the Arab countries and the role of financial surpluses in promoting Arab monetary integration.**
Abdul Munim Al-Sayyed Ali. In: *Arab monetary integration: issues and perspectives.* Edited by Khair El-Din Haseeb, Samir Makdisi. London, Canberra: Croom Helm, 1982, p. 299-330.

This paper examines the flow of trade and of economic resources in general among the Arab countries, assesses their balance of payment positions, analyses the flow of financial resources among them, and considers the role of financial surpluses in helping to achieve closer Arab monetary integration. It provides figures on various aspects of Bahrain's trade.

676 **Arabanks: the International Yearbook 1981/82.**
Paris: Edires France, 1981. 323p.

A thorough guide to the banks of the Arab world. Bahrain's banks are listed on p. 9-32.

677 **Bahrain Monetary Agency Annual Report.**
Bahrain: Bahrain Monetary Agency, 1974- . annual.

A useful annual report on the state of Bahrain's economy, which also provides information on aspects other than finance. It is divided into sections on international development, domestic economic development, financial development, Agency activities, and a list of financial institutions in Bahrain.

678 **Banking and investment 1980: *Khaleej Times* special report.**
Dubai: Khaleej Times, Galadari Printing and Publishing Establishment, 9 December 1980. 30p.

A report on banking in the Gulf. Bahrain's financial scene is analysed on p. 13-17. Here Bahrain is described as the Arab nation's banker, and it is argued that the key to its banking success has been its offshore banking units. Additional short articles provide information on the increasing role of the Japanese in Bahrain's financial scene, and on the activities of the recently founded Arab Banking Corporation.

Finance and Banking

679 Offshore financial centres.
John Chown, revised by Mary Cook. London: Financial Times
Business Publications, 1981. 4th ed. 285p.

Following an introductory chapter on the characteristics of offshore banking
centres this detailed publication analyses the various offshore centres of the
world. Bahrain is discussed in chapter 13 which provides details of control and
supervision, banking, currency and foreign exchange control, legal entities and
taxation.

680 Banking in the Gulf.
Kevin Fenelon. *Banker*, vol. 120 (Nov. 1970), p. 1,198-210.

Banking in Bahrain is discussed mainly on p. 1,207-09 of this account. It notes
that the first bank in Bahrain was the Eastern Bank established in 1920. The
British Bank of the Middle East was then established in Bahrain in 1943, to be
followed 13 years later by the Bank of Bahrain. Around 1960 the Arab Bank
moved into the islands, and in the 1960s these four banks dominated Bahrain.
With increasing oil revenues since then banking has expanded.

681 A hundred million dollars a day: inside the world of Middle East money.
Michael Field. London: Sidgwick & Jackson, 1975; New York:
Praeger, 1976. 240p.

This book is primarily concerned with the money of the four major Arabian
peninsula oil producers, Saudi Arabia, Kuwait, Abu Dhabi and Qatar. There are
also, though, several mentions of Bahrain in connection with its bank deposits,
foreign assets, oil production and reserves, and infrastructural developments.

682 Finance in the Arab world: a special report.
The Times (London), 6 March 1981, p. I-XII.

This useful report on finance and banking in the Arab world covers such subjects
as the location of Arab investments, the role of Islamic principles in banking, and
aid. The major Arab banking states are each described in turn, and the section on
Bahrain (p. VI) is mainly concerned with its offshore banking units.

683 Gulf Banking and Finance.
Manama: Al Hilal Publishing and Marketing Group, Jan. 1981- .
monthly.

The only financial magazine published in the Gulf. It includes many interesting
articles and notes on banking in Bahrain and other Gulf Co-operation Council
countries. Circulation 5,500. Free controlled circulation in the GCC and bookshop sales. A banking directory associated with this magazine is to be produced
in 1983 and this will list every bank in the Gulf, including foreign and locally
incorporated banks, financial data, boards of directors, shareholders, addresses,
relevant subsidiaries, affiliates and associates worldwide. Each month the
directory will be updated as an insert in *Gulf Banking and Finance*.

684 **Arab monetary integration: issues and perspectives.**
Edited by Khair El-Din Haseeb, Samir Makdisi. London,
Canberra: Croom Helm, 1982. 475p.

A collection of papers resulting from a seminar held in Abu Dhabi in November
1980. Bahrain is specifically discussed in the papers by Karim Nashashibi and
Abdul Munim Al-Sayyed Ali.

685 **Towards a Gulf Monetary Area.**
Jawad Hashim. In: *Issues in development: the Arab Gulf states.*
Edited by May Ziwar-Daftari. London: MD Research and
Services, 1980, p. 187-201.

The purpose of this article is to present a case for the establishment of a Gulf
Monetary Area by a group of countries bordering the Arab Gulf. It provides some
figures for Bahrain's money supply, consumer prices, exchange rates, and international reserves in the 1970s.

686 **Public finance prospects and policies for Bahrain, 1975-1985.**
Jared E. Hazleton. Beirut: Ford Foundation, 1975. 123p.
bibliog.

An analysis and projection of Bahrain's revenue and expenditure policies, written
in the mid-1970s. It argues that at that time Bahrain needed to make a careful
assessment of its long run development needs, that it needed to evaluate its
revenue structure to determine the extent to which additional revenues could be
generated, and that it needed to improve its budgeting procedures. Four appendixes provide useful statistics on the state's economy, demographic structure,
petroleum sector, and public finance.

687 **Middle East Financial Directory 1981.**
London: Middle East Economic Digest in association with the
Arab Banking Corporation, 1981. 5th ed. 314p.

In this financial directory of the Arab world, Bahrain is described on p. 5-21
where details are given on its central bank authority, commercial and investment
banks (including representative offices and offshore banking units), specialized
banks, and other financial institutions.

688 **The development of banking in Bahrain.**
Alan E. Moore. In: *Issues in development: the Arab Gulf states.*
Edited by May Ziwar-Daftari. London: MD Research and Services,
1980, p. 138-53.

This account traces the growth of banking in Bahrain from the opening of the
first branch of the Eastern Bank in 1921 to the emergence of Offshore Banking
Units in the late 1970s. It is a comprehensive and useful study of the development
of banking in Bahrain.

Finance and Banking

689 **Bahrain looks to a secure future.**
John Whelan, Martin Roth. *Middle East Economic Digest*,
vol. 26, no. 16 (16 April 1982), p. 20-21.

A report on Bahrain's role as the banking centre of the Gulf. It notes that, since
the establishment of the Gulf Co-operation Council in 1981, Bahrain has become
a major recipient of its benefits, and that it is planning five major new projects for
the 1980s: the Arabian Gulf University, the $350 million Gulf Petrochemical
Industries Company ammonia/methanol plant, the $300 million Arab Iron and
Steel Company pelletizing plant, the $555 million Bahrain-Saudi Arabia causeway,
and the $1,000 million Heavy Oil Conversion Corporation project.

690 **Recent financial trends in the Gulf.**
R. J. A. Wilson. Durham, England: University of Durham,
Centre for Middle Eastern and Islamic Studies, 1981. 39p.
(Economic Research Paper, no. 9).

An evaluation of the growth of the financial sector in the Gulf following the
collapse of Beirut as a financial centre and the 1974 quadrupling of oil prices.
Bahrain is characterized as a money market centre, and much attention is paid in
the text to the offshore banking units established there following government
legislation in 1975.

**The U.K. and Arabia: a commemorative issue to mark the visit of
H.M. Queen Elizabeth II.**
See item no. 602.

**Trade and exchange regimes and the exercise of monetary policy in
the Arab countries.**
See item no. 699.

Trade

691 **Arab-British Chamber of Commerce: Annual Directory 1983.**
London: Arab-British Chamber of Commerce, 1983. 275p.
English; 196p. Arabic.

Provides a general survey of Arab companies, details of each Arab country, and general and commercial information on the region. Bahrain is discussed on p. 45-54, where information is given on its development planning, banking and finance, oil and gas, industry, foreign trade, business and basic data.

692 **Commercial directory of Kuwait & Gulf states 1978/79.**
Kuwait: Arab Advertising Agency, 1978. various paginations.

The fifth edition of this directory of firms in the Gulf. The section on Bahrain provides information on its physical and social geography, economy, history and business, as well as over 100 pages of traders and advertisers.

693 **Export corridors of the world: Bahrain.**
The Times (London), 30 May 1974, p. I-IV.

The fourth in a series of special reports on export corridors of the world. It covers Bahrain's new status as a haven for industry, its gas and oil industries, the drydock plan, Mina Sulman, airport expansion, the shrimp industry, and land reclamation for industrial purposes.

694 **Business opportunities in the Gulf states: Bahrain, Kuwait, Oman, Qatar, U.A.E.**
Andrew Hayman. London: Metra Consulting Group, 1981.
246p. 7 maps.

After an introduction, summary, background discussion and analysis of the economy of the region, there are two chapters, on infrastructure and on industry, agriculture and minerals, in which each country is surveyed in turn. The final chapters analyse banking, trade, social services, investment, and the business environment in the Gulf. Appendixes include lists of useful addresses and contracts placed by the Gulf states in 1980. It provides much useful information on the economic changes that have recently taken place in Bahrain.

Trade

695 **Hints to exporters: Bahrain and Qatar.**
London: British Overseas Trade Board, 1980/81. 76p. 2 maps.
bibliog.

This useful guide provides information on Bahrain divided into the following main
sections: general information, travel, hotels, telecommunications, economic
factors, import and exchange control regulations, and methods of doing business.

696 **Implications of regional development in the Middle East for U.S.
trade, capital flows and balance of payments: a summary report
of findings of National Science Foundation, RANN, grant no.
APR75-22411.**
Ragaei El Mallakh, Fred R. Glahe, Mihssen Kadhim, Carl McGuire,
Barry Poulson. Boulder, Colorado: International Research
Center for Energy and Economic Development, 1977. 64p.

A description of regional co-operation in the Middle East, and an evaluation of
the implications of development in the region for the United States' economy.
The ASRY drydock is mentioned as an example of regional co-operation, and
some figures are provided on Bahrain's trade with the USA.

697 **Cargoes of the East: the ports, trade and culture of the Arabian
Seas and western Indian Ocean.**
Esmond Bradley Martin, Chryssee Perry Martin. London: Elm
Tree Books, 1978. 244p. 5 maps.

A thorough and well-illustrated account of the history of the dhow trade of the
western Indian Ocean. Bahrain is specifically discussed in chapter 9 (p. 164-72),
where details are given of its traditional pearl trade, dhow building past and
present, and the dhow trade of Bahrain. It notes that Bahrain is the third
most active dhow port on the Arabian side of the Gulf.

698 **Middle East Trade.**
London: Middle East Trade Publications, 1961- . 10 times a year.

Covers a variety of subjects relating to trade and the construction industry in the
Middle East. Main articles are in Arabic but there are English summaries.

699 **Trade and exchange regimes and the exercise of monetary policy
in the Arab countries.**
Karim Nashashibi. In: *Arab monetary integration: issues and
perspectives.* Edited by Khair El-Din Haseeb, Samir Makdisi.
London, Canberra: Croom Helm, 1982, p. 103-24.

This paper aims to illustrate some of the problems facing economic integration
in the Arab world. Bahrain is described as having a liberal trade régime, and it
notes that prior to 1979 Bahrain, Qatar and the UAE attempted to co-ordinate
their exchange-rate policies. It also notes that there are 61 banks in Bahrain, of
which 42 are offshore.

700 **The Gulf pattern 1977-1982: trade, ports, economies.**
Peat, Marwick, Mitchell & Co. for Gray Mackenzie & Co.
London: Gray Mackenzie & Co., 1978. 129p.

A consideration of economic trends in the Gulf, which is concerned with maritime trade. Within each of the chapters on population and immigration, economic background, oil, gas and petrochemicals, industry and mining, agriculture, trade forecasts, transport infrastructure, and freight transport, there is a section on Bahrain. Details of the port of Mina Sulman, including a map, are given on p. 115.

701 **Doing business in Saudi Arabia and the Arab Gulf states.**
N. A. Shilling. New York: Inter-Crescent Publishing and
Information, 1975. 308p. 7 maps. bibliog.

A useful study of the Arabian peninsula, paying particular attention to the identification of markets; the economic frameworks in terms of laws and policies; the incentives, advantages and pitfalls of business; and practical ways in which to succeed in the area.

702 **Doing business in Saudi Arabia and the Arab Gulf states: 1977 supplement.**
Nancy A. Shilling. New York: Inter-Crescent Publishing and
Information, 1977. 147p. bibliog.

This useful volume supplements and updates information presented in *Doing business in Saudi Arabia and the Arab Gulf states* (above). The chapter on Bahrain (p. 3-20) includes the following sections: overview; government; budgets, revenue and development 1975-77; infrastructure; bottlenecks relating to port congestion, the airport and cement shortages; industry, in terms of legal and commercial developments; tendering; banking and finance, including details on the Real Estate Bank, the Gulf International Bank, the Bahrain Monetary Agency, Offshore Banking Units, and regulations; imports; exports; cost of living; labour, covering labour law, shortages, work permits, wages, and contract labour; banks; holidays; and a short bibliography.

703 **Ancient trading centres of the Persian Gulf VII: Bahrein.**
A. W. Stiffe. *Geographical Journal*, vol. 18, no. 3 (Sept. 1901),
p. 291-94.

A short account of the history and antiquities of Bahrein, noting its freshwater springs and paying particular attention to the Portuguese conquests of the islands.

704 **Trade contacts in Arab countries.**
London: London Chamber of Commerce and Industry, 1976.
249p.

Part 1 provides a list of useful addresses, High Commissions, and chambers of commerce in Arab countries. Part 2 is a directory of countries covering ministries, banks, industrial concerns and trading companies.

Trade

705 Marketing in the Middle East.
G. Vassiliou. London: Graham & Trotman, 1980. 158p.

An analysis of the marketing climate in the Middle East and a description of the prevailing conditions in the region. There are three sections: the first deals with the market and its people, the second concentrates on the organization of the market and the constituent parts of the marketing game, and the third examines the development of marketing processes in the region. It provides numerous marketing statistics on Bahrain.

706 Trade and investment in the Middle East.
Rodney Wilson. London: Macmillan, 1977. 152p.

An analysis of recent trends in Middle Eastern trade and investment, which considers their implications for both the region itself and also for the world at large. It is specifically concerned with the region's factor endowment, the development of the agrarian economy, import substitution, tariff and exchange rate policies, intra-regional trade and factor mobility, and with the relationships between the Middle East and the international economy. It notes that in Bahrain there are no quantitative restrictions on imports, apart from goods from Israel and the then Rhodesia, and that, together with Saudi Arabia, Kuwait, the UAE, Qatar and Oman, Bahrain accepts the obligations of Article VIII, Sections 2, 3 and 4 of the International Monetary Fund agreement on convertibility, which in practice means that these countries' currencies can be freely converted in world money markets.

Harappan trade in the Arabian Gulf in the 3rd millenium B.C.
See item no. 231.

New archaeological evidence for maritime trade in the Persian Gulf.
See item no. 232.

A short survey of a still topical problem: the third millenium Arabian Gulf trade mechanism seen in the light of the recent discoveries in southern Iran.
See item no. 233.

Seafaring merchants of Ur?
See item no. 269.

Towards an integrated history of culture change in the Arabian Gulf area: notes on Dilmun, Makkan and the economy of ancient Sumer.
See item no. 272.

Gun-running in the Persian Gulf.
See item no. 317.

Iran: the contemporary state.
See item no. 581.

U.K. & the Gulf 1971-1981: a MEED special report.
See item no. 606.

The external economic and monetary position of the Arab countries and the role of financial surpluses in promoting Arab monetary integration.
See item no. 675.

Industry

707 **Arab dry dock underlines Saudi influence.**
Lloyd's List, 31 March 1978, p. 4-5.
A report on the planning and early operations of the Arab Shipbuilding and
Repair Yard's drydock in Bahrein, which it describes as 'the brainchild of the
Saudi Oil Minister'.

708 **Bahrain takes steps to diversify industry through projects
financed by oil revenue.**
Robert Barth. *International Monetary Fund Survey*, 7 Nov.
1977, p. 344-45.
A report on Bahrain's economic diversification, concentrating on the smelter
operated by Aluminium Bahrain, the Arab Shipbuilding and Repair Yard's drydock, the offshore banking units established since 1975, the expansion of Mina
Sulman, and other infrastructural developments.

709 **Construction in the Arab world: a special report.**
The Times (London), 5 Sept. 1980, p. I-VIII.
Bahrain is mentioned in several places in this report on the Middle Eastern
construction industry, which includes a specific discussion of the bids submitted
for the Saudi Arabia-Bahrain causeway.

710 **The role of the Gulf in the future development of the world
aluminium industry.**
P. U. Fischer. In: *Engineering and development in the Gulf.*
Bahrain Society of Engineers. London: Graham & Trotman,
1977, p. 139-52.
Argues that the Gulf has many assets which make the establishment of further
aluminium industry attractive. Bahrain was the first Gulf state to produce
aluminium for the world market.

711 **Arab industrial integration: a strategy for development.**
Elias T. Ghantus. London: Croom Helm, 1982. 240p. bibliog.

This study by the Assistant Secretary General of the General Union of Chambers of Commerce, Industry and Agriculture for Arab Countries, aims to take into consideration the differing economic settings of the individual Arab countries in a strategy for integrated industrial development. Part 1 develops a theoretical framework for the study of economic integration among developing countries, and part 2 examines the specific case for integration among the Arab Middle East countries. Among several general mentions of Bahrain it notes that, with respect to refined oil, Bahrain has the highest dependence on export markets of any country in the Arab Middle East.

712 **Gulf Construction & Saudi Arabia Review.**
Manama: Al Hilal Publishing and Marketing Group, June 1980- . monthly.

Provides a wide range of information on the construction industry in Bahrain and other Gulf Co-operation Council countries. Circulation 11,300. Free controlled circulation in the GCC and limited bookshop sales.

713 **Gulf construction: *Khaleej Times* special report.**
Dubai: Khaleej Times, Galadari Printing and Publishing Establishment, 31 Jan. 1982. 66p.

A report on the construction industry in the Gulf, which includes a special section on Bahrain (p. 49-52). This concentrates on the expected boom in construction associated with the building of the causeway linking Bahrain to Saudi Arabia.

714 **Gulf Construction Materials and Maintenance: Directory.**
Manama: Al Hilal Publishing and Marketing Group, 1982- . annual. c.300p.

Provides a listing of approximately 20,000 companies relevant to the construction industry in the Gulf. Information on Bahrain was given on p. 51-83 in 1983.

715 **Gulf states: industrial planning, a common concern.**
Arab Economist, no. 136, vol. 13 (Jan. 1981), p. 21.

A brief analysis of planning in Arabia. It notes that in Bahrain there is now co-operation going on with the World Bank to work out a consultation program for industrial development.

Industry

716 **Industrialisation in Arab countries: patterns, options and strategies.**
Z. Y. Hershlag. In: *Arab industrialisation and economic integration.* Edited by Roberto Aliboni. London: Croom Helm, 1979, p. 13-89.

This study discusses the overall regional and individual national industrial structures of the Arab countries, and analyses their prevailing and potential industrial trends. The joint Arab venture of the Arab Shipbuilding and Repair Yard Company in Bahrain is mentioned briefly, as is the establishment in 1976 of the Arabian Gulf Organisation for Industrial Consulting which was set up with the support of Saudi Arabia, Kuwait, the UAE, Qatar, Bahrain, Oman and Iraq.

717 **Application of surplus oil revenues of OAPEC for development use.**
Usameh F. Jamali. In: *Engineering and development in the Gulf.* Bahrain Society of Engineers. London: Graham & Trotman, 1977, p. 213-24.

Notes OAPEC's support of the Arab Ship Building and Repair Yard whose drydock was being constructed at Bahrain.

718 **Manufacturing industry in the lower Gulf, 1980: *Khaleej Times* special report.**
Dubai: Khaleej Times, Galadari Printing and Publishing Establishment, 17 Sept. 1980. 50p.

A report on the nature of manufacturing in Bahrain, Qatar, the UAE and Oman. Bahrain is specifically discussed on p. 37-40, where its pioneering role in industrial diversification, its desire for Gulf co-ordination, the Bahrain Aluminium Extrusion Company, the United Building Factories, Maskati Brothers paper and plastic factory, and the Bahrain and Kuwait Company for Light Industries and Commerce are described.

719 **Problems confronting the establishment of a heavy industrial base in the Arab Gulf.**
John Townsend. In: *Social and economic development in the Arab Gulf.* Edited by Tim Niblock. London: Croom Helm, 1980, p. 95-105.

An analysis of the overall strategy of the oil-producing Arab nations of the Gulf for heavy industry, and an interpretation of the major constraints preventing a rapid transformation of the Arab Gulf into an industrial region. It discusses the Arab Ship Repair Yard and the ALBA aluminium smelter in Bahrain.

720 **Industrial development in the Arab Gulf states.**
Louis Turner. In: *Issues in development: the Arab Gulf states.*
Edited by May Ziwar-Daftari. London: MD Research and Services,
1980, p. 210-20.

A study of industrialization in the Gulf which observes that, after Qatar, Bahrain
has the next most interesting history of diversification away from the oil industry.
It briefly mentions the coming on stream of the ALBA aluminium smelter in
1971, the opening in 1978 of OAPEC's drydock company (ASRY – the Arab
Shipbuilding and Repair Yard), and the acceptance in Bahrain of Offshore
Banking Units.

721 **Middle East industrialisation: a study of Saudi and Iranian
downstream investments.**
Louis Turner, James H. Bedore. Farnborough, England:
Saxon House, for the Royal Institute of International Affairs,
1979. 219p. bibliog.

This analysis studies Saudi Arabian and Iranian industrial development and
diversification, and its influences on the countries of the Middle East, West
Europe, the United States and Japan. It concentrates on oil refining and petrochemical industries. Bahrain's aluminium smelter is mentioned as a competitor to
Saudi Arabia's planned aluminium plant in the Eastern Province, and OAPEC's
Arab Shipbuilding and Repair Yard, which opened in Bahrain in 1977, together
with Bahrain's oil refinery are also noted briefly.

722 **The Arabian Year Book.**
Edited by Rashid Wazaifi. Kuwait: Dar Al Seyassah Press,
1978- . annual.

Provides details of businesses throughout the Gulf states. It gives an introduction
to Bahrain together with a commercial and industrial guide to the country. The
volume concludes with a who's who of the Gulf.

723 **The development of offshore oilfields in the U.A.E.**
Rodney J. A. Wilson. In: *Issues in development: the Arab Gulf
states.* Edited by May Ziwar-Daftari. London: MD Research and
Services, 1980, p. 160-69.

A study of the UAE's recent offshore oil developments, which observes that
Dubai's gas-powered aluminium smelter duplicates that already established in
Bahrain which has so far proved profitable.

724 **The rising costs of industrial construction.**
Rodney J. A. Wilson. In: *Issues in development: the Arab Gulf states.* Edited by May Ziwar-Daftari. London: MD Research and Services, 1980, p. 65-75.

This paper argues that cost constraints are likely to restrict industrial progress in the Gulf in the 1980s. It provides figures to show the high rate of inflation in Bahrain during the 1970s, and also observes that Bahrain's shipping fleet rose from 9 ships to 32 ships from 1970 to 1978 with a corresponding increase in gross tonnage from 2,969 tonnes to 7,161 tonnes.

The U.K. and Arabia: a commemorative issue to mark the visit of H.M. Queen Elizabeth II.
See item no. 602.

Bahrain looks to a secure future.
See item no. 689.

The significance of ASRY to the future industrial development of Bahrain.
See item no. 785.

Oil Industry

725 **Oil policies of the Gulf countries.**
William D. Anderson. In: *Conflict and cooperation in the Persian Gulf.* Edited by Mohammed Mughisuddin. New York, London: Praeger, 1977, p. 60-78.

This paper argues that two sets of conflicts have shaped the oil policies of Gulf states in the 1970s: those between Western concession-holding oil companies and their Gulf host countries, and those among the Gulf countries themselves. It notes that Bahrain, like Saudi Arabia, became a preserve of US companies, with Socal and Texaco owning the Bahrain Petroleum Company, and that Bahrain, like Dubai, Iraq and Iran, had sustained itself above dire poverty before oil revenues became important.

726 **The Middle East: oil, politics and development in the Middle East.**
Edited by John Duke Anthony. Washington, DC: American Enterprise Institute for Public Policy Research, 1975. 109p.

A collection of seven papers with some commentaries resulting from a conference on world energy problems held at the University of Toronto in January 1974. It includes scattered references to Bahrain.

727 **Aramco handbook: oil in the Middle East.**
Dhahran, Saudi Arabia: Arabian American Oil Company, 1968. rev. ed. 279p. 23 maps. bibliog.

Although mainly concerned with Aramco's work in Saudi Arabia, this volume includes material on the development of Bahrain's oil industry, archaeological investigations undertaken on the islands, the capture of the islands by the Al Khalifah in 1783, details on the oil concessions, refinery and pipeline to Saudi Arabia, and the creation and growth of the Bahrain Petroleum Company. The first part of the book is devoted to an historical introduction to the Middle East, concentrating on the Gulf, and provides much background material to the society and culture of the region.

728 **Arab states of the Persian Gulf.**
Thomas C. Barger. In: *Energy policies of the world,* vol. 1.
Edited by Gerard J. Mangone. New York: Elsevier, 1976,
p. 121-204.

An attempt to trace the historical and social factors that affect the policies of
Arab states of the Gulf, especially with respect to the oil industry. It analyses
pricing, production, and participation in that industry in the Gulf, the formation
of the Organization of Oil Producing and Exporting Countries, and the Arab
embargo of 1973. It notes that in 1974 with proved oil reserves of 0.34 billion
barrels and production of 0.07 million barrels per day, Bahrain's oil reserves were
expected to last for only 13 years. Bahrain's oil policy is specifically discussed
on p. 190-91.

729 **Oil and Bahrain.**
J. H. D. B[elgrave]. *The World Today,* vol. 7, no. 2 (Feb. 1951),
p. 76-83.

An account of the social and economic impact of the discovery of oil in Bahrain
in 1932. The author suggests that Bahrain had a progressive outlook long before
the Bahrain Petroleum Company started its operations in 1931. It argues that
the moral consequences of oil development have not been as bad as is often
suggested, and that the material benefits are obvious.

730 **Wells of power, the oilfields of south-western Asia: a regional
and global study.**
Olaf Caroe. New York: Macmillan, 1951. 240p. 4 maps. bibliog.

In addition to an account of the early days of Bahrain's oil industry this book
notes that fresh water springs exist on the islands, that they are the main centre of
the Gulf's pearl fisheries, that Persia lays claim to them, and that they were the
centre of British administration in the Gulf.

731 **The evolution of oil concessions in the Middle East and North
Africa.**
Henry Cattan. Dobbs Ferry, New York: Oceana Publications,
1967. 173p. 2 maps.

A thorough study of the history of oil concessions in the Middle East with several
references to Bahrain. It includes an appendix which notes the main oil concessions and concessionaires in each country in the region.

732 **OPEC and the international oil industry: a changing structure.**
Fadhil J. Al-Chalabi. Oxford, England: Oxford University Press,
for OAPEC, 1980. 165p.

A survey and analysis of the main structural changes in the international oil
industry during the last 35 years, with special emphasis on the changes of the
1970s. It is divided into four main parts, which concentrate on extraction,
marketing, and pricing of oil, and the administration of OPEC. A final chapter
discusses the interdependence between nations in terms of energy and development.

733   **OPEC oil report: second edition, November 1979.**
Edited by Bryan Cooper. London: Petroleum Economist, 1979.
2nd ed. 292p. 15 maps.

A thorough account of OPEC's operations. Part one covers OPEC's revenues, oil prices, dependency of consuming countries on OPEC oil, transport and movement of OPEC oil, natural gas and LNG (liquid natural gas), export refineries and petrochemicals, and the outlook for energy to the year 2000. Part two provides a country by country account of OPEC activities. Bahrain, though not a member of OPEC, is mentioned briefly in the section on Saudi Arabia, in connection with the early refining of Saudi oil in Bahrain and the 1945 construction of the submarine pipeline from the mainland to Bahrain.

734   **Oil and security in the Arabian Gulf.**
Edited by Abdul Majid Farid. London: Croom Helm, 1981.
162p.

A selection of papers resulting from the symposium on oil and security in the Arab Gulf organized by the Arab Research Centre in London in October 1980. The papers by Fred Halliday, Robert J. Hanks, James E. Akins, Robert Pranger, Douglas Hurd, Michel Jobert, Mohammed El Rumaihi, and the penultimate chapter on the Gulf War all mention Bahrain.

735   **Ölinseln in Persergolf.** (Oil islands in the Persian Gulf.)
Von Erhard Gabriel. *Geographische Rundschau*, vol. 22, no. 8
(Aug. 1970), p. 309-15.

This paper on the creation of oil islands in the Gulf, notes that, unlike Kharg, Das and Lavan islands, Bahrain was previously inhabited and possessed a traditionally important economy.

736   **Oil, debt and development: OPEC in the Third World.**
Paul Hallwood, Stuart W. Sinclair. London: George Allen &
Unwin, 1981. 206p. bibliog.

An investigation into the relationships between the member countries of OPEC and other less developed countries. It argues that while there are elements of both co-operation and competition in these relationships, it is competition which tends to dominate. Although Bahrain is not a member of OPEC, its trade with member countries of OPEC and its labour market are discussed.

737   **Oil companies and governments. An account of the international oil industry in its political environment.**
J. E. Hartshorn. London: Faber & Faber, 1967. 2nd rev. ed.
410p. 5 maps. bibliog.

An analysis of the relationships between governments and oil producers prior to the mid-1960s. It briefly mentions Socal's concession in Bahrain.

738 **The impact of the oil industry on the Persian Gulf shaykhdoms.**
Rupert Hay. *Middle East Journal*, vol. 9, no. 4 (autumn 1955),
p. 361-72.

A discussion of the social and political effects of the discovery of oil in Kuwait,
Bahrain, Qatar and the Trucial States. It notes that the oil industry has brought
great prosperity to Bahrain following its discovery by the Bahrain Petroleum
Company in 1932, but it also argues that this new wealth has made surprisingly
little difference to the manner of life of the population due to their strict adher-
ence to the precepts of Islam.

739 **Petroleum developments in Middle East countries in 1979.**
D. O. Hemer, J. F. Mason, G. C. Hatch. *American Association of
Petroleum Geologists, Bulletin,* vol. 64, no. 11 (1980),
p. 1,836-61.

Provides information on recent oil developments in all of the countries of the
Middle East.

740 **Il petrolio nella geografia politica della penisola d'Arabia.** (The
political geography of oil in the Arabian peninsula.)
V. Langella. *Annali Istituto Orientale di Napoli*, vol. 14, no. 1
(1964), p. 202-32.

An analysis of the political geography of oil in Arabia.

741 **Saudi Arabia: its people, its society, its culture.**
George A. Lipsky. New Haven, Connecticut: Human Relations
Area Files, 1959. 367p. 4 maps. bibliog. (Survey of World
Cultures).

An introduction to Saudi Arabia based on the research used for the production of
the United States government handbook of the area. It includes several mentions
of Bahrein, in particular in connection with the discovery of oil there in 1932
and its consequent exploitation.

742 **Oil in the Middle East: its discovery and development.**
Stephen Hemsley Longrigg. London, New York, Toronto:
Oxford University Press, 1954. 3rd ed., 1968. 519p. 9 maps.

Provides information on the emergence of Bahrain's oil industry between 1923
and 1966, and the role played by the Bahrain Petroleum Company (Bapco). It
notes the beginnings of oil drilling on the island in 1931, the completion of the
pipeline from Dhahran to Bahrain in 1945, the increase in throughput of Bahrain's
refinery resulting from the Secod World War demands for oil by Britain, the role
of Bapco in increasing the country's prosperity in the post-war period, and the
beginnings of offshore exploration in the 1960s.

743 **OAPEC: an international organization for economic cooperation and an instrument for regional integration.**
Abdelkader Maachou, translated by Anthony Melville. Paris: Berger-Levrault, 1982. 198p. bibliog. (Mondes en Devenir — Points Chauds).

An account of the development of the Organization of Arab Petroleum Exporting Countries, from its origins on 8 January 1968 to the end of the 1970s. Bahrein was admitted to OAPEC in 1970. Appendixes include details of the agreement establishing OAPEC and statistics relating to the oil production, consumption and refining of its member countries in 1977-78.

744 **The oil industry in the Middle East.**
Keith McLachlan. In: *Change and development in the Middle East: essays in honour of W. B. Fisher.* Edited by John I. Clarke, Howard Bowen-Jones. London, New York: Methuen, 1981, p. 95-112.

An investigation of the evolution, location, effects of, reserves, exports, ownership and prospects of the oil industry in the Middle East. It notes that Bahrain became an oil producer in 1934, that its history of trade made it well placed to convert its oil income into viable alternative assets, and that its oil reserve position is now deteriorating.

745 **Oil production, revenues and economic development: prospects for Iran, Iraq, Saudi Arabia, Kuwait, United Arab Emirates, Oman, Qatar and Bahrain.**
Keith McLachlan, Narsi Ghorban. London: Economist Intelligence Unit, 1974. 59p. map. (QER Special, no. 18).

Bahrain is discussed briefly on p. 55 of this report on the state of the Gulf Oil industry following the rapid increase in oil prices after October 1973. It envisages the decline of Bahrain's oil industry as its reserves give out.

746 **Claims to the oil resources in the Persian Gulf: will the world economy be controlled by the Gulf in the future?**
Farin Mirvahabi. *Texas International Law Journal,* vol. 11 (1976), p. 75-112.

An overview of the major legal issues relating to oil production in the Persian Gulf area. It notes that in March 1975 the government of Bahrain took over the remaining 40 per cent private ownership of the Bahrain Petroleum Company, which had previously been divided equally between Standard Oil of California and Texaco. A section on the Law of the Sea in relation to the Gulf describes the Saudi-Bahrain agreement of 1958, which was the first bilateral agreement demarcating the submarine boundaries of two Gulf states and which was drawn up on the basis of the median line. The Iranian claim on Bahrain is also discussed briefly. In its conclusion the paper suggests that Bahrain has sufficient non-petroleum resources to remain economically viable without its oil production.

747 **OAPEC: the Organization of Arab Petroleum Exporting Countries News Bulletin.**
Kuwait: OAPEC Information Department, 1975- . monthly.

This provides a primary source of information on OAPEC's activities and gives an account of the changes taking place in Bahrain's petroleum industry.

748 **O.A.P.E.C. partnership creates the world's finest dry docks.**
Voice (of the Arab world), (11 Aug. 1976), p. 13.

A brief account of the then proposed Arab Shipbuilding and Repair Yard's dry-dock at Bahrain.

749 **OPEC and the petroleum industry.**
Mana Saeed al-Otaiba. London: Croom Helm, 1975. 192p. bibliog.

An analysis of the role of OPEC divided into two parts, the first on the formation of OPEC and its composition, and the second on OPEC's policies. Although Bahrain is not a member of OPEC, it notes that the Red Line agreement may have restricted competition in the purchase of Bahrain crude in the late 1930s, and that the American insistence that the Europeans followed an open-door policy after World War I enabled American companies to obtain petroleum rights in Bahrain.

750 **Oil and state in Arabia.**
Edith Penrose. In: *The Arabian peninsula: society and politics.* Edited by Derek Hopwood. London: George Allen & Unwin, 1972, p. 271-85.

An investigation of the effects of the exploitation of oil on the political, social and economic structures of states in Arabia. It notes that oil was discovered in Bahrain in 1932 and that exports began in 1934. From the beginning of oil income in Bahrain, one-third of the oil revenue went to the Shaikh for his personal and family needs, a further third went to current government expenses and to development, and the final third was reserved for overseas investment against future needs.

751 **Middle East oil and changing political constellations.**
Don Peretz. In: *OPEC and the Middle East. The impact of oil on societal development.* Edited by Russell A. Stone. New York: Praeger, 1977, p. 21-35. (Praeger Special Studies in International Politics and Government).

This account of changing political allegiances and the use of the oil weapon in the Arab-Israeli conflict notes that Bahrain joined OAPEC in 1970.

752 **Petroleum and Arab economic development.**
Kuwait: Organization of Arab Petroleum Exporting Countries,
1978. 226p.

Contains the following articles translated from the Arabic quarterly *Oil and Arab
Cooperation*: 'Petrochemical development in OAPEC area – aims and impact',
Abdul Aziz Al Wattari; 'The needs and requirements for directing oil financial
surpluses into regional Arab investments', Hikmat Nashashibi; 'New possibilities
for oil producer-consumer relations', Ali Ahmed Attiga; 'The future of petroleum-
nuclear balance in the OAPEC countries', Yusef R. Rashid and Adnam Shihab
Eldin; 'The Arab companies established under the auspices of OAPEC', Ahmed
Kesmat Al Geddawy; 'The evolving attitudes of industrial nations and their
impact on the oil producers', Hussein Abdallah; and 'Fifteen years of international
development assistance', Abdlatif Y. Al-Hamad. These articles all concern Bahrain
as a member of OAPEC, and the article by Ahmed Kesmat Al Geddawy provides
specific information about the Arab Shipbuilding and Repair Yard company
based in Bahrain.

753 **Arabian oil ventures.**
H. St. J. B. Philby. Washington, DC: Middle East Institute,
1964. 134p.

Philby's last book, recording how the oil concession of Saudi Arabia was made. It
includes scattered references to Bahrain and notes that during 1939 Saudi oil was
being sent to be refined in Bahrain at the rate of 700 tons a day.

754 **Géopolitique du pétrole et stratégie des grandes puissances
dans le golfe Persique.** (The geopolitics of oil and the strategy
of the great powers in the Persian Gulf.)
Jean-Paul Pigasse. *Stratégie*, no. 19 (July-Sept. 1969), p. 47-91.

An analysis of the significance of the oil-producing nations of the Gulf, situated at
one of the most important strategic crossroads in the world, and their relationships with the USA and the USSR.

755 **Development of the oil industry in the Persian/Arabian Gulf
1901-1968.**
George Rentz. In: *Middle East focus: the Persian Gulf.* Edited
by T. Cuyler Young. Princeton, New Jersey: Princeton University
Conference, 1969, p. 39-64.

An historical account of the oil industry in the Gulf. It notes that in 1914,
following the discovery of oil in Iran, the ruler of Bahrain pledged not to give an
oil concession to anyone without the permission of the British government. The
negotiations preceding the Bahrain Petroleum Company's discovery of oil in
Bahrain in 1932 are also described.

Oil Industry

756 **The preliminary oil concessions in Trucial Oman, 1922-1939.**
Rosemarie J. Said [Zahlan] . *International Interactions*, vol. 3,
no. 2 (1977), p. 113-34.

An analysis of the political and economic factors influencing the granting of oil
concessions in the north-east of the Arabian peninsula. It includes discussions on
the D'Arcy Exploration Company, the Anglo-Persian Oil Company, Petroleum
Concessions Ltd., and California Arabian Standard Oil Company. Attention is given
to conflict between the American and British interests in the area. Bahrain is
mentioned as the first country to strike oil, in 1932, and consequently the first to
achieve an economic renaissance.

757 **Arab oil and gas directory 1982.**
Edited by Nicolas Sarkis. Paris: Arab Petroleum Research
Centre, 1982. 519p.

Bahrain's oil industry is discussed on p. 67-78 of this extensive and detailed
account of the oil industry in the Middle East. Information is provided on the
historical background, reserves and drilling, oil production, gas production and
utilization, refining, petrochemicals, transport, drydock facilities, revenues
and budget, and aluminium industry in Bahrain.

758 **Erdölfördergebiete und Oasenlandwirtschaft im arabischen
Trockenraum: Die Provinz al-Hasa/Saudi Arabien.** (Oil-producing
regions and oasis agriculture in the Arabian arid zone: the
province of al-Hasa in Saudi Arabia.)
Fred Scholz. *Geographische Rundschau*, vol. 32, no. 12 (Dec.
1980), p. 523-26.

Although mainly on al-Hasa, this paper also mentions Bahrain in connection with
pearling and oil, and it includes an interesting satellite photograph of the islands
together with a map of the oil installations of the area.

759 **Twenty-five years of Middle East oil: BAPCO operations in
Bahrain.**
G. Sell. *Institute of Petroleum Review*, no. 142, vol. 12 (1958),
p. 333-36.

An account of the first 25 years of oil activity in Bahrain. It provides information
on Bahrain's refinery, drum plant, marine terminal, staff, training and safety.

760 **Middle East oil: a study in political and economic controversy.**
George W. Stocking. Nashville, Tennessee: Vanderbilt
University Press, 1970; London: Allen Lane/Penguin Press, 1971.
485p. bibliog.

An analysis of the controversies that have developed between oil companies and
the countries of the Middle East. It commences with a survey of the political
and economic environment in which the original oil concessions were granted.
This is followed by a study of the terms of the concessions, an analysis of how
national and collective actions have tried to resolve the conflicts, an investigation
of how oil pricing, production costs and profits have influenced the controversies,
and it concludes with observations on the future of the oil industry in the Middle
East. The concession granted to Major Frank Holmes by the Sheikh of Bahrain,
and the subsequent creation of the Bahrain Petroleum Company by Standard of
California to exploit the oil resources of Bahrain are briefly mentioned.

761 **OPEC and the Middle East. The impact of oil on societal
development.**
Edited by Russell A. Stone. New York: Praeger, 1977. 264p.
(Praeger Special Studies in International Politics and Government).

Although this book is concerned specifically with OPEC, of which Bahrain is not
a member, the state is nevertheless mentioned briefly in the paper by Don Peretz.

762 **Future of petrochemicals in the Gulf.**
M. Taheri. In: *Engineering and development in the Gulf.* Bahrain
Society of Engineers. London: Graham & Trotman, 1977,
p. 199-212.

An evaluation of the future situation of chemical feedstocks when Gulf oil
production may have to be reduced to 40 per cent of its 1975 levels.

763 **Oilfields of the world.**
E. N. Tiratsoo. Beaconsfield, England: Scientific Press, 1976.
2nd rev. ed. 384p. 34 maps.

Bahrein's Awali field is described on p. 151 of this general text on the oilfields of
the world.

764 **Oil: the biggest business.**
Christopher Tugendhat, Adrian Hamilton. London: Eyre
Methuen, 1968. rev. ed., 1975. 404p. 6 maps. bibliog.

A survey of the development of the oil industry. It briefly notes the granting of
the concession to Holmes and the subsequent discovery of oil in Bahrain on 31
May 1932.

Oil Industry

765 **Oil companies in the international system.**
Louis Turner. London: George Allen & Unwin for the Royal
Institute of International Affairs, 1978. 240p. bibliog.
An investigation of the relationships between the major multinational oil companies and national governments. It concludes that these companies have only been a marginal influence in the political arena. The British government is noted as having tried to prevent Socal entering Bahrain, and the pre-war oil discoveries there are seen as being significant in alerting other companies to the potential of the Gulf region.

766 **Oil, social change and economic development in the Arabian peninsula.**
John Vianney. *Levante*, vol. 15, no. 4 (1968), p. 45-48.
A brief account of change in Arabia following the initial discovery of oil in Bahrein in 1932.

767 **Negotiations for oil concessions in Bahrain, El Hasa (Saudi Arabia), the Neutral Zone, Qatar and Kuwait.**
Thomas E. Ward. USA: printed for private circulation by Ardlee Service, New York, 1965. 296p. 5 maps.
A thorough and detailed account of the oil concession negotiations on the Arabian side of the Gulf. It provides full details of the 1925 exclusive prospecting permit granted to the Eastern and General Syndicate Ltd. by the Shaikh of Bahrain, the 1927 option contract given to Eastern Gulf Oil Company, its transfer to the Standard Oil Company of California in 1928, the incorporation of the Bahrain Petroleum Company Ltd. in 1929, the transfer of oil rights to that company in 1930, the exclusive concession of 1934 granted to the Bahrain Petroleum Company Ltd., and the subsequent supplementary concession signed in 1940.

The petroleum geology and resources of the Middle East.
See item no. 79.

Persian Gulf — past and present.
See item no. 290.

The Middle East: a political and economic survey.
See item no. 302.

Journey into chaos.
See item no. 429.

Oil, power and politics: conflict in Arabia, the Red Sea and the Gulf.
See item no. 446.

Persian Gulf oil in Middle East and international conflicts.
See item no. 447.

Politics in the Gulf.
See item no. 449.

Oil, Arabism and Islam: the Persian Gulf in world politics.
See item no. 454.

Persian Gulf — contrasts and similarities.
See item no. 466.

Oil politics in the Persian Gulf region.
See item no. 481.

L'Arabie à l'âge du petrole. (Arabia in the oil age.)
See item no. 492.

The legal framework for oil concessions in the Arab world.
See item no. 516.

Persian Gulf oil and the world economy.
See item no. 522.

Arabs, oil and history: the story of the Middle East.
See item no. 592.

Oil and security in the Gulf: an Arab point of view.
See item no. 593.

Middle Eastern oil and the western world: prospects and problems.
See item no. 596.

Eastern Arabia, Kuwait and Bahrain.
See item no. 654.

Quarterly Energy Review: Energy in the Middle East.
See item no. 665.

Agriculture and Fisheries

768 **The farmer's perception of soil for agriculture in Bahrain.**
J. H. Ahmed, J. C. Doornkamp. *Third World Planning Review,*
vol. 3, no. 3 (Aug. 1981), p. 275-88.

This report notes that, although they are generally illiterate, the farmers show a
high degree of awareness of soil conditions in Bahrain. The following weaknesses
in the present agricultural system are also noted: the land tenure system under
which 70 per cent of farmers are on rented land with short leases, the small establishment of professional staff in the Agricultural Directorate, the saline groundwater, and poor land drainage in low coastal areas. It provides some agricultural
statistics for the late 1970s.

769 **The date palm in Bahrain.**
Riaz Ahmed. Bahrain: Directorate of Agriculture, 1977. 25p.
in English; 25p. in Arabic. bibliog. (Extension Unit Publication,
no. 2).

A useful introduction to the date palm in Bahrain. It provides details of its
history, importance, layout and transplanting, irrigation, manuring, intercropping,
pruning, pollination, thinning, harvesting, yield, marketing, curing, varieties,
utilization, insect pests and diseases, and it concludes with a section on the
decline of Bahrain's date industry.

770 **Agriculture and the use of water resources in the Eastern
Province of Saudi Arabia.**
H. Bowen-Jones. In: *Issues in development: the Arab Gulf
states.* Edited by May Ziwar-Daftari. London: MD Research and
Services, 1980, p. 118-37.

This briefly notes that the Eocene and the younger Neogene-Quaternary water-
bearing rocks of the Eastern Province stretch eastwards into Bahrain.

771 **Agriculture in Bahrain, Kuwait, Qatar and UAE.**
H. Bowen-Jones. In: *Issues in development: the Arab Gulf
states.* Edited by May Ziwar-Daftari. London: MD Research and
Services, 1980, p. 46-64.
A thorough account of past and present agriculture in the countries of the Gulf. It
notes that 6,000 hectares of land in Bahrain are available for agriculture and that
the groundwater is derived from three aquifers extending eastward from Saudi
Arabia. It suggests that agriculture in Bahrain is a residual activity which is under
great socio-economic pressure and also suffers from great physical resource limitations.

772 **The developing agriculture of the Middle East.**
R. M. Burrell, S. Hoyle, K. S. McLachlan, C. Parker. London:
Graham & Trotman, 1976. 74p.
The fourth chapter, which is on Saudi Arabia, includes a map of agricultural
developments in Arabia and the Gulf on which Bahrain is illustrated.

773 **Fisheries of the Arabian peninsula.**
William J. Donaldson. In: *Change and development in the
Middle East: essays in honour of W. B. Fisher.* Edited by John
I. Clarke, Howard Bowen-Jones. London, New York: Methuen,
1981, p. 189-98.
There are several mentions of Bahrain in this account of Arabian fisheries. It notes
that Bahrain has had a large shrimp-fishing company since 1959, but that it has
recently met with financial difficulties.

774 **Fishing in Arabia.**
Donald S. Erdman. *Scientific Monthly*, vol. 70, no. 1 (Jan.
1950), p. 58-65.
An account of fishing around Bahrain, giving some details of the main types of
fish and boats involved during the 1940s.

775 **Middle East Agribusiness.**
Redhill, England: International Trade Publications, 1981- .
bimonthly.
Provides much up-to-date information on agricultural production, processing,
storage, distribution, marketing and related activities in the Middle East. In
English with a short Arabic section.

Agriculture and Fisheries

776 **Fisher-folk and fish-traps in al-Baḥrain.**
R. B. Serjeant. *Bulletin of the School of Oriental and African Studies,* vol. 31, no. 3 (1968), p. 486-514.
A thorough and detailed account of the methods of fishing in al-Baḥrain. It includes an appendix on the star-calendar used in the islands, and also discusses the social cleavage between the Arabs of tribal descent in al-Baḥrain and the Shī'ah Baḥārnah.

777 **Memoir on Bahreyn.**
R. W. Whish. *Transactions of the Bombay Geographical Society,* vol. 16 (June 1860-Dec. 1862), p. 40-47.
This memoir accompanies a chart of a survey of Bahreyn Harbour and the Khaurel-Bab, which was undertaken by the author while he was stationed on Her Majesty's steamer *Mahi,* Indian Navy, which was cruising between Bahreyn and Demmam watching the movements of the chiefs of those places. It also makes some observations on the agriculture and geology of the islands, noting the freshwater springs there to be found.

Bahrain: a special report.
See item no. 11.

Geology, geomorphology and pedology of Bahrain.
See item no. 90.

The travels of Ibn Baṭṭūta A.D. 1325-1354.
See item no. 141.

Transport

778 **Arab ports: tap ship jam (special report: Arab shipping).**
Arab Economist, vol. 7, no. 78 (July 1975), p. 38-48.
A general report on Arab shipping in the mid-1970s. It argues that one of the
most serious bottlenecks in the Arab world at this time was the low capacity of
its ports and harbours. Several mentions of Bahrain are included.

779 **The Arab Shipbuilding and Repair Yard Co. on the occasion of
the inauguration of the A.S.R.Y. drydock Dec. 15, 1977.**
OAPEC News Bulletin (special supplement), vol. 3, no. 12
(Dec. 1977). unpaged.
An account of the establishment of ASRY, its operations, the site of the drydock,
the maritime works, the shore works, and its technical training school, published
to coincide with the inauguration of the drydock in 1977. It includes a list of the
firms and organizations involved in the construction and running of the drydock.

780 **Arab shipping 1983: a Seatrade guide.**
Colchester, England: Seatrade Publications, 1983. 6th ed. 200p.
The sixth edition of this guide which itemizes each vessel over 1,000 grt under an
Arab flag. Introductory papers cover the following aspects of the maritime scene:
Arab shipping policy, the emerging Arab hull market, changing incentives for a
seagoing career, and Arab liner shipping. Bahrain's maritime sector is summarized
on p. 32-39, which includes sections on state and other organizations, owners,
agents and marine services, and ports.

781 **Arab transport, a means for economic expansion.**
Arab Economist, no. 113, vol. 11 (1979), p. 16-19.
An analysis of the recent expansion in the attention paid to transport in the Arab
world. Bahrain's roles as a sea port and airport are briefly mentioned.

782 **Bahrain opens the A.S.R.Y. yard.**
Norwegian Shipping News, no. 1 (13 Jan. 1978), p. 21-22.
A brief report on the opening and construction of the Arab Shipbuilding and
Repair Yard's drydock at Bahrain.

783 **Bahrain's international airport 1932-1971.**
No publication details [Bahrain: Directorate of Civil Aviation, 1972].

Provides details of the history of Bahrain's international airport, and in particular its development to take Boeing 747 aircraft. It shows numerous photographs of the airport, including several of the original *barasti* (palm branch) hut which formed the first airport terminal building. The first civil registered aircraft landed in 1932, and the new 12,000 foot runway was inaugurated in 1971.

784 **Arab dhows of eastern Arabia.**
Richard Le Baron Bowen. Rehoboth, Massachusetts: privately printed, 1949. 54p. map. bibliog.

An account of the evolution, construction and sailing of the Arab dhow. It pays particular attention to the Arab use of the Lateen rig. Bahrein is frequently mentioned as a centre of the dhow trade and a place where dhows are built. A copy can be inspected in the London School of Oriental and African Studies Library, ref. Pam. Near East E.

785 **The significance of ASRY to the future industrial development of Bahrain.**
A. M. Caetano Carriera. In: *Engineering and development in the Gulf.* Bahrain Society of Engineers. London: Graham & Trotman, 1977, p. 71-84.

An evaluation of the likely impact of the OAPEC sponsored Arab Shipbuilding and Repair Yard Company (ASRY) on Bahrain and other countries of the Gulf.

786 **Ports of the Arabian peninsula: a guide to the literature.**
H. Dodgeon, A. M. Findlay. Durham, England: Centre for Middle Eastern and Islamic Studies, Durham University, 1979. 49p. (Occasional Papers Series, no. 7).

A useful bibliography on ports and trade in Arabia. It is divided into sections on introductory works, historical development, modern port development, official publications, and periodicals. It includes a place-name index, which provides several references to Bahrain's Mina Sulman and the Arab Shipbuilding and Repair Yard.

787 **The tanker crisis: causes, effects and prospects to 1985.**
H. P. Drewry (Shipping Consultants). London: H. P. Drewry (Shipping Consultants), 1976. 132p.

An analysis of the depressed tanker market prospects from 1975-1985. This crisis is seen as being due to a great extent to the general incentives available to owners to expand their fleets which obscured long-term cash flow prospects. Bahrain is mentioned mainly in the context of its role as a small Middle Eastern oil producer.

788 **Gulf states invest heavily in shipbuilding and repairing despite market trends.**
W. D. Ewart. *Middle East Economic Digest*, vol. 20, no. 14 (2 April 1976), p. 7-11.
An analysis of the heavy investment within the Gulf in ship repairing facilities. It provides details of the Arab Shipbuilding and Repair Yard's drydock at Bahrain, and the work undertaken by the Bahrain Ship Repairing and Engineering Company.

789 **Arab shipping 1982.**
Gary Gimson. Colchester, England: Seatrade Publications, 1982. 5th ed. 200p. 22 maps.
This comprehensive analysis of Arab marine interests itemizes each vessel over 1,000 grt under an Arab flag, in a regular format. Five short introductory chapters on the maritime scene cover the following topics: flags of convenience, liners, tankers, livestock and bunkers. This is followed by a country-by-country survey of the Arab region with Bahrain being described on p. 35-41. Brief information is provided on the state's marine government organizations, ship owners, agents, marine services and ports. For a later edition see *Arab shipping 1983*, listed earlier in this section.

790 **Gulf dockyards struggle to get going: merger seems only hope for A.S.R.Y. and Dubai.**
Middle East, no. 37 (Nov. 1977), p. 92-94.
An account of the teething problems of ASRY and the Dubai Dry-Dock Company.

791 **Gulf ports: congestion eases but handling remains the main problem.**
Middle East Economic Digest, vol. 21, no. 28 (13 July 1977), p. 3-4.
This brief report notes the efforts made by the Gulf ports, and in particular Mina Sulman in Bahrain, to eliminate congestion in 1977.

792 **Gulf Shipping and Transport.**
Manama: Al Hilal Publishing and Marketing Group, Jan. 1981- . monthly.
Provides regular coverage on shipping and transport in the Gulf region. Circulation 5,800 in Gulf Co-operation Council countries. Free controlled circulation in GCC countries and bookshop sales. An annual directory is also produced, with Bahrain's transport industry being listed on p. 17-27 in 1983.

Transport

793 **The dhow: an illustrated history of the dhow and its world.**
Clifford W. Hawkins. Lymington, Hampshire, England:
Nautical Publishing, 1977. 143p. 2 maps. bibliog.

A thorough and well-illustrated study of the dhow. After introductory chapters on the seas where dhows are found, and on ship construction, the various different locations where dhows sail are described in turn, beginning with Kuwait and then discussing Dubai, Aden and India. It concludes with a glossary of terms associated with dhows and an appendix provides details of oars, masts, yard, sails and measurements, as well as line drawings of all of the different types of dhow found in the region.

794 **British routes to India.**
Halford Lancaster Hoskins. London: Frank Cass, 1928, 1966.
494p. map.

An analysis of the development of transport routes to India by Britain in the 19th century. It notes that in 1834 Egyptian forces briefly occupied Bahrein, before being ousted as a result of British protests. British forces themselves then took possession of the islands in 1839 and maintained Bahrein as a base for their operations.

795 **Arab seafaring in the Indian Ocean in ancient and early medieval times.**
George Fadlo Hourani. Princeton, New Jersey: Princeton
University Press, 1951. 131p. 7 maps.

A general history of the ships used by the Arabs until the later mediaeval period, and also of the trade routes of the Indian Ocean. It equates Dilmun with al-Bahrayn and notes that one of Alexander the Great's ships explored the coast of the Gulf and observed pearl fisheries at al-Bahrayn. Various exploits of sailors from al-Bahrayn in the mediaeval period are also recorded. It provides an interesting summary of the types of ships, their construction, the methods of sailing, and of trading activities in the period before AD 1000.

796 **Dhows.**
David Howarth, photographs by Robin Constable. London:
Quartet Books, 1977. 159p.

A detailed and well-illustrated account of the Arab ships of the Gulf. It provides information on the history of the boats, the main types of 'dhow', their construction, sails and rigging, piracy and the slave trade, navigation, and trades and cargoes, and it concludes with a section on the future in which the author suggests that the building and sailing of 'dhows' may soon drift out of Arab hands and into those of Pakistanis and Indians. There are several mentions of Bahrain.

797 **The future of Gulf ports.**
Anne M. Hughes. *Geography*, vol. 64, no. 1 (Jan. 1979), p. 54-56.
A brief evaluation of the economic future of the ports of the Gulf. It notes that just over 62 per cent of the berths at Bahrein's port of Mina Sulman were required for the import of construction materials, and also observes that Bahrein has attempted to become a specialist in ship repairing and servicing.

798 **Transportation in Eastern Arabia.**
Alexander Melamid. *Geographical Review*, vol. 52, no. 1 (Jan. 1962), p. 122-24.
This brief report notes that, despite the growth of land transportation, scheduled air traffic in the early 1960s was still limited to flights from Bahrein and Ad Dawhah to Abū Zaby and Ash Shāriqah.

799 **The Middle East: feature.**
International Freighting Weekly, 10 Nov. 1982, p. 12-34.
A special report on road, air and sea transport concentrating on the Gulf. It includes reports on the 25-kilometre causeway joining Saudi Arabia and Bahrain, which is due for completion in or before January 1986, and the recent slump in air freight trade to Bahrain's international airport.

800 **The Arab navigation.**
'Allāma Syed Sulaimān Nadvi, translated by Syed Ṣabāḥuddīn 'Abdur Raḥmān. Lahore: Sh. Muhammad Ashraf, 1966. 153p.
This short introduction to the history and techniques of Arab navigation is based on a series of lectures given by the author in 1931. Bahrein is mentioned in several places as an important port and centre of commerce in the Gulf, from early Islamic times through to the 20th century.

801 **Persian Gulf pilot comprising the Persian Gulf and its approaches from Ras al Hadd, in the south west, to Cape Monze, in the east.**
London: HM Stationery Office, for the Hydrographic Department, Admiralty, 1932. 8th ed. 328p.
Contains full sailing directions for the Gulf. An introductory chapter provides information on such features as ports and anchorages, towns, population, trade, pearl fisheries, weather, tides, visibility, fuel and piracy. The waters around Bahrain are described on p. 203-14.

802 **Present trends show urgency of pan-Arab action on ports.**
Middle East, vol. 46 (1978), p. 72-73.
Argues that co-ordinated planning for port facilities is essential in the Gulf and notes that Bahrain was planning to add six berths to Mina Sulman in the late 1970s.

Transport

803 **The Persian Gulf dhows: new notes on the classification of mid-eastern sea-craft.**
A. M. J. Prins. *Persica*, vol. 6 (1972-74), p. 157-78.
A useful discussion of the types of boat used in the Gulf and of its ports.

804 **Ship repairing in Arabian Gulf ports.**
Shipping World and Shipbuilder, no. 3,929, vol. 170 (1977), p. 71, 73.
An account of work in progress on the Arab Shipbuilding and Repair Yard's facility in Bahrain, the record year achieved in 1976 by the Bahrein Slipway Co. Ltd. when 202 vessels were slipped, and the work of the Bahrain Ship Repairing and Engineering Co.

805 **Shipping in the Middle East: special report.**
Middle East Economic Digest, vol. 15, no. 7 (1971). 8p.
A special report on ports and shipping in the Middle East.

806 **Civil aviation in the Gulf: the role of commercial interests in the issue of traffic rights.**
Elda I. Stifani. *Arabian Studies*, vol. 3 (1976), p. 29-50.
This article notes the inadequacy of conventional international law to counter-balance the weight of commercial competition, and argues that there needs to be greater interdependence between the air transport systems of the Gulf states. It mentions that Gulf Air is jointly owned by Bahrain, Qatar, the United Arab Amirates and Oman, and that Bahrain's 13,000-foot runway was completed in 1971.

807 **Port congestion: waiting times fall as port authorities try rough tactics.**
John Whelan. *Middle East Economic Digest*, vol. 21, no. 8 (25 Feb. 1977), p. 3-4.
An account of port congestion in the Gulf and Arabian peninsula. It notes that the waiting time at Bahrain was 30 days in February 1977.

Leading the Saudis into temptation.
See item no. 441.

Cargoes of the East: the ports, trade and culture of the Arabian Seas and the western Indian Ocean.
See item no. 697.

The Gulf pattern 1977-1982: trade, ports, economies.
See item no. 700.

O.A.P.E.C. partnership creates the world's finest dry docks.
See item no. 748.

Employment and Manpower

808 **The labour market performance in some Arab Gulf states.**
Henry T. Azzam. In: *Issues in development: the Arab Gulf states.* Edited by May Ziwar-Daftari. London: MD Research and Services, 1980, p. 27-45.

This paper argues that without expatriate manpower the economies of the Gulf countries would not have been able to grow at the rate that they have achieved in recent years. It includes many mentions of Bahrain's labour force, and notes in particular that, in contrast to Kuwait, Qatar and the UAE, Bahrain has a majority of nationals in its labour force.

809 **Recent developments in labor relations in Bahrayn.**
Willard A. Beling. *Middle East Journal*, vol. 13, no. 2 (spring 1959), p. 156-69.

A study of the development of labour legislation in Bahrayn. It notes the protests, violence and riots in 1953 and 1954, which were provoked initially by Sunni Shi'i differences, and which were followed by an island-wide protest strike by Shi'i workers in December 1954. As a result in July 1956 a Labour Exchange was established, in October 1957 the industrial compensation law was approved by the ruler, and in November 1957 he also approved a new labour law to come into effect in January 1958. The paper concludes that the re-establishment of a strong labour movement would be closely related to politics and Arab nationalism.

810 **Arab manpower: the crisis of development.**
J. S. Birks, C. A. Sinclair. London: Croom Helm, 1980. 391p. map. bibliog.

The structure of this book is based on a thematic analysis of labour markets in individual countries of the Arab world. These state-by-state studies are drawn together by international comparisons and examinations of linkages between national labour markets. The result is an important regional analysis of manpower in the Arab Middle East. The state of Bahrain is classified as a pseudo-capital-rich state and is analysed in detail in chapter 8. It argues that Bahrain has never been able to afford expatriate staff on a wide scale, due to its slender oil reserves, and that adjusting to the reality of these meagre resources in the 1980s may be a traumatic experience. It also provides information on Bahrain's demography, education, economic development, and government revenue and expenditure in the 1970s.

Employment and Manpower

811   **Aspects of urban employment.**
J. S. Birks, C. A. Sinclair. In: *The changing Middle Eastern city.*
Edited by G. H. Blake, R. I. Lawless. London: Croom Helm;
New York: Barnes & Noble, 1980, p. 77-91.
Bahrain is used as an example of a capital-rich country in this assessment of urban employment patterns in the Middle East. In contrast to Kuwait, Qatar and the United Arab Emirates, the expatriate component of the work force is less than one half of the total number of economically active in Bahrain.

812   **Economic and social implications of current development in the Arab Gulf: the Oriental connection.**
J. S. Birks, C. A. Sinclair. In: *Social and economic development in the Arab Gulf.* Edited by Tim Niblock. London: Croom Helm, 1980, p. 135-60.
A study of the reasons behind, and consequences of, labour migrations in the Gulf. It notes that, although Bahrain has a modest income when compared, for example, with Kuwait and the UAE it behaves in the labour market as a capital-rich state, with approximately 40 per cent of its labour force consisting of non-nationals. One of the earliest major enclave contracts in the region was the construction of the drydock in Bahrain using South Korean labour, and this is seen as a successful project, with the departure of the Koreans on completion of the project contrasting favourably with the aftermath of the construction of the ALBA smelter when many of the migrants who had been employed building the plant remained.

813   **International migration and development in the Arab region.**
J. S. Birks, C. A. Sinclair. Geneva: International Labour Office, 1980. 175p. bibliog.
A thorough and detailed study of the nature and patterns of migration in the Middle East. Bahrain, a labour importing country, is discussed specifically on p. 74-75. It notes that, because Bahrain is poorer than several of its neighbours, the country has a relatively small migrant labour force. In 1975 migrants represented 40 per cent of the workforce, but between 1971 and 1977 the Arab share of the immigrant population fell from 45 to 14 per cent while that of the Asian immigrants rose from 32 to 64 per cent.

814   **International migration project country case study: the state of Bahrain.**
J. S. Birks, C. A. Sinclair. Durham, England: University of Durham, Department of Economics, 1978. 45p.
A detailed analysis of Bahrain's labour market. An introductory chapter is followed by chapters on labour supply, labour demand, and present migration patterns. It concludes that although Bahrain is small and poor, by comparison with her neighbours in the Gulf, the state is probably the most developed in the Arabian peninsula. In the 1970s the Arab share of employment in Bahrain fell dramatically, to be replaced in importance by Asian labour. Although Bahrain's expatriate labour force is small, the authors argue that her labour market has responded to external factors in a way comparable to her more wealthy neighbours.

815 **The nature and process of labour importing: the Arabian Gulf states of Kuwait, Bahrain, Qatar and the United Arab Emirates.**
J. S. Birks, C. A. Sinclair. Geneva: International Labour Office, 1978. 87p. bibliog. (World Employment Programme Research Working Paper, WEP 2-26/WP 30).

This useful publication is divided into sections on labour supply, economic development and labour demand, the labour market, and present migration patterns and expatriate communities. It notes that Bahrain's population has risen from about 90,000 in the 1941 census when 16 per cent were non-nationals to 182,300 in 1965 with 21 per cent non-Bahrainis, and 216,100 in 1971 when just less than 18 per cent were non-nationals. Bahrain has possessed a modern education system for longer than any other country in the Gulf, and 60 per cent of Bahraini men are recorded as being literate. The paper argues that because Bahrain's economy is more mature and complex than other states in the Gulf, and also because of its very small oil reserves, it might be showing patterns of labour demand that will be exhibited in other areas of the Gulf by the end of the century. By 1977 Asians provided 67 per cent of the working-age population of Bahrain.

816 **Some aspects of the labour market in the Middle East, with special reference to the Gulf states.**
J. Stace Birks, Clive A. Sinclair. *Journal of Developing Areas*, vol. 13, no. 3 (April 1979), p. 301-18.

An investigation of the manpower shortages and consequent high levels of expatriate labour to be found in the capital-rich Arab states. It estimates that of the countries of the Gulf Bahrain had the highest percentage of nationals in its workforce in 1975 at 60.4 per cent. Of its 56,000 non-nationals 73.4 per cent were Asians, Omanis or Iranians. A crisis is forecast when the traditional labour supplies of the Gulf states run dry.

817 **Recruitment and training of labor: the Middle East oil industry.**
David Finnie. *Middle East Journal*, vol. 12, no. 2 (1958), p. 127-43.

An account of the labour organization of the Middle East oil industry in the 1950s. It provides details of the composition of Bahrain Petroleum Company's workforce 1952-54.

818 **Bahrain to iron out pressing job needs.**
Ann Fyfe. *Middle East*, no. 54 (April 1979), p. 90-91.

Notes that discussions in Bahrain on unemployment problems, the cost of living and women's role in society are becoming increasingly pegged on the eventual opening of the causeway linking Saudi Arabia to Bahrain.

819   **Education and manpower in the Arabian Gulf.**
      Robert Anton Mertz. Washington, DC: American Friends of the
      Middle East, 1972. 226p.

A study on the requirements of education and manpower in the Gulf undertaken
in 1971 and 1972. Chapter 1 (p. 3-33) is devoted to Bahrain and provides information on the state's economic position, population growth, enrolment in
education 1961/2-1971/2, secondary enrolment, expanding technical and scientific
education, educational finance, and various aspects of the nature of its labour
force.

820   **Migrant workers in the Arab Middle East.**
      Third World Quarterly, vol. 4, no. 3 (July 1982), p. 530-31.

A short summary of migration patterns in the Gulf area. Bahrain is noted as a
capital-rich country importing mostly Asian labour.

821   **Migration and employment in the Arab world: construction as
      a key policy variable.**
      R. Paul Shaw. *International Labour Review*, vol. 118, no. 5
      (1979), p. 589-605.

An account of labour migration in OAPEC countries noting the severe data
limitations inherent in such a study. It notes that in Bahrain in 1971 18.6 per cent
of the non-agricultural labour force was employed in construction, and that in
1976 non-nationals comprised 43.4 per cent of the total labour force of 83,000.

822   **Impact of technical change on the structure of the labour force
      in the ECWA region.**
      Nadia M. El-Shishini. In: *Technology transfer and change in the
      Arab world.* Edited by A. B. Zahlan. Oxford, England; New
      York: Pergamon Press, 1978, p. 205-21.

Notes that 58 per cent of total employment in Bahrain was in the tertiary sector
in the early 1970s, and that the percentage of the population of Bahrain that was
urban rose from 61.4 per cent in 1950 to 80.0 per cent in 1975.

823   **The Arab brain drain.**
      Edited by A. B. Zahlan. London: Ithaca Press for the United
      Nations, 1981. 309p.

The proceedings of a seminar on the Arab brain drain, organized by the United
Nations Economic Commission for Western Asia in Beirut 4-8 February 1980.
The papers by Ibrahim Ibrahim and Alfonso Mejia mention Bahrain.

Arab migrations.
See item no. 402.

L'immigration dans la péninsule arabique. (Immigration in the Arabian peninsula.)
See item no. 407.

Migration and labour force in the oil-producing states of the Middle East.
See item no. 410.

Labour markets and citizenship in Bahrayn and Qatar.
See item no. 413.

The modernization of labor and labor law in the Arab Gulf states.
See item no. 506.

Statistics

824 **Government of Bahrain: Annual Report.**
Bahrain: Government of Bahrain, 1937-71. annual.

A report of government activities (written until 1952 by Charles Belgrave) during the period of British control, covering such things as education, welfare, agriculture, the postal services, and budget. In addition to government statistics it provides information on certain aspects of social and political change on the islands. The annual reports were preceded by a condensed report on the administration of the Bahrain government from 1926 to 1937, also written by Charles Belgrave.

825 **Statistical Abstract.**
Bahrain: Directorate of Statistics, [1971-]. annual.

Provides statistical information on Bahrain, divided into twelve sections on the following: area and climate, population, vital statistics, education, health services, oil, transport and communications, justice, finance, electricity and water, foreign trade and miscellaneous statistics.

826 **Statistical Yearbook.**
New York: United Nations, 1948- . annual.

Provides up-to-date summary economic and social statistics for many countries of the world, including Bahrain, for which details on fishing, oil and gas, petroleum refining, trade, transport, communications, national accounts, consumption and energy are given.

The Middle East: a handbook.
See item no. 2.

Bahrain: a MEED special report.
See item no. 31.

The Middle East and North Africa.
See item no. 49.

Bahrain.
See item no. 68.

Die Arabische Halbinsel: Länder zwischen Rotem Meer und Persischen Golf. (The Arabian peninsula: lands between the Red Sea and the Persian Gulf.)
See item no. 73.

Demographic Yearbook.
See item no. 406.

Environment

827 **Urban water problems.**
Peter Beaumont. In: *The changing Middle Eastern city*. Edited
by G. H. Blake, R. I. Lawless. London: Croom Helm; New York:
Barnes & Noble, 1980, p. 230-50.
This paper evaluates the water resource problems that rapid urbanization has
caused in the Middle East. It notes that Bahrain, in company with Saudi Arabia
and Sudan, has urban water use values in excess of 400 litres/capita/day.

828 **'Big Brother' threatens Arabs with catastrophe.**
Sunday Times (London), 10 April 1983, p. 11.
A detailed report on the extent of the oil slick emanating from Iran's offshore
Nowruz oilfield early in 1983, and its threat to Bahrain.

829 **The environmental history of the Near and Middle East since
the last Ice Age.**
Edited by William C. Brice. London, New York, San Francisco:
Academic Press, 1978. 384p. 55 maps.
Bahrain is mentioned in the chapters by C. E. Larsen and G. Evans, and T. Al-
Asfour in this account of the changing environments of the Middle East.

830 **Effluent re-use: how the Gulf states balance benefits and risks.**
World Water (Jan. 1981), p. 32-35.
An account of effluent re-use in the Arab Gulf states.

831 **Water resources in the Arab Middle East and North Africa.**
Christiaan E. Gischler. Cambridge, England: Middle East and
North African Studies Press, 1979. 132p. 7 maps. bibliog.
An analysis of the occurrence of groundwater and the technology involved in its
utilization in the Arab world. It notes that the Umm er Radhuma limestone
aquifer extends under Bahrain, and that submarine springs exist to the north-east
of the island. An annexe provides basic statistics relating to Bahrain's water
balance.

832 **Dust haze at Bahrain.**
J. Houseman. *Meteorological Magazine*, no. 1,063, vol. 90
(Feb. 1961), p. 50-52.
Notes that the dust frequency closely fits the climatological régime of Bahrain.
From November to February the moistening of the desert surface almost com-
pletely prevents dust haze. From May through June and July the dust is at its
worst, coinciding with the north-west Shamal wind of 15-20 knots associated with
the monsoon low over India and Persia, which brings dust from Iraq to Bahrain.

833 **Middle East Water and Sewage.**
Redhill, England: Fuel and Metallurgical Journals, July 1977- .
bimonthly.
Each issue normally contains a section on current news about water and sewage in
the Middle East as well as articles on a wide range of topics related to water. It
provides much useful information on the development of desalination plants in
Bahrain.

834 **Discomfort in Bahrain.**
A. E. Turner. *Weather*, vol. 33, no. 9 (Sept. 1978), p. 334-38.
Provides details of Bahrain's weather, and describes the levels of discomfort,
based on an index of discomfort ranging from a wet-bulb temperature of 25°C to
35°C over the years 1966-76.

835 **A comparison of effective temperatures at Bahrain and Sharjah.**
G. A. Watt. *Meteorological Magazine*, no. 1,155, vol. 97 (Oct.
1968), p. 310-14.
Notes that Sharjah has a more pleasant climate than Bahrain in the summer due
to the prevalence in Sharjah of a dry katabatic wind during the morning, and
that afternoon weather conditions are similar in both locations.

836 **An index of comfort for Bahrain.**
G. A. Watt. *Meteorological Magazine*, no. 1,144, vol. 96
(Nov. 1967), p. 321-27.
An analysis of 'effective temperatures' (derived from the scale devised by the
American Society of Heating and Ventilating Engineers) of Bahrain over the
period 1962-66. It provides a brief description of the country's weather.

Area handbook for the peripheral states of the Arabian peninsula.
See item no. 5.

Bahrain Surface Materials Resources Survey.
See item no. 82.

**The Bahrain Surface Materials Resource Survey and its application to
regional planning.**
See item no. 83.

Environment

Geology, geomorphology and pedology of Bahrain.
See item no. 90.

Soil map of the world 1:5,000,000. Volume VII: South Asia.
See item no. 97.

Agriculture and the use of water resources in the Eastern Province of Saudi Arabia.
See item no. 770.

Education

837 **Development of education in Bahrain, 1940-1965.**
Abdul-Malik Yousuf Al Hamer. Bahrain: Oriental Press, 1969.
122p. bibliog.
An analysis of the development of education in Bahrain from the origins of formal education in 1919 to the end of the 1960s. It includes a description of the historical evolution of the system of education and provides information about teachers' backgrounds, opinions on education, and aspirations.

838 **The education and training of technician engineers in the Gulf.**
Donald Longman, C. H. Nicholls, J. P. Sharp, W. G. Philips.
In: *Engineering and development in the Gulf.* Bahrain Society of Engineers. London: Graham & Trotman, 1977, p. 59-70.
This paper is divided into four sections, each written by one of the authors: academic standards and finance, industrial liaison, mechanical and electrical engineering, and civil engineering and building construction. It concentrates on the achievements of the Gulf Technical College established on its present site in 1970, and it observes that Bahrain has been forunate in possessing the energy and foresight to plan a progressive secondary technical education system which is feeding many students into the College.

839 **Education in the Arab states in the light of the Abu Dhabi conference 1977.**
Abdelhadi Tazi. [Geneva] : Unesco, 1980. 81p.
This booklet presents the educational problems of the Arab countries in their socio-economic context, and shows how the present situation could develop. It also reproduces the complete text of the declaration and recommendations adopted by the fourth regional conference on education in Arab countries organized by Unesco in association with the Arab Educational, Cultural and Scientific Organization, and held in Abu Dhabi 7-14 November 1977. It provides a number of statistics on education in Bahrain.

Education

840 **Arabian days.**
Sheikh Hafiz Wahba. London: Arthur Barker, 1964. 184p.

An account of the Arabian peninsula by Saudi Arabia's first Minister of Education, who was later Ambassador from Ibn Saud at the Court of St. James. It notes differences of opinion between Bahreinis and Kuwaitis, pearling in Bahrein, the establishment of two schools there in 1920, and the creation of the first municipality in the same year.

Journey into chaos.
See item no. 429.

Arab manpower: the crisis of development.
See item no. 810.

The nature and process of labour importing: the Arabian Gulf states of Kuwait, Bahrain, Qatar and the United Arab Emirates.
See item no. 815.

Education and manpower in the Arabian Gulf.
See item no. 819.

A critical analysis of school science teaching in Arab countries.
See item no. 842.

Arab education 1956-1978: a bibliography.
See item no. 902.

Science and Technology

841 **Arab telecommunications: Financial Times survey.**
Financial Times, 6 Jan. 1981, p. 9-12.
An account of the recent changes and developments in telecommunications technology throughout the Arab world.

842 **A critical analysis of school science teaching in Arab countries.**
J. E. Arrayed. London: Longman; Beirut: Librairie du Liban, 1980. 254p.
This study by the Undersecretary of the Ministry of Education in Bahrain is in three parts. The first examines the nature and aims of science teaching in the Arab countries and how these have changed since the early 1960s. The second part contains a review and examination of some current Arab efforts at the regional level to develop their school science. The third part examines in detail the need and possibilities for future developments of Arab school science in Bahrain, and it concludes with suggestions concerning the strategy and the lines of action that the country can follow in order to bring about the required changes.

843 **Engineering and development in the Gulf.**
Bahrain Society of Engineers. London: Graham & Trotman, 1977. 228p.
A collection of papers presented at the first seminar of the Bahrain Society of Engineers. The papers by Lord Llewelyn-Davies; Donald Longman, C. H. Nicholls, J. P. Sharp and W. G. Philips; A. M. Caetano Carriera; P. J. Lambeth, J. B. Kuipers, R. Roff and A. Jumah; P. U. Fischer; M. Taheri; Usameh F. Jamali; and P. J. B. Clarricoats discuss Bahrain.

844 **The importance of telecommunications in a developing country.**
P. J. B. Clarricoats. In: *Engineering and development in the Gulf.*
Bahrain Society of Engineers. London: Graham & Trotman, 1977, p. 225-28.
Notes that before the coming of the satellite terminal in Bahrain, high frequency radio communications provided the main form of worldwide communications for the country.

Science and Technology

845 **The Persian Gulf submarine telegraph of 1864.**
Christina Phelps Harris. *Geographical Journal*, vol. 135, no. 2
(June 1969), p. 169-90.
An account of the development of the Persian Gulf submarine telegraph from
Basra to Rishahr, Ru'us al Jibal, and then Gwadur. It notes that one of the earlier
plans had considered sending the cables via Bahrain.

846 **Solar energy in the Arab world: policies and programs.**
M. Ali Kettani, M. A. S. Malik. Kuwait: Organization of Arab
Petroleum Exporting Countries, 1979. 199p. map. bibliog.
This book is an outcome of a study commissioned by OAPEC to investigate the
potential of solar energy in the Arab world. It notes that the Bahrain National
Oil Company started a solar energy programme in 1977 in association with the
Kuwait Institute for Scientific Research in which the basic research and develop-
ment would be undertaken in Kuwait. An extensive bibliography is included.

847 **High voltage insulation for Bahrain and the problem of desert
pollution.**
P. J. Lambeth, J. B. Kuipers, R. Roff, A. Jumah. In: *Engineering and development in the Gulf*. Bahrain Society of Engineers.
London: Graham & Trotman, 1977, p. 113-37.
An investigation into the problems of pollution flashover and the provision of
insulation for overhead transmission lines in Bahrain. Salt-laden winds present
particular insulation problems in the Gulf area, and it suggests that flat disc
insulators with nine suspension discs at 66KV operation should provide satisfactory
performance.

848 **Telecommunications in the Arab world: a special report.**
The Times (London), 2 Feb. 1981, p. 17-19.
This report on telecommunications notes that Bahrain has as many as 22 tele-
phones per 100 of its population.

849 **The status of science and technology in the Western Asian region.**
United Nations Economic Commission for Western Asia, NRST
Division, presented by R. Van der Graaf. In: *Technology transfer
and change in the Arab world*. Edited by A. B. Zahlan. Oxford,
England; New York: Pergamon Press, 1978, p. 51-94.
Provides some statistics relating to Bahrain's trade and technical staff during the
early 1970s, and also notes that Bahrain is establishing a National Research Centre
in co-operation with Jordan's Royal Scientific Society. This institute will have
departments of mechanical engineering, computer sciences, economics, and
documentation.

850 **Middle East science: a survey of subjects other than agriculture. A report to the Director General Middle East Supply Centre.**
E. B. Worthington. London: HM Stationery Office, 1946. 239p. 5 maps. bibliog.

The report of a survey into the problems related to the non-agricultural resources, including water resources, and problems with a biological basis affecting the population in the Middle East. It notes Bahrein's sweet water springs, high humidity, oil exploration, pearl fisheries, and the hospital maintained there by the Reformed Dutch Church of America in the 1940s.

851 **Science and science policy in the Arab world.**
A. B. Zahlan. London: Croom Helm, 1980. 205p.

An investigation into scientific activity and research in the Arab world. It notes that in November 1978 the Bahrain Engineering Society organized a conference on construction in the Arab world.

852 **Technology transfer and change in the Arab world: a seminar of the United Nations Economic Commission for Western Asia.**
Edited by A. B. Zahlan. Oxford, England; New York: Pergamon Press for the United Nations, 1978. 506p.

The proceedings of a seminar on technology transfer and change in the Arab world organized by the Natural Resources, Science and Technology Division of the United Nations Economic Commission for Western Asia during October 1977. The papers by R. Van der Graaf, Elia T. Zureik, and Nadia M. El-Shishini mention Bahrain.

853 **Values, social organization and technology change in the Arab world.**
Elia T. Zureik. In: *Technology transfer and change in the Arab world.* Edited by A. B. Zahlan. Oxford, England; New York: Pergamon Press, 1978, p. 185-203.

Notes that in 1973 Bahrain had 395 engineers and scientists per 100,000 population and that 78.0 per cent of these were non-nationals.

Impact of technical change on the structure of the labour force in the ECWA region.
See item no. 822.

The education and training of technician engineers in the Gulf.
See item no. 838.

The Arts

854 **Arabian fantasy.**
Herbert Chappell, photographs by Robin Constable. London:
Namara Publications/Quartet Books, 1976. 144p.

The author, together with David Fanshawe, visited Bahrain to make a film of a musical score in which Fanshawe has combined his own music with field recordings of traditional musicians. The resulting book provides an extensively illustrated introduction to Bahrain, with particular emphasis on its music and pearl fishing.

855 **A history of Arabian music to the XIIIth century.**
Henry George Farmer. London: Luzac, 1973. 264p. bibliog.

First published in 1929, this is an historical analysis of the development of Arabian music prior to the fall of the 'Abbāsids. It notes that in the second century AD, as a result of the Arab migration from South Arabia, a group of tribes confederated under the title of the Tanūkh settled in Al-Baḥrain, and that Islam reached Al-Baḥrain before the death of the Prophet Muḥammad.

856 **Bahrain: protection of cultural property and development of a museum in Bahrain.**
A. Ghosh. Paris: Unesco, 1968. 20p. (Serial no: 787/BMS.RD/ CLT).

Provides an account of the archaeology of Bahrain, the scope for future archaeological work, the need for an archaeological organization, antiquarian law, and the proposals for the establishment of a museum in Bahrain.

857 **Warm images of Bahrain.**
Duncan Gilchrist, photographs by Philip Hartas. Printed London and Wisbech, England: Balding & Mansell, 1977. unpaged.

A collection of poetry and photographs written by an expatriate with over 20 years of involvement in the life and progress of Bahrain.

858   **The music of the Arabian Gulf.**
Molly Izzard.   *Dilmun: a Journal of Archaeology and History in Bahrain*, no. 9 (1980), p. 4-9.
A short, illustrated introduction to the music and musical instruments to be found in the Gulf.

859   **Bait al-Mu'ayyad: a late nineteenth-century house of al-Baḥrayn.**
Geoffrey King.   *Arabian Studies*, vol. 4 (1978), p. 27-46.
An architectural survey of a house at Samāhīj on al-Muḥarraq.

860   **Traditional architecture in Kuwait and the northern Gulf.**
Ronald Lewcock, with an introduction by Zahra Freeth.
London: Art and Archaeology Research Papers, 1978. 172p. map. bibliog.
A well-illustrated account of architecture in Kuwait, covering houses, mosques, forts, other building types, doors, and wind towers. Bahrain is mentioned in several places in connection with the historical relations between the countries of the Gulf. It also notes that Bahrain has a distinctive type of door, and characteristic mid-wall wind catchers.

861   **A literary history of the Arabs.**
R. A. Nicholson.   Cambridge, England: Cambridge University Press, 1969. 506p. bibliog.
An introduction to Arab literature, first published in 1907. It mentions the 6th-century poet Ṭarafa b. al-'Abd, who was a member of the tribe of Bakr and lived at Bahrain.

862   **Architecture of Bahrain.**
Rashid Al-Oraifi.   Manama: Tourist Gallery, 1978. 42p. English; 53p. Arabic. (Bahrain Heritage Series, 1).
A survey of buildings in Bahrain, which the author divides into five styles: Dilmun period, *barastis* (palm branch houses), village and farming communities, large homes built in the late 19th and early 20th centuries, and modern. It includes numerous drawings and photographs of buildings in each style.

863   **The art of Arabian costume.**
Heather Colyer Ross.   Fribourg, Switzerland: Arabesque Commercial SA, 1981. 188p. 2 maps. bibliog.
A comprehensive and illustrated account of Arabian dress. It is divided into chapters on the historical background, influences on the costumes, traditional Arab costume, people of the Arabian peninsula, body ornament, and arts and crafts. Although mainly concerned with Saudi Arabia there are several mentions of Bahrain, and it notes in passing that many skilled weaponry jewellers are located in Bahrain. The regional style of clothes in Bahrain is discussed in detail on p. 84 where the traditional importance of pearls is mentioned.

864 **Conservation of the character and Islamic heritage of Arab towns.**
Ebrahim Uthman. Bahrain: Bahrain Central Municipal Council
Technical and Engineering Department, n.d. unpaged. 3 maps.

An introduction to the architecture and planning of Arab towns, with particular
emphasis on Bahrain. It is well illustrated, with drawings and photographs, and
discusses traditional housing, the reasons for the loss of character of Arab towns,
means of preserving characteristics of Arab towns, building materials and
implements, *areesh* (palm branch) houses, traditional decoration, *keshteel* (wind-
towers), and mosques.

The Persian Gulf states.
See item no. 23.

Al Watheeka. (The document.)
See item no. 393.

Sports and Recreation

865 **Falconry in Arabia.**
     Mark Allen. London: Orbis Publishing, 1980. 143p. 2 maps.
     bibliog.
An essential, and beautifully illustrated, text for those interested in falconry in
Arabia. Bahrain is not a main hunting ground, nor is it an area where hawks are
trapped, but the book notes that the Al-Isa tribe of Bahrain flies hawks.

866 **Gardening and pot plants in the Gulf.**
     Sheila M. Glashier. Privately printed. n.d. 64p. [Copies available
     from 42 Pinewood Road, Hordle, Lymington, Hampshire,
     England, or Family Bookshop, Manama, Bahrain].
A useful guide to the potential and problems of gardens in the Gulf. As well as
information on planning gardens it provides details on how to grow successfully
vegetables and herbs, trees, bushes and shrubs, lawns and pot plants.

867 **Gulf Travel Trade.**
     Manama: Al Hilal Publishing and Marketing Group, June 1979- .
     monthly.
This trade journal provides information on hotels, travel, airlines and travel agents
in the Gulf. Circulation 5,200. Free controlled circulation in Gulf Co-operation
Council countries.

868 **Gulf Traveller.**
     Manama: Al Hilal Publishing and Marketing Group, Dec. 1981- .
     biannual.
A travel magazine for people of the Gulf. It provides information on a variety of
destinations from America to the Far East. Circulation 8,600 in Gulf Co-operation
Council countries.

Sports and Recreation

869 **The Amiri Arabian stud of Bahrain.**
Compiled by Danah Al Khalifa, edited by Richard Silvey, Mariam bint Isa Al Khalifa. Bahrain: Danah Al Khalifa, 1980. 112p. map.

An account of the history of the Amiri Arabian stud of Bahrain, which lists all of the horses subdivided by their family or strain.

870 **Games of Bahrain.**
Rashid Al-Oraifa. Manama: Rashid Al-Oraifa Art Gallery, 1979. unpaged. (Bahrain Heritage Series, 3).

A comprehensive introduction to the children's games of Bahrain. It describes 54 games, each of which is illustrated with photographs or line drawings. In Arabic and English.

871 **Leisure, recreational and sporting facilities in the Arab states of the Gulf.**
Philip Stephens. London: London Chamber of Commerce and Industry, 1977. 33p.

This report aims to indicate to British architects, consultants, contractors, and suppliers the scale of the development of leisure, recreational and sporting facilities in the Arab states of the Gulf. Bahrain is discussed on p. 4-7, where it is noted that Shaikh Hamad bin Isa has shown a keen personal interest in the development of sports. Brief details are provided of the Muharraq Sports Complex, Isa Town Stadium, the Manama Race Course Complex, and some other small developments. It also notes the emphasis on leisure-orientated hotels, supported by the country's relatively cosmopolitan outlook and liberal alcohol laws.

Al Hilal guide to living and working in Bahrain.
See item no. 41.

Mass Media

872   **Al-Baḥrain.** (Bahrain.)
Manama: Ministry of Information, 1978- . weekly.
An Arabic publication relating to current affairs in Baḥrain. Circulation 5,000.
From 1972 to 1978 it was known as *Al-Baḥrain Al-Youm* (Bahrain Today) and in
1970-71 as *Huna al-Bahrain* (This is Baḥrain).

873   **Bahrain News.**
Manama: Ministry of Information, [1971-] . weekly.
An English and Arabic news weekly.

874   **Gulf Daily News.**
Manama: Gulf Daily News, 1978- . daily.
A daily tabloid of normally about 20 pages covering news and numerous aspects
of life in Bahrain. It also provides occasional magazines on such subjects as
banking, shipping, industry and construction. Circulation c.10,000.

875   **Gulf Mirror.**
Manama: Gulf Publishing, 1971- . weekly.
A weekly tabloid on general topical and social affairs. There are five editions for
Bahrain and Kuwait, Saudi Arabia, Qatar, the UAE and the Sultanate of Oman.
Circulation 17,000.

876   **Al-Hiya al-Tijariya.** (Commerce Review.)
Manama: Bahrain Chamber of Commerce and Industry,
Oct. 1961- . monthly.
An Arabic review of business, commerce and economics in Bahrain. Circulation
3,000.

877   **Al-Jarida al-Rasmiya.** (Official Gazette.)
Manama: Ministry of Information, 1971- . weekly.
The Arabic official government gazette.

878   The Arab press: news media and political process in the Arab
      world.
      William A. Rugh.   Syracuse, New York: Syracuse University
      Press; London: Croom Helm, 1979. 205p.
Provides details of media statistics, newspapers, the media system, expatriate
journalists, radio and television, the news agency, and foreign radio listeners in
Bahrain. It argues that the press in Bahrain is consistently loyal and supportive of
the régime in power.

879   **Sada al-Usbou.** (Weekly Echo.)
      Manama: Sada al-Usbou, 1969- . weekly.
An Arabic weekly covering general topical and social events. Circulation 20,000.

This is Bahrain.
See item no. 63.

Bibliographies

880 **The states of the Arabian Peninsula and Gulf littoral: a selected bibliography.**
John Duke Anthony. Washington, DC: Middle East Institute, 1973. 21p.

A partially annotated bibliography of Arabia focusing primarily on material pertinent to the area's governmental systems, political dynamics, internal relations and economics. No indexes.

881 **The contemporary Middle East, 1948-1973: a selective and annotated bibliography.**
George N. Atiyah. Boston, Massachusetts: G. K. Hall, 1975. 664p.

Includes 6,491 references on the contemporary Middle East, most of which are annotated. It is divided into nine main sections: 1) The Middle East, 2) The Arab-Israeli conflict, 3) The Arab countries, 4) The Arabian peninsula, 5) The Fertile Crescent, 6) The Nile valley, 7) The Maghrib, 8) Turkey, and 9) Iran. Sections 1-3 and 8, 9 are subdivided by subject matter or discipline, and sections 4-7 by country and then by subject matter of discipline. Author and subject indexes.

882 **Bahrain Historical and Archaeological Society reference library book list.**
Bahrain: Bahrain Historical and Archaeological Society, 1983. 45p.

A list of all the books, articles and typescripts held by the Bahrain Historical and Archaeological Society on the following subjects: archaeology in Bahrain, general archaeology, the history of Bahrain, natural history, maps and films. It provides one of the most complete bibliographies on Bahrain's archaeology and history.

883 **Arab culture and society in change: a partially annotated bibliography of books and articles in English, French, German and Italian.**
Compiled by the staff of CEMAM 'Centre d'Etudes pour le Monde Arabe Moderne'. Beirut: Dar el-Mashreq, 1973. 318p.

A bibliography with nearly 5,000 entries concerned with the period 1914-73, divided into chapters on acculturation; townsmen, countrymen and nomads; cultural reaction to economic change; condition of women; marriage and family; youth; education; the Arabic language; pluralism, ethnic and religious; political ideology; Islam and modern thought; Islam in modern society; Islam and the state; Islam and modern law; and a final supplementary miscellany. It includes author, personal-name, regional, and selected subject indexes.

884 **The emergence of Arab nationalism from the nineteenth century to 1921: a bibliography.**
Frank Clements. London: Diploma Press, 1976. 290p.

This annotated bibliograpjy is divided into three main sections: the struggle between the Arabs and the Turks, the peace settlement and its consequences, and the Fertile Crescent under the mandate system. It provides some useful references concerning Turkish influence in Arabia. Author and title index.

885 **Le Golfe persique: introduction bibliographique.** (The Persian Gulf: bibliographical introduction.)
Mohammed-Reza Djalili. Geneva: Centre Asiatique, Institut Universitaire de Hautes Etudes Internationales, 1979. 92p.

This bibliography is divided into three parts: the first covers general works, the second individual countries around the coasts of the Gulf, and the third the major problems of the Gulf. Bahrein is detailed specifically on p. 42-44.

886 **A bibliography of articles on the Middle East, 1959-1967.**
Compiled by Uri Dotan, edited by Avigdor Levy. Tel Aviv, Israel: Mif'al Haschichpul, 1970. 227p. (Shiloah Center's Teaching and Research Aids, 2).

This bibliography, aimed particularly at the Israeli reader, includes 2,902 entries in Western languages, Arabic and Hebrew, and has an author index. A few entries for Bahrain are included on p. 182-87 covering Kuwait and the Gulf states.

887 **Saudi Arabia and the Gulf states.**
Wendy Fiander. London: Statistics and Market Intelligence Library, 1979. 48p. (Sources of Statistics and Market Information, 7, revised).

An annotated bibliography of Bahrain, Kuwait, Qatar, Saudi Arabia and the UAE divided into sections on general background, business conditions, directories, and statistics. Bahrain is specifically referred to in references 33-41, 110-12, and 151-56.

888   **Bibliography on southwestern Asia.**
Henry Field.   Coral Gables, Florida: University of Miami Press,
1953-62, vols. 1-7, with supplements 1-8, 1968-72.

An anthropological bibliography of the area ranging from Istanbul to the Hindu
Kush on the north and from Aden to the Makran coast on the south, from the
Suez Canal on the west to the eastern boundary of Afghanistan. It has an author
index, and is divided into sections on anthropogeography subdivided into anthropology, archaeology, geology, agriculture, cartography, astronomy, medicine, art,
music and poetry, and on natural history subdivided into zoology, anthropods,
birds, fish, mammals, mollusks, reptiles, amphibians and botany. Subject indexes
are published separately.

889   **Analytical guide to the bibliographies on the Arabian peninsula.**
C. L. Geddes.   Denver, Colorado: American Institute of Islamic
Studies, 1974. 50p.

An annotated guide to 70 bibliographies published in European languages prior to
1974 on the Arabian peninsula.

890   **A bibliography of the avifauna of the Arabian peninsula, the
Levant and Mesopotamia.**
W. A. C. Griffiths.   England: Army Bird-watching Society, 1974.
101p. map.

An extensive list of 734 publications on avifauna in the region noted in the title.
It also includes appendices on further related bibliographies, a geographical index,
a bibliography of Socotra and Abd-el-Kuri islands, a list of type specimens, a list
of sources of unpublished papers, and a key to abbreviated titles of publications.

891   **Arab Islamic bibliography. The Middle East Library Committee
guide based on Giuseppe Gabrieli's *Manuale di bibliografia
musulmana.***
Edited by Diana Grimwood-Jones, Derek Hopwood, J. D. Pearson,
with the assistance of J. P. C. Auchterlonie, J. D. Latham, Yasin
Safadi.   Hassocks, England: Harvester Press; Atlantic Highlands,
New Jersey: Humanities Press, 1977. 292p.

An Arab Islamic bibliography based on Gabrieli's work, divided into sections on
bibliographies; encyclopaedias and reference works; Arabic grammars; genealogies,
biographical dictionaries and who's whos; the press and periodicals; maps and
atlases of the Arab world; Arabic geographical names; Festschrifts and commemorative volumes; scientific expeditions; orientalism and orientalists; institutions;
Arabic manuscripts; Arabic papyri; archives; Arabic epigraphy; Muslim numis-
matics; Arabic printing and book production; libraries; and booksellers. There is
an index of authors, with titles of anonymous works.

892 **Middle East and Islam: a bibliographical introduction.**
Edited by Diana Grimwood-Jones. Zug, Switzerland: Inter
Documentation Company Ag., rev. and enlarged ed., 1979. 429p.

A broad bibliographical introduction to the Middle East divided into five main
sections on reference works, history and Islamic studies, subject bibliographies,
regional bibliographies, and language and literature. Bahrain is generally included
in sections on Arabia. Author index only.

893 **Bibliography of the Arabian peninsula.**
Harry W. Hazard, Robert W. Crawford, *et al*. New Haven,
Connecticut: Human Relations Area Files, 1956. 256p.

A list of articles and books compiled for the American Geographical Society on
the subject of Arabia. No index.

894 **Selected bibliography on Kuwait and the Arabian Gulf.**
Soraya M. Kabeel. Kuwait: Kuwait University Libraries Depart-
ment, May 1969. 104p. (Kuwait University Libraries Department
Bibliographic Series, no. 1).

A selective bibliography of periodical articles, books, references and other
material on Kuwait, Bahrain, Muscat, Oman and Qatar. For Bahrain 106 references
are found on p. 60-65.

895 **Source book on the Arabian Gulf states: Arabian Gulf in general,
Kuwait, Bahrain, Qatar and Oman.**
Soraya M. Kabeel. Kuwait: Kuwait University Press, 1975.
427p.

This useful introduction to the region is divided into three parts: a general introductory survey providing economic, historical and geographical information on
each country, a bibliographical survey, and a general index.

896 **The Islamic Near East and North Africa: an annotated guide to
books in English for non-specialists.**
David W. Littlefield. Littleton, Colorado: Libraries Unlimited,
1977. 375p.

A guide aimed to stimulate the interest of the non-expert reader in various aspects
of the region from c.600 AD to the present. It is divided into two sections, the
first on general works, including history, politics, language and literature, society
and religion, and the second on individual countries. One specific reference to
Bahrain is found on p. 178, but other references to the state are also to be found
elsewhere in the chapter on the Arabian peninsula.

897 **Bibliography of the Arabian peninsula.**
Eric Macro. Coral Gables, Florida: University of Miami Press,
1958. 80p.

A bibliography compiled mainly between 1945 and 1950. Author index only.

898 **A guide to manuscripts and documents in the British Isles relating to the Middle East and North Africa.**
Compiled by Noel Matthews, M. Doreen Wainwright, edited by J. D. Pearson. Oxford, England: Oxford University Press, 1980. 482p.

A guide to the locations of manuscripts relating to the Middle East to be found in libraries and record offices throughout Britain. It is divided up by the towns and cities in which the libraries are located, and the index contains references to Bahrain's court proceedings, India Office records, oil, the Political Agency, the Persian claim to the islands, and the activities of the correspondent of *The Times* in Bahrain.

899 **The status of the Arab woman: a select bibliography.**
Samira Rafidi Meghdessian. London: Mansell, 1980. 176p.

After general introductions on the cultural and social background of the Middle East, conferences and seminars on the Arab woman, women in Islam and the law, women in the Arab Middle East, and women in North Africa, references are listed for each country in the region. For Bahrain 10 references are given on p. 97-98. Subject and author index.

900 **Middle East Journal.**
Washington, DC: Middle East Institute, 1947- . quarterly.

In addition to varied articles on the Middle East, this journal includes a chronology of recent events, a section of book reviews, and a bibliography of periodical literature.

901 **The security of Gulf oil: an introductory bibliography.**
David Newman, Ewan Anderson, Gerald Blake. Durham, England: University of Durham Centre for Middle Eastern and Islamic Studies, 1982. 55p. (Occasional Papers Series, no. 13).

A collection of 750 references on the security of the Gulf divided into sections on general references, internal politics, superpower rivalry and interests, the oilfields, sealanes and the Straits of Hormuz, the Indian Ocean and the Cape route. No index.

902 **Arab education 1956-1978: a bibliography.**
Veronica S. Pantelidis. London: Mansell, 1982. 552p.

A thorough guide to sources of information on education in the 21 member states of the Arab League as of 1978. After a general section on the Arab world, the countries are listed separately. Author, title and subject index.

Bibliographies

903 **Index Islamicus.**
     J. D. Pearson. Cambridge, England: W. Heffer & Sons, 1958
     (1906-55); 1962 (supplement 1956-60); 1967 (supplement
     1961-65). London: Mansell Information/Publishing, 1972 (third
     supplement 1966-70), 1977 (fourth supplement 1971-75).
A catalogue of articles on Islamic subjects in periodicals and other collective
publications.

904 **The Quarterly Index Islamicus: current books, articles and papers
     on Islamic studies.**
     Edited by J. D. Pearson. London: Mansell Information/Publishing,
     Jan. 1977- . quarterly.
Lists articles from a wide range of periodicals by country.

905 **A book world directory of the Arab countries, Turkey and Iran.**
     Anthony Rudkin, Irene Butcher. London: Mansell; Detroit,
     Michigan: Gale, 1981. 143p.
A directory of libraries, booksellers, publishers, institutional publishers, newspapers and periodicals in the Middle East. Bahrain is covered on p. 5-7 where 24
entries are included.

906 **Oman and southeastern Arabia: a bibliographic survey.**
     Michael Owen Shannon. Boston, Massachusetts: G. K. Hall,
     1978. 165p.
A bibliography listing 988 publications on Oman and the surrounding Arab
territories. It has a subject, author and title index.

907 **Theses on Islam, the Middle East and North-west Africa
     1880-1978 accepted by universities in the United Kingdom and
     Ireland.**
     Peter Sluglett. London: Mansell, 1983. 147p.
A list of 3,051 theses arranged by subject. Includes a very short subject index, and
a thorough author index.

908 **The central Middle East: a handbook of anthropology and
     published research on the Nile valley, the Arab Levant, southern
     Mesopotamia, the Arabian peninsula, and Israel.**
     Edited by Louise E. Sweet. New Haven, Connecticut: Human
     Relations Area Files, 1971. 323p. map. bibliog.
Bahrain is mentioned in chapter 4 of this selection of anthropological essays and
bibliographies.

909   Arabia in early maps: a bibliography of maps covering the
       peninsula of Arabia printed in western Europe from the invention
       of printing to the year 1751.
       G. R. Tibbetts.   Naples, Italy: Falcon Press; New York &
       Cambridge, England: Oleander Press, 1978. 175p. 22 maps.
       bibliog.
A bibliography of maps of the Arabian peninsula from that of Ptolemaeus in 1477
to Jean Baptiste Bourguignon D'Anville's map of 1751. By the mid-16th century
Bahrain is regularly depicted on these maps.

910   A brief guide to sources for Middle East studies in the India
       Office Records.
       Penelope Tuson.   London: India Office Library and Records,
       1982. 35p. bibliog.
Provides a general introduction to the Middle East sources in the India Office
Records. Those specifically relating to Bahrain are noted on p. 24 where there is
also a short note summarizing the nature of British political administration in
Bahrain.

911   The Arabian peninsula: a selected, annotated list of periodicals,
       books and articles in English.
       Prepared under the direction of the US Library of Congress Near
       East Section, Division of Orientalia. Washington, DC: US Govern-
       ment Printing Office, 1951. Reprinted, New York: Greenwood
       Press, 1969. 111p.
Emphasis in this bibliography of 719 entries is placed on the geography, ethno-
logy, economy and politics of Arabia. Author index only.

Middle East — review and bibliography of geomorphological
contributions.
See item no. 87.

Wildlife in Bahrain: Bahrain Natural History Society annual reports
from 1978-1979.
See item no. 198.

The Arab world: a guide to business, economic and industrial information sources.
See item no. 653.

Ports of the Arabian peninsula: a guide to the literature.
See item no. 786.

Index

The index is a single alphabetical sequence of authors (personal and corporate), titles of publications and subjects. Index entries refer both to the main items and to other works mentioned in the notes to each item. Title entries are in italics. Numeration refers to the items as numbered.

227

228

229

234

238

E

East India Company 313
Eastern and General Syndicate 767
Eastern Arabian frontiers 339
Eastern Bank 680, 688
Eastern Gulf Oil Company 767
Ebert, C. H. V. 91
Economic crises 74
Economic 'development' 3, 8, 15-18,
    22, 35, 40, 48, 50-51, 64-65, 73,
    106, 428, 440, 491, 610, 615-616,
    618, 620, 626-627, 636, 654,
    657, 660, 677, 694, 702, 810
*Economic development and regional
    cooperation: Kuwait* 648
*Economic development of the United
    Arab Emirates* 649
Economic planning 615-616, 624,
    631, 642, 691, 715
Economic potential 616
Economies of the Middle East 672
Economist Intelligence Unit 92
Economy 2-3, 7-8, 11-13, 15-17,
    21, 35, 39, 41, 44-46, 49-50,
    54-56, 58-59, 69-70, 74, 111,
    125, 167, 175, 327, 336, 338,
    380, 420, 451, 465, 486-487,
    609, 613, 615, 617-618, 620-623,
    625, 628, 631, 636, 640, 643,
    652-653, 660, 666, 668, 677,
    692, 700, 746, 819
  19th century 75, 162, 316, 389
  1940s 71
  bibliographies 880, 911
  diversification 11, 410, 532, 708,
    718, 720
  English-Arabic dictionary 414
  Gulf integration 490, 623, 657-658
  impact of immigration 407, 413
  influence of Iran-Iraq war 666
  influence of oil 52, 64-65, 77, 410,
    427, 448, 645, 729, 738
  periodicals 22, 486, 613, 655-656,
    662-663
  private sector 55-56, 508
  prospects 47, 629
  services sector 56, 74, 625, 628
  statistics 620, 628, 686
  traditional 65, 80, 128, 369, 379,
    434, 496, 735
Edrisi 100
Education 2, 3, 5, 12, 15, 23, 35, 37,
    54, 58, 61, 173, 316, 326, 380,

    409, 429, 444, 519, 614, 623,
    629, 810, 815, 819, 824-825,
    837-840, 842
  bibliographies 902
  Gulf Technical College 838
  Gulf University 55
  influence on politics 488
  influence on society 491, 568
  Ministry 842
  school teachers for United Arab
    Emirates 638
  teachers 638, 837
  technical 838
  university sector 55, 689
  Yusuf Kanoo School of Continuing
    Education 444
*Education in the Arab states in the
    light of the Abu Dhabi conference
    1977* 839
Effluent 830
Egypt
  relations with Bahrain, 19th century
    337-338, 340-341, 351, 398, 794
Eisele, F. R. 66
El-Chihabi, Moustapha 417
El-Hakim, A. A. 505
El Mallakh, R. 648-651, 696
El-Rumaihi, M. G. 434, 593, 659, 734
El-Shishini, N. M. 822, 852
Eldin, A. S. 752
Elections 488, 553
Electricity 35, 825, 847
Embassies 9, 25, 619
*Emergence of Arab nationalism from
    the nineteenth century to 1921:
    a bibliography* 884
Emergency services 9
Emery, K. O. 93
*Les émirats du golfe Arabe: le Kowëit,
    Bahrëin, Qatar et les Emirats
    Arabes Unis* 64
*Les émirats du Golfe: histoire d'un
    peuple* 379
Employment 68, 380, 490, 623, 629,
    808, 813, 816, 819, 821
  'Bahrainization' 616, 666
  construction industry 821
  female 61
  non-Arab 462, 813-815
  oil industry 644
  pearling 348, 390, 434, 611
  'Ten Thousand' scheme 666
  women 61
Empty quarter 86

239

250

Map of Bahrain

This map shows the more important towns and other features.

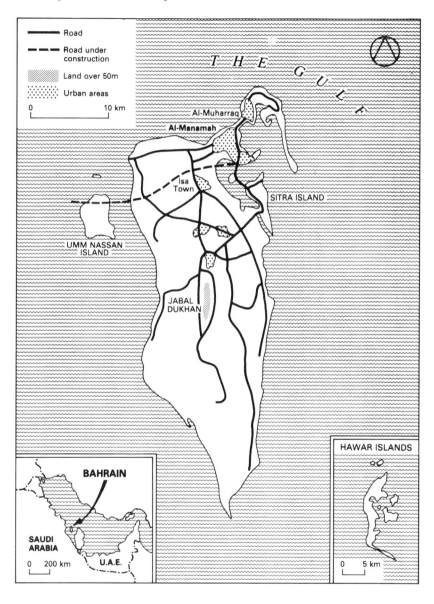